CINEPHILIA IN THE AGE OF DIGITAL REPRODUCTION

CINEPHILIA IN THE AGE OF DIGITAL REPRODUCTION

Film, Pleasure and Digital Culture, Vol.2

Edited by Scott Balcerzak & Jason Sperb

WALLFLOWER PRESS

LONDON & NEW YORK

A Wallflower Book
Published by
Columbia University Press
Publishers Since 1893
New York • Chichester, West Sussex
cup.columbia.edu

A complete CIP record is available from the Library of Congress

ISBN 978-0-231-16216-6 (cloth : alk. paper)
ISBN 978-0-231-16217-3 (pbk. : alk. paper)
ISBN 978-0-231-85017-9 (e-book)

Columbia University Press books are printed on permanent
and durable acid-free paper.
This book is printed on paper with recycled content.
Printed in the United States of America

c 10 9 8 7 6 5 4 3 2 1
p 10 9 8 7 6 5 4 3 2 1

CONTENTS

The following is a collection of essays on the fluid, unbroken presence of cinephilia in an age of digital reproduction. As such, this eclectic mix of work reflects the different agendas and forms through which critics and scholars have tackled the issue of cinephilia in our current historical moment. How is cinephilia still present, and what does it present to us? Most are original articles written for this collection. Some are reproductions of published work with the author's expressed consent. Others still began as blog posts or essays with online journals. Though each piece is different in form and content, the collective research here speaks to the enduring, and also diverse, work cinephilia does in the age of digital reproduction.

NOTES ON CONTRIBUTORS

Scott Balcerzak is Assistant Professor of Film and Literature in the Department of English at Northern Illinois University. He is the co-editor, with Jason Sperb, of *Cinephilia in the Age of Digital Reproduction: Film, Pleasure and Digital Culture, Vol. 1* (2009) and has published articles on film and performance for such journals as *Camera Obscura* and *Post Script*.

Chris Cagle is Assistant Professor of Film and Media Arts at Temple University. He has published articles in the journal *Screen* and in the recent edited volumes *Media Convergence History* (2009) and *Hollywood Reborn: Movie Stars of the 1970s* (2010). His current research and book project is on the Hollywood social problem film and the postwar film industry.

David Church is a PhD candidate in Communication and Culture at Indiana University. He is the editor of *Playing with Memories: Essays on Guy Maddin* (2009), and his work has also appeared in *Cinema Journal*, the *Journal of Film and Video*, *Participations* and several other books on cinema culture.

Susan Felleman is Associate Professor at Southern Illinois University Carbondale, where she teaches Cinema Studies, and in the programs of Women, Gender and Sexuality Studies and Art History and Visual Culture. She is the author of *Botticelli in Hollywood: The Films of Albert Lewin* (1997), *Art in the Cinematic Imagination* (2006), and other writings on art and film. She is currently completing a manuscript entitled *Real Objects in Unreal Situations: Modern Art in Fiction Films*.

Adrian Martin is Professor of Film and Television Studies, Monash University in Melbourne, Australia. He is the author of six books, the latest being *A Secret Cinema* (2012), co-editor, with Jonathan Rosenbaum, of *Movie Mutations: The Changing Face of World Cinephilia* (2003) and author of numerous essays and chapters in edited anthologies. He is also co-editor of LOLA (www.lolajournal.com).

Kristi McKim is Assistant Professor of English and Chair of the Film Studies Program at Hendrix College, Arkansas. She is the author of *Love in the Time of Cinema* (2011) and is currently completing a manuscript entitled *Cinema as Weather: Stylistic Screens and Atmospheric Change*.

James Morrison is Professor of Literature and Film Studies at Claremont McKenna College. He is the author, co-author, or editor of nine books, including, most recently, *Hollywood Reborn: Film Stars of the 1970s* (2010) and *Everyday Ghosts* (2011), a novella.

Ted Pigeon is author of the blog 'The Cinematic Art' and also writes for *Slant Magazine*'s blog, *The House Next Door*. He received his Bachelor's and Master's from Villanova University, Philadelphia.

Catherine Russell is Professor of Film Studies at Concordia University, Montreal. She is the author of many books and articles, most recently *Classical Japanese Cinema Revisited* (2011). She has published extensively on Japanese Cinema, experimental and ethnographic cinemas, Canadian cinema, narratology and Walter Benjamin. She is presently co-editor of the *Canadian Journal of Film Studies*.

Greg Singh teaches Media and Cultural Studies at the University of the West of England, and is an Associate Lecturer in Audio Cultures at Buckinghamshire New University. He is the author of *Film After Jung* (2009) and he is currently working on his second book-length publication which deals with the emotional work of cinema. He has published on several film-related subjects, including cinephilia, depth psychology and the cinematic encounter, CGI and neo-noir.

Steve Spence is Associate Professor of Media Studies at Clayton State University, Atlanta. His chapter in this collection is drawn from an unpublished manuscript entitled *Digitizing Martin Luther King: New Media and the African American Freedom Struggle*. Another, article-length selection from this work is available in the fall 2011 issue of *Public Culture*.

Jason Sperb is Assistant Professor of Film Studies in the Department of English at Michigan State University. He is the co-editor, with Scott Balcerzak, of *Cinephilia in the Age of Digital Reproduction: Film, Pleasure and Digital Culture, Vol. 1* (2009) and the author of *Disney's Most Notorious Film: Race, Convergence and the Hidden Histories of Song of the South* (2012).

ACKNOWLEDGEMENTS

The editors wish to express gratitude to the following individuals, without whom *Cinephilia in the Age of Digital Reproduction: Film, Pleasure and Digital Culture, Vol. 1* and *Vol. 2* would not have thrived in the manner they have: Dudley Andrew, Robert Burgoyne, Zach Campbell, Christian Keathley, Chris Cagle, Corey Creekmur, Barry Keith Grant, Catherine Grant, Joan Hawkins, Barbara Klinger, Paula Massood, Lloyd Michaels, Jenna Ng, James Naremore, Eyal Peretz, Ted Pigeon, Robert Ray, Jonathan Rosenbaum, Catherine Russell, Girish Shambu, Steven Shaviro, Vivian Sobchack, Chuck Tryon, Maureen Turim, Gregory Waller, and Kristin Whissel.

Chapter 1 by James Morrison originally appeared as 'After the Revolution: On the Fate of Cinephilia', *Michigan Quarterly Review* 44: 3, 393–413, 2005. Chapter 11 by Adrian Martin originally appeared as 'Turn the Page: From Mise en scène to Dispositif', in *Screening the Past*, issue 31 (July 2011), http://screeningthepast.com.

REMAPPING CINEPHILIA

Jason Sperb & Scott Balcerzak

Since the earliest movements of the Paris cine-clubs in the early to mid-twentieth century, *cinephilia* has denoted a deep, even limitless passion for cinema that has included consuming, producing, defining, sharing, discussing, and writing about films. Yet, for a while, it seemingly went underground. When several of the contributors to *Cinephilia in the Age of Digital Reproduction: Film, Pleasure and Digital Culture, Vol. 1* first met on a panel discussing digital visual effects at the Society for Cinema and Media Studies (SCMS) Conference in Vancouver, British Columbia, during the spring of 2006, cinephilia was still reemerging as a topical conversation piece. What are by now the usual critical suspects were just gaining visibility then. Christian Keathley's touchstone *Cinephilia and History, or The Wind in the Trees* (2006) had been released only a few months earlier, while Marijke de Valck's and Malte Hagener's *Cinephilia: Movies, Love, and Memory* (2005), along with Adrian Martin and Jonathan Rosenbaum's *Movie Mutations: The Changing Face of World Cinephilia* (2003), were both starting to find a hungry critical audience. Girish Shambu was still just one of many anonymous upstart film bloggers instead of one of the few bona fide stars in the cinephiliac blogosphere. Not surprisingly then, when Yoram Allon, Commissioning Editor of Wallflower Press, suggested a two-volume collection of essays on the subject, we expanded the topic to include online communication, digitised home viewing, and computer-generated and enhanced onscreen imagery, in relation to the historically volatile concept of cinephilia. The initial timing of the two-volume collection's inception over five years ago would prove in the long run to be both prescient and frustrating.

As editors, we had now initiated a large-scale, long-term project to understand the complications and possibilities of cine-love in the digital age, where the experience of both watching and discussing movies had been irreversibly changed. Yet, in retrospect, we were perhaps not completely wise to how cinephilia within and beyond our discipline was an area of interest still in flux. On a rainy March afternoon in 2008, we returned to the topic of twenty-first-century cinephilia at the annual SCMS meeting in Philadelphia, PA. Much had changed since our first visit to the conference in 2006, where we introduced the topic as, primarily, a focus on cinematic engagement and digital imagery on a panel called 'Cinephilia in the Age of Digital Reproduction'. We had now returned to the world's largest gathering of film and media scholars with a broader understanding of the issue than we had two years earlier. We were older and more knowledgeable concerning the issue's scope. Yet, we had set out on the right path. And the years since have confirmed our initial sense that the subject of cinephilia would return in a big way.

In the time between the production of *Cinephilia in the Age of Digital Reproduction, Vol. 1*, and work on the present volume, cinephilia has since become a major trend among film critics and scholars. In the *Critical Inquiry* article, 'The Core and Flow of Film Studies' (2009), Dudley Andrew identified how digital media's reshaping of cinephilia was one of the major shifts in film studies (citing volume one, along with *Cinephilia: Movies, Love, and Memory* and *Movie Mutations* as important benchmarks in that trend). Meanwhile, major film journals dedicated sections and even whole issues to the movement. In *Framework* (2009), Jonathan Buchsbaum and Elena Gorfinkel edited a special issue on the subject entitled, 'Cinephilia Dossier: What is Being Fought for in Today's Cinephilia(s)?'. This collection featured the provocative contributions of such distinguished critics and scholars as Jonathan Rosenbaum, Dudley Andrew, Laura Mulvey, Chris Fujiwara and Nicole Brenez, as well as new work from volume one contributors Adrian Martin, Girish Shambu, and Zach Campbell. *Cinema Journal* also dedicated a special dossier to cinephilia (2010), compiled by Mark Betz and featuring new work by past contributor and fellow SCMS panelist Jenna Ng. Rosenbaum even revisited the subject in his recent book, *Goodbye Cinema, Hello Cinephilia: Film Culture in Transition* (2010) – a collection of his film criticism writing from the last forty years. In his introduction, Rosenbaum outlines the gains and losses of film culture's move to the Internet, a trend he approaches with guarded optimism. As these developments indicate, the question facing cinephiles today seems to be as much *what can be done* with cinephilia as it is how one might choose to define cinephilia. As editors of *Cinephilia in the Age of Digital Reproduction* we quickly discovered that volume two must work within that *history* of these trends of which it is by now also a part. Cinephilia remains a common, but still fertile, critical ground, and so we faced a key question. Where to take volume two?

RECONTEXTUALISING VOLUME ONE

The 2008 SCMS panel was designed to serve as a bridge between the two volumes by featuring the work of volume one contributors Robert Burgoyne and Jason Sperb alongside volume two contributors Catherine Russell and Ted Pigeon. Meanwhile, past and present contributors such as Zach Campbell and Susan Felleman were also in attendance. As chair, Scott introduced the workshop as linking the conceptual basis of each volume. The first book examined experiential aspects of a cinephilic existence by organising the works in the following classifications: contexts, affects, ontologies, and bodies. The second book, as it was then announced, was to veer towards the pragmatics of cinephilia, practical usages of cine-love, to examine different avenues of thought onto themselves. If volume one explored the productive arenas of the abstract, volume two would plant twenty-first-century cinephilia – and whatever one wished to classify as reflecting such a movement – into the realm of more material knowledge. In essence, cinephilia was to be employed to examine cultural studies, new theory, and educational approaches. At the time, it felt like a logical progression. Since the first volume featured experiential categorisations, volume two surely should move beyond the hypothetical into the practical, while still respecting the knowledge accumulated through the former.

The panel went smoothly, with all the participants engaging in a worthwhile discussion of cinephilia as a cultural movement and as a personal investment. Yet, in retrospect, the transition in topic marked by the event was overly simplistic – a premature rush by the editors to classify a difference between the two volumes motivated in equal parts by the complicated logistics of publishing pressures and healthy doses of youthful arrogance. For volume one, we had set out to define cinephilia, the digital, and its confluences in an extensive introduction called 'Presence of Pleasure'. There, we outlined some background on the project and on the popular cinephilia movements of the twentieth century. In the second half, we ultimately foregrounded our discussions of 'Cinema (and Cinephilia) in the Age of Digital Reproduction' into three distinct categories: digital imagery, DVDs, and Blogs. The introduction continually stressed the fluidity of all these technologies and classifications, writing that the book's use of the word *digital* 'does not represent any particular technological development as it is a configuration for the complex, even contradictory, potential that such developments promise' (2009: 26). With this volatility in mind, did we really believe that our first volume could so clearly define cinephilia in such a technological environment? How could we believe our second volume could seamlessly move into practical employments of these definitions? Did we really think, at the 2008 panel, we could do anything but scratch the surface of this topic with volume one? Were we ever so young?

If we were to do another panel based on these volumes, we would take into account our own initial reactions to the first book once it came to print. With its release, we both found ourselves blogging on what we saw as its successes and limitations. Under its achievements, we both were enormously proud of the intelligent and original work of the contributors. Therefore, the limitations were squarely suggested in our roles as editors – or as Jason so fruitfully defined us on his blog *Jamais Vu*, 'stewards for cinephilia'. As he wrote concerning his own personal involvement, 'I do not "own" cinephilia, not even my own often half-thought and ephemeral discussions on them, but I am responsible for it, for help-ing to shape what it has, what it will and what it will *not* become' (2009b). With our roles as *stewards* to the topic of cinephilia, we both initially acknowledged the concern of any work of technologically-focused scholarship – the inability to keep the topic truly current. As Scott wrote on *Dr. Mabuse's Kaleido-Scope*: 'in so many words, the most frustrating aspect of doing a technology-focused col-lection is that the length of the publication process ultimately makes some topics feel conspicuously missing. For example, Blu-Ray and Netflix are not mentioned despite both feeling intensely significant to questioning cinema culture today' (2009a). In short, the *digital* (if we are to use the word to encompass both tech-nological innovation and its cultural impact) evolves at a rate that makes the lulls in any print publication process feel all the more frustrating. This becomes the case especially when harsh economic situations enforce further delays upon the publication process.

While this annoyance was understandable, Jason blogged about something more problematic when considering our roles as stewards: 'a big problem with the collection's focus is that it conceives of cinephilia's influence in such a wide scope of possibility that invariably many people will not find what they are hop-ing to find in the collection, because they are defining "cinephilia in the age of digital reproduction" much differently than Scott and I originally did' (2009a). In other words, as the project evolved from its original focus in 2005–06 on digital imagery (though admitting the endless possibilities of a twenty-first-century cine-philia), we also highlighted our own limitations as editors and stewards. Since many of the contributions were from the earliest stages of the project, a good portion of the first book focused on CGI digital imagery as opposed to, for exam-ple, the equally significant development of digitised home viewing. As such, we never could really *define* cinephilia in the digital age; we could only bring forth a worthwhile collection of ideas to understand the issue in our current cinematic moment.

But, of course, this approach ultimately made the project succeed on another level, one that benefitted greatly from the good fortune we had locating talented writers for both volumes. As Jason blogged, 'the collection is a strong compila-tion of distinguished and promising scholars, as well as a vital contribution (a crucial snapshot in time) from some of the leading cinephiles in the English-speaking world' (2009a). In other words, 'cinephiliac stewardship' has been a rewarding role to play and the thought-provoking writings of the contributors speak for themselves.

PRESENT CONTRIBUTIONS

With these reflections in mind, we provide volume two not so much as an elaboration but as a vital continuation of this 'crucial snapshot in time' of a twenty-first-century cinephilia – as it exists in the worlds of critical, scholastic, and online discourses. As one can tell by taking a quick look over the table of contents of this book, we do not so much take a step forward to employ previous definitions as much as step backwards, and sideways, to clarify, solidify, and (most importantly) challenge the assumptions of volume one. This approach can be seen in our movement away from the theoretical conditions (contexts, affects, ontologies, and bodies) that organised the first volume. We organised this book in a three-section structure that reflects such theory in practice: histories of cinephilia, international cinephilias, and transmedia cinephilias.

The first section on the 'Histories' of cinephilia begins with a republished piece from James Morrison, entitled 'After the Revolution', which first appeared in *Michigan Quarterly Review* (2005). This article offers one of the first substantive documentations of what cinephilia meant as movie-going began to shift from theatres to homes. Morrison's work grounds our larger collection here with the pointed question, 'What *was* cinephilia?', recognising that the historical underpinnings of the term had changed since the days of Susan Sontag. If the term endures, Morrison suggests, it may be through the commodified fetishising and consumption of the home video market. In 'The Virtual Spaces of Civil Rights', Steve Spence argues that the emergence of digital effects is part of a larger continuation of our cinephiliac relationship to mediated history, of our desire to collapse past with the present. This becomes particularly apparent in various recent digital recreations of the civil rights movement in America in the mid-twentieth century. Next, David Church offers a revelatory and meticulously researched history on the distribution of pornographic 'stag' films, historic artifacts of lustful moments past, which have now resurfaced through the internet. Vintage porn sites reveal much, Church argues, about our own cinephiliac relationship to the past, and in particular to the cinematic presence of death. Finally, Jason Sperb uses the occasion of Michel Gondry's quirky *Be Kind Rewind* (2008) to construct an elegy to his own personal cinephilia in favor of the more communal and historical one which the film champions. The film's representation of cine-love both resists, and reinforces, cinema's relationship with newer media technologies, with the ambivalent cultural impact of modernity, and with the history of twentieth-century America's (mediated) physical spaces. The result is an *off-modern cinephilia* that rejects linear narratives of social and technological progress and instead embraces the cinema's ability to wander in all directions, and proliferate through numerous platforms.

In the second section, 'International Cinephilias', Catherine Russell begins with an analysis of Wong Kar-Wai's *In the Mood for Love* (2000), showing that cinephilia's 'use-value' can be in how it helps motivate the production of film knowledge and history. Using the concept of the 'cinematic phantasmagoria', Russell sees cinephilia as both a fantasy of cinephiliac spectatorship and a form of ritualistic movie consumption, whereby we engage with open-ended texts and film history rather than passively consume it. In 'A Home for Cinephilia', Kristi McKim looks at Bernardo Bertolucci's *The Dreamers* (2003), a cinephiliac touchstone text that also anchors Morrison's article. She identifies a 'sensual history' for cinephilia here, whereby the pleasure and bliss of cinephiliac citation, films referencing other films, constitutes an affective relationship to movie history. Similarly, Susan Felleman examines Adrian Lyne's *Unfaithful* (2002) in relationship to its counterpart, Claude Chabrol's *La femme infidèle* (1968), as a meditation on America's historically cinephiliac relationship with French cinema. This relationship, meanwhile, is often constituted in the memories of filmmakers, stars and audiences.

Finally, the section on 'Transmedia Cinephilias' explores the ways in which movies, other media, cinephilia and film criticism intersects in the digital age. Prominent film blogger Ted Pigeon's article, 'Revisioning Critical Space in the Digital Age', articulates how the Internet allows greater access for the cinephile, as an active consumer of film, to navigate the vast critical spaces between the great divide of film criticism and academic scholarship. These are two traditionally separate approaches to cinema which such venues as blogging can now unite under the watchful guidance of the cinephile. Chris Cagle, in 'Academic Blogging and Disciplinary Practice', also discusses the practical impact of blogging, this time on academic film studies. He offers one of the first truly insightful accounts of this innovative form of writing's role and value for the film and media academic, documenting the different uses – such as sharing work-in-progress – that blogging offers. Cagle importantly reminds us that blogging only works as one limited part of a larger intellectual commitment to writing about film. Then, in 'The Kitsch Affect', Greg Singh revisits the collection's original muse: digital visual effects, exploring how memory and nostalgia complicate our temporal relationship to the flat ahistoricism of such images, while its visual excess problematises its crucial status as a commodity. Singh too documents the cinephiliac relationship to film history, the role it plays in constructing our sense of a cinematic past and in bonding our affective relationship to the product. Finally, Adrian Martin returns with a companion piece to his volume one contribution, entitled, 'Turn the Page'. Like Singh, Martin examines the nature of the digital image, positing a theory of ontology that moves beyond Bazinian indexicality, so long at the heart of cinephiliac spectatorship, and embraces the fundamentally materialist apparatus of film in an increasingly inter-media age, which digital cinema foregrounded once and for all.

The reader will note the chapters are much more focused on the historical, institutional and political use-values of cinephilia than volume one. Essentially, this reflects an intended shift from the ontologies and experiential cinephilias of the first collection. It also suggests an implicit polemical charge as interested in the material contexts for cinephilia as in defining its subjectivities or ephemera. The reader may also note that along with this shift from the personal, there is necessarily less blog content than seen in volume one, other than in more distanced, reflexive ways (Pigeon, Cagle, Sperb). During the long process of constructing this project, the editors have noted that the full promise of the turn-of-the-century blogging moment has, in many ways, passed since the earliest seeds of *Cinephilia in the Age of Digital Reproduction* were first conceived in 2005. Everyone blogs, or at least tries to, and yet that ubiquity merely highlights the limitations of the form. Moreover, social networking (primarily Facebook and Twitter) has emerged since then as a key venue that often connects communities of film fans in more immediate (yet, undoubtedly, fleeting) ways than the web log. In addition to providing a platform for film criticism amateurs and professionals to articulate their thoughts and interact with one another, blogging seems to work best as that which initiates larger, more substantive projects, such as the impressive contributions offered by authors here. And it is our suspicion that the Internet will soon put forth, if not already (MUBI, perhaps?), a new digital venue for cinephilia in the near future quite different in form and function from that earlier style. The (digital) histories of cinephilia remain to be written.

REFERENCES

Andrew, Dudley (2009) 'The Core and Flow of Film Studies,' *Critical Inquiry*, 35, 879–915.

Andrew, Dudley and Mary Anne Lewis (2009) 'Writing on the screen': An interview with Emmanuel Burdeau. *Framework: The Journal of Cinema and Media*, 50, 1–2, 229–34.

Balcerzak, Scott (2009) 'Initial Responses to *Cinephilia in the Age of Digital Reproduction* – Part Two', *Dr. Mabuse's Kaleidoscope*. Available at: http://dr-mabuses-kaleido-scope.blogspot.com/2009/08/initial-responses-of-cinephilia-in-age.html

Balcerzak, Scott and Jason Sperb (2009) 'Presence of Pleasure,' in Scott Balcerzak and Jason Sperb (eds) *Cinephilia in the Age of Digital Reproduction: Film Pleasure and Digital Culture. Vol. 1*. London: Wallflower Press, 7–29.

Buchsbaum, Jonathan and Elena Gorfinkel (2009) 'Introduction', *Framework: The Journal of Cinema and Media*, 50, 1–2), 176–80.

Brenez, Nicole (2009) 'For an insubordinate (or rebellious) history of cinema', *Framework: The Journal of Cinema and Media*, 50, 1–2, 197–201.

Campbell, Zachary (2009) 'On the political challenges of the cinephile today', *Framework: The Journal of Cinema and Media*, 50, 1–2, 210–13.

De Valck, Marike and Malte Hagener (eds) (2005) *Cinephilia: Movies, Love, and Memory*. Amsterdam: Amsterdam University Press.

Fujiwara, Chria (2009) 'Cinephilia and the imagination of filmmaking', *Framework: The Journal of Cinema and Media*, 50, 1–2, 194–6.

Keathley, Christian (2006) *Cinephilia and History, or the Wind in the Trees*. Bloomington: Indiana University Press.

Martin, Adrian (2009) 'Cinephilia as war machine'. *Framework: The Journal of Cinema and Media*, 50, 1–2, 221–5.

Mulvey, Laura (2009) 'Some reflections on the cinephilia question', *Framework: The Journal of Cinema and Media*, 50, 1–2, 190–3.

Ng, Jenna (2010) 'The myth of total cinephilia', *Cinema Journal*, 49, 2, 146–51.

Rosenbaum, Jonathan (2010) *Goodbye Cinema, Hello Cinephilia: Film Culture in Transition*. Chicago: University of Chicago Press.

Rosenbaum, Jonathan and Adrian Martin (eds) (2003) *Movie Mutations: The Changing Face of World Cinephilia*. London: British Film Institute.

_____ (2009) 'Reply to Cinephilia Survey'. *Framework: The Journal of Cinema and Media*, 50, 1–2, 181–2.

Shambu, Girish (2009) 'What is being fought for by today's cinephilia(s)?', *Framework: The Journal of Cinema and Media*, 50, 1–2, 218–20.

Sperb, Jason (2009a) 'Initial Responses to 'Cinephilia in the Age of Digital Reproduction', *Dr. Mabuse's Kaleidoscope*. Available at: http://dr-mabuseskaleidoscope.blogspot.com/2009/08/initial-responses-to-cinephilia-in-age.html

_____ (2009b) 'The Stewardship of Ideas', *Jamais Vu: Thoughts on Film and Media*. Available at: http://lightpalimpsest.blogspot.com/2009/06/stewardship-of-ideas.html

HISTORIES OF CINEPHILIA

CHAPTER ONE

AFTER THE REVOLUTION: ON THE FATE OF CINEPHILIA
James Morrison

'One cannot live without Rossellini!'

– Bertolucci's Before the Revolution

In 1995, the year of cinema's centenary, Susan Sontag published a now well-known essay for the occasion. From the title – 'A Century of Cinema' – one might have surmised that the piece was a fond tribute to the quintessential art of the 1900s. Instead, after a breezy recounting of some high points in film history, it turned into a subdued elegy for a medium in decline. (First published in Germany, the essay was subsequently reprinted in the *New York Times Magazine* under a title that left little room for doubt: 'The Decay of Cinema'.) Others, elsewhere, were already mourning the death of cinema – and had been, in one way or another, for nearly the whole hundred years of film's existence. What Sontag lamented was the death of *cinephilia*, and that difference may be what caused her essay to strike a chord the other dirges missed. All the chatter about the death of cinema was somehow predictable, especially at the onset of new digital media that posed direct challenges to the primacy of film, and it had a more generally familiar ring, harking back to now-quaint debates about the death of opera at the end of the nineteenth century, or proclamations concerning the exhaustion of literature in the 1960s. But Sontag was talking about something else. 'If cinephilia is dead', she wrote, 'then movies are dead … no matter how many movies, even very good ones, go on being made' (1996: 61). Despite the conditional form of the sentence, it still had the air of a dour, final pronouncement. Especially considering Sontag's enduring cultural authority, it seemed quite official: Something important had waned, was gone, without ever having been properly recognised until after its crucial influence had already passed.

What *was* cinephilia? It was a particular *way* of loving movies: eclectic, voracious, attuned to the importance of film as a force in everyday life, impassioned, if a little sentimental, undiscriminating in its pursuit of a new movie high – a form of addiction that hoped never to be sated. The cinephile might have loved and sought great movies, masterpieces, but was fervently committed foremost to an aesthetic of amplitude, of tireless ranginess, that could admit anything – not to demean masterpieces by mixing them up with tripe, but to experience the rush of discovering the masterpiece amid the tripe. Anyone can spot a masterpiece, a *Grand Illusion* (1937) or *Earrings of Madame de...* (1953), a *L'Avventura* (1960) or *Persona* (1966), but only a cinephile could uncover the glories, all the more wondrous for being hidden, of minor, even failed work that might be refashioned, if only by force of will, into greatness of another kind, perhaps even a better kind because of the heady exertions its conversion demanded: an *Elena and Her Men* (1956) or *Rise of Louis XIV* (1966) or *The Exile* (1947), a *Zabriskie Point* (1970) or *The Touch* (1971) – this last Ingmar Bergman's worst film by far, but an object of potential reverence to those cinephiles for whom a truly awful movie was almost as good as a really great one, and infinitely preferable to a simply mediocre one. On the other hand, since the ultimate object of the cinephile's love was the image itself, the *idea* of the image, it may be that there was no such thing as a mediocre movie. For the true cinephile, books might be mediocre; movies were sublime.

Cinephilia was a form of cultism, an art of seeing in movies what others didn't see – the beauty of form in Hitchcock's *Under Capricorn* (1949), say, or the tenderness under the surface of some of Buñuel's seemingly cruelest films, the diffuse elegance of Stan Brakhage, the wayward intellect of Otto Preminger. It was itself a form of intellect, though intellectuals from Graham Greene to Jean Epstein to Nicola Chiaromante to Guillermo Cabrera Infante to Roland Barthes to Gilles Deleuze – to, for that matter, Sontag herself – could stand accused of slumming whenever they indulged it. But it was, principally, a commitment to intellect as vehement passion, finding powerful stimulation where those who considered intellect merely a facet of rational cognition would find only tedium. It embraced moments of intensity even in the most banal films (*pace* Epstein's notion of *photogénie*), and made of those intensities a private, shared mythology. The cinephile might have commanded an encyclopedic knowledge of film, but it would rarely boast anything like the logical order of an actual encyclopedia, this being intellect of a *new* order, responding to new needs, and answerable chiefly to the lure of images, not the rule of words. Cinephilia was frequently garrulous, as in such representative samples as the film writing of Vachel Lindsay, Blaise Cendrars, or Manny Farber, or more recently that of David Thomson in the 1970s (collected in the books *America in the Dark* [1978] and *Overexposures* [1981]), or Geoffrey O'Brien's *The Phantom Empire* in 1993, perhaps the last gasp of a certain strain of cultivated cinephilia. But the words poured forth most often as stream-of-consciousness, with the hopeful obstinacy of free association and with a crabby restlessness indicating a keen awareness that even the poetry of certain words could never adequately convey the poetry of any image.

And maybe, come to think of it, it wasn't true that anyone could recognise a masterpiece. After all, the philistines at Cannes booed *L'Avventura* off the screen in 1960, and it took the cinephiles, with some unexpected help from the critical establishment, to put it back in the canon where it belonged. Part of the history of cinephilia is a history of recovery, a slow process of persuading the general audience, the non-cinephiles, of the value of what was overlooked or neglected or scorned. It is, therefore, a history of surpassing masterpieces subject to initial abuse: Dreyer's *Gertrud* (1964), say, or Hitchcock's *Marnie* (1965), or the films of John Cassevetes from *Shadows* (1959) to *A Woman Under the Influence* (1974), all works from the heyday of cinephilia. The urge of the cinephile was to rescue such works, to restore them to the greatness that was proper to them, while also protecting them, keeping them from the grasp of the uncomprehending masses. This was a curator's impulse, but the cinephile's archive was a chaotic one, a vast hodgepodge of titles from many places and times (though mostly America and Europe), and to be admitted you had to leave your ordinary standards of taste at the door, accept the vital and joyous subversion of traditional cultural hierarchies, and suspend normative attitudes of evaluation.

Cinephiles were often literally curators and archivists – Henri Langlois of the French Cinémathèque was the best example, Richard Roud of the New York Film Festival (and Langlois's biographer) another – but at the peak of cinephilia, they were rarely critics, the cabal at *Cahiers du cinéma* notwithstanding. During the 1960s in the United States, a lively film culture flourished, though largely in the shadow of its European cousins. Not surprisingly, this culture was principally centered in New York, and it would not be inaccurate to call aspects of this marginal renaissance cinephiliac, but this was also the period of the emergence of a quite consolidated bloc in American film criticism, monolithic if not exactly unified, consisting of figures such as Dwight Macdonald, Andrew Sarris, John Simon, Stanley Kauffmann, Pauline Kael, and a few others. Of these only Sarris and Kael leaned toward cinephilia – Sarris in his cultish, neo-auteurist eclecticism, Kael in her brittle but earthy promotion of a pop aesthetic of energetic vulgarity – but like the rest, both remained highly dependent on a notion of traditional standards and nursed biases no true cinephile would have maintained (against avant-garde cinema, for instance). The rest of these critics upheld a lofty conception of film as art that was really meant to preserve an even loftier realm of art as such. With its monomaniacal drive to uncover and to cherish whatever was most distinctive in film, and to pursue ruthlessly the challenges the new medium posed to old-fashioned ideas about art, cinephilia clearly endangered that very preserve. One of those critics, Stanley Kauffmann, famously designated this age 'the film generation'; though Kauffmann celebrated this development in 1966, within a year or two he was anything but wholehearted in his approval of a new youth culture weaned on film and therefore increasingly indifferent, as he saw it, to other arts, to culture itself, to politics, to society. When he later bemoaned the apparent inexorability of this rising tide, so much at odds with what he represented himself, he was talking about cinephilia.

Near the beginning of Bernardo Bertolucci's film *The Dreamers* (2003) – among other things an ode to cinephilia – a lonely young American in the Paris of 1968 haunts the Cinémathèque, lapping up movies, always sitting in the front rows so that, as he says, he can capture the image before anyone else. Near the end, he goes back with a date – a young French woman with whom, together with her brother, he has been having an unruly yet frolicsome ménage-à-trois – and they sit in the rear of the auditorium. Only those without dates, he explains, sit in the front. The film unfolds; it's Frank Tashlin's *The Girl Can't Help It* (1957), a cinephile's delight – and the boy and the girl make out in the dark, oblivious to the pleasures on the screen. Bertolucci keeps his camera close to them, as if that proximity were sufficient to communicate the responsiveness to their youthful passions he clearly means to convey, but he also cuts away restlessly to the film, as if wanting us to pay attention to what they're missing. It is not entirely clear whether Bertolucci expects us to groove on these kids' tempestuous sexuality or to notice how self-absorbed it is, but by putting us in the position of having to choose, as it were, between two kinds of cinematic pleasure – that of the literal sexual content that the movies have always made so richly available, or that of the voluptuary formalisms of an auteur like Tashlin – Bertolucci raises basic questions about the role of eroticism in movie love and, by extension, of sexuality in society.

Whether cinephiliac or not, anyone watching movies will eventually be placed in the position of voyeur. The sight of people kissing was among the first to be chronicled on film – in Edison's *The Kiss* (1896) – and it escalated over decades to become a pivotal image of the movies, if not the definitive one, marking tumultuous turning points (in, say, *Gone With the Wind* [1939] or *Vertigo* [1958]), bringing about or securing whole climaxes (in typical romances, or less typical screwball comedies like *Bringing Up Baby* [1938], or in earnest melodramas like *Brief Encounter* [1945], where the kissing is kept chaste to signify a greater seriousness), and growing more zealous through the years, despite ever-vigilant censors, until being superseded at last by images of actual intercourse, simulated or otherwise. The migration of such images of flagrant carnality from pornography into the more general and putatively respectable sphere of 'legitimate' cinema was a transition assisted by directors like Bertolucci himself in the 1960s and 1970s, and it is a history everyone knows, even if it remains in large part a shadow history, like that of cinephilia. What Bertolucci draws attention to in *The Dreamers* – some thirty years after *Last Tango in Paris* (1972), an ultimately masochistic gesture in the direction of sexual liberation – is not so much the narcissism inherent in taking movies as a substitute for sex. After all, Bertolucci's whole career suggests that he would happily approve of narcissism if it succeeded as a means to self-fulfillment – except that, in his work, it never does.

Rather, in a mode of sensual nostalgia that revels in its own simultaneous naïveté and cynicism, Bertolucci lays bare the exclusionary mechanisms of cinematic voyeurism. Watching lovers on the screen, why aren't we constantly aware of our own profound removal from their passions, and how can we go on loving movies when we know how cruelly they leave us out, especially once we have come up against the blunt inevitability of our own participation in the world they can only reflect?

As a cinematic figure, the ménage-à-trois addresses itself to the subject of voyeurism quite directly, and Bertolucci's lissome threesome recalls a whole movie history of such trios, particularly those of the French New Wave – Truffaut's *Jules and Jim* (1962) or Godard's *Band of Outsiders* (1964), to name only two of the most obvious examples. Each of these films implies that the love of movies is an extension of eroticism beyond the dualism of traditional heterosexuality, with its compulsory rituals of coupling. In *The Dreamers*, the young American, Matthew (Michael Pitt), sports the undersised blazer and too-tight trousers of a Belmondo wannabe, and he walks with a gangly, off-centered strut that could come of seeing *Breathless* (1961) too many times but remaining unsure whether one isn't really still closer to James Dean after all – or whether, worse yet, there *is* no viable model on which to fashion oneself. The brother and sister, Theo (Louis Grarrel) and Isabelle (Eva Green), are more sophisticated types who start out sniping at each other like the siblings in Cocteau's *Les Enfants Terribles* (1950). (The standard English translation of Cocteau's novel gives the title as *The Holy Terrors*, and the novel by Gilbert Adair on which *The Dreamers* is based is called *The Holy Innocents*; Bertolucci's film was released in France under the title *Les Innocents*.) Once their mutual contempt is revealed as incestuous desire, however, they settle down into latter-day versions of the doe-eyed and angst-ridden semi-delinquent and the sagacious but neurotic, leonine temptress – in other words, Jean-Pierre Léaud and Jeanne Moreau, seen through a glass, lightly.

What is most suggestive about the three is how unpersuasive they are as figures of counterculture youth circa May 1968, how unconvincing, really, they seem called upon to be. Much about the evocation of period atmosphere in the film has an impersonally distilled, semiotic quality – background details and the overall surround presented not so much as a set of actual objects but as a sequence of ready-made signs, a bust of Mao placed here, a book by Susan Sontag or a copy of *Cahiers du cinéma* strewn there – and the actors appear less as characters than as highly embodied signifiers. Whatever the intent, one effect of this is to indicate a kind of mimetic rupture, prompting awareness that the young people playing these roles, representative as they may be of something in contemporary youth, are simply not very much like the young people who might have watched those movies, chanted those slogans, or joined those protests in the distant time and place the film tries to recapture. This sense of disconnection paradoxically amplifies the movie's nostalgia, suggesting how far past that time now is, and how very distant that place.

Bodies being a principal object of voyeurism, cinematic or otherwise, it is the bodily presence of the three players that Bertolucci keeps returning to, and in the sense that the ménage-a-trois enacts or replicates the erotics of spectatorship in the cinema, the director uses it to comment on the voyeuristic gaze he elicits. The film's conceit is to place these three in an opulent apartment as the riots of May 1968 roil about them, and to let us watch (or make us watch, as the case may be) their private games of transgression, involving teasing cinematic fantasies and blunt sexual realities that, in turn, can function only as fantasy for the viewer. Bertolucci seems to be asking us to think about the relation of the 'personal' to the 'political' against the backdrop of the very history that notoriously altered that relation forever. At first playful, if charged with sadism, the kids' games grow more and more hermetic, more and more removed from the social turmoil brewing just outside. A standard take on May '68 is that it gave new credence to notions of *cultural* politics, forging the link between personal, cultural affiliations or preferences (left or right, black or white, colonial or anticolonial, male or female, gay or straight, to cite the oppositions most commonly associated with the period) and political action. According to conventional wisdom, this was the decisive moment when a politics based on class gave way to one allied with larger issues of identity, but by the time the three young people in Bertolucci's movie join the riots, their escapades have become so insular, so narcissistic, we can see little connection between their private conflicts and their public protests. Yet Bertolucci does not appear to be slamming the pretensions of the idle rich, exposing the impulse behind the protests as just another version or outcome of bourgeois ennui (like Louis Malle in *May Fools* [1990]). Rather, he seems to be interested in exploring the limits of cultural politics, especially in relation to the cinema as a begetter of private fantasy, a vehicle of identity formation, and a cultural form with real social effects.

In the films of the French New Wave, the ménage-à-trois was perhaps the most common objective-correlative for what were perhaps the most characteristic themes or moods of the movement: jealousy, envy, resentment (or its more exact French equivalent, *ressentiment*). Moviegoing itself played a key role in the treatment of these themes, for one of the things that made the New Wave seem so modern, so up to the minute, so casually self-reflexive, was the fact that where characters of previous films rarely went to the movies, the characters in films of the New Wave often did – and often in threes, like the mother, father, and son in *The Four Hundred Blows* (1959) setting off for the cinema in a rare moment of happiness. (That happiness was not just rare but short-lived, since moviegoing in New Wave films often had clear sadomasochistic connotations.) It wasn't just that the ménage-à-trois was already a movie cliché, one that the characters of these films were as keen to reenact as they were to take on the personae of the film stars they adored, and for much the same reasons of cultural identification. At some level, movies like *Jules and Jim* and Godard's *Pierrot le fou* (1965) and Rivette's *Paris Belongs to Us* (1966) and Chabrol's *La Femme Infidel* (*The Unfaithful Wife* 1969), all films about triangulated desire, express an awareness that this centrifugal force is basic to the movie-going experience. In the ménage-à-trois – at least as these films portray it, especially Bertolucci's – one is both participant and watcher; at the movies, as a passive observer, one is always in some fashion the excluded other in a transaction of physical, visual pleasure, the outcast third in a dyadic compact that still teasingly coaxes one's attentions: the pair of lovers gamboling on the screen, or the lone body that solicits the camera itself in a kind of surrogate coupling of which the viewer can only pretend to be part. (Bertolucci makes us aware of this dynamic in *The Dreamers* by systematically showing each member of the triangle enviously watching the other two in pairs.) The tragic sense of the films of the New Wave has a great deal to do with just this kind of abjection; the movies end in disaster when it becomes clear that the ménage-à-trois arrangement, far from compensating for the losses of cinematic or everyday voyeurism, merely repeats them, as in *Jules and Jim* – or more simply, when you realise you'll never really be Bogey, or that life isn't a musical, or that the guns that seem like such nifty trinkets on the screen produce real blood (or at least, *pace* Godard, quantities of red paint) when used on actual flesh. For all the ambivalent love of movies these films express – until May 1968, that is – they are largely engaged in exposing the fantasy life engendered by the movies as sterile and destructive.

Bertolucci's movies take up many of the same issues, often in more traditionally political terms. His first important film, *Before the Revolution*, was released in 1964 (when he was twenty-four, a year younger than the Welles of *Citizen Kane* [1941]), only five years after the New Wave had announced itself with such brash confidence. From the start Bertolucci's work was in a pan-European mode closer in style to that of the younger French directors than it was to Bertolucci's fellow Italians. Especially in the work of Fellini or Antonioni, in films like *8½* (1963) or *L'Avventura*, the Italian cinema was in the process of edging over from the neo-realism of the postwar era to a tempered modernism postulated to boost that country's own competing version of a new wave. Bertolucci was very much a part of this transition, but his films of the 1960s ally themselves to the more anarchic and roguish spirit of the French New Wave – so much so that he became virtually an honorary member of that movement.

For the first decade of his career Bertolucci's work seems split between an allegiance to radical political critique under the influence of Godard, and a lushness of style – inimical to Godard's early work – that constantly threatens to undermine the films' avowed ideologies. The tension is reflected as early as the first sequence of *Before the Revolution*, in which a character is comically torn between going to a screening of Howard Hawks' *Red River* (1948) or joining the Communist Party. This conflict between a luxuriant sensuality, often tied to love of cinema, and the implicit demand for a rigorously progressive politics finds an analogue in the subjects of Bertolucci's films, which tend to concern passive, callow characters forced to choose between opposing ways of life or political allegiances, a schism typically framed as a clash between sexuality and social responsibility. In *The Conformist* (1970) Bertolucci follows a long line of popular representation in implying a causal link between homosexuality and fascism: Seduced by the family chauffeur as a young boy, the film's main character dubiously commits to fascism as a man, recalling his childhood trauma as an underlying source of this allegiance. Though the film associates homosexuality with apolitical decadence, it revels in a style with clear associations to high-camp aesthetics. *The Dreamers* all but eliminates the explicit homosexual content of the novel on which it is based, but it too thrives on a free-floating homoeroticism.

While the sexual politics of Bertolucci's films remain deeply ambiguous, they often concern, as in *Before the Revolution*, the confrontation of erotic fantasy with a reality principle typically construed as politics itself. To the extent that cinephilia contains a crucial ingredient of erotic fantasy, it becomes a suggestive vehicle of that theme in both *Before the Revolution* and *The Dreamers*. Bertolucci's constant recurrence to the notion of sex as social emancipation suggests that he takes that idea with some degree of seriousness, even if it never succeeds as a possibility in his work. For Godard, for whom sex is associated with bourgeois individualism, such an idea would be anathema; for Truffaut, for whom sex is old-fashioned romance, it would be irrelevant, romance having a way of working itself out in his films as comedy, tragedy, or farce in a process impervious to social agendas. In that sense Bertolucci is the best equipped of the three to deal with the sociocultural implications of the erotics of cinephilia, even if his perennial recourse to sexuality as theme always remains willfully unresolved.

In *The Dreamers*, sex and cinephilia are aligned as dimensions of the personal with potentially liberating social effects. With its implication of naïve idealism, the title of the film alone points to the failure of this potential, and the mode of the film's nostalgia for the period it evokes is a kind of gingerly but affectionate elegy, rife with circumspect, and retrospective, awareness of just what the youthful exuberance of its characters, and their high hopes for the future, came to so quickly. The long, mournful last shot of the film portrays the very beginning of this cultural revolution as foredoomed, and the film is animated by the contradictory energies that infuse Bertolucci's work as a whole. The filmmaker is avidly attracted to these characters' attitudes even though the whole point of the film is to exhibit their limitations; he deeply wants cinephilia to liberate the sensibility and sex to free the body, but he knows now that they can't. Perhaps he always knew it: the heady blend of romanticism and self-conscious skepticism in his work was already present in *Before the Revolution*, in the main character's diagnosis of himself as afflicted with 'nostalgia for the present' (a phrase later appropriated by Fredric Jameson and others to define aspects of the postmodern condition). What he means – and what the film in its fierce extravagance portrays – is that his desire to capture reality, to make direct and powerful contact with contemporary experience, is so fervent that it becomes a form of blockage. It is a lesson Bertolucci has certainly embraced by now as a matter of course – that the most feverish desire becomes an end in itself, and renders its objects insignificant – and the reversionary nostalgia of *The Dreamers* is of the old-fashioned kind, for a past longed for because it was delectably imperfect, and is now irretrievably gone.

Cinephilia itself, of course, was a form of desire; as Bertolucci's film makes clear, it was very nearly libidinal in the vivacity of its appetites, which were intensified all the more by the open recognition of its objects as pure phantasm. In *The Dreamers*, the movies are seen as a sphere of public fantasy that lends itself to private reverie and appropriation, and the characters in the film co-opt movies fanatically, successively, for purposes of alliance, coalition, contention, identification, variance, self-fashioning. They think of movies not as displaced eroticism but as actual sex, masturbatory yet orgiastic, and they act out their favorite scenes to integrate the movies into their daily lives as ritual, forging a cult of movie history – so passionately that it rises above mere trivia – which they use to test others' worth, and their own. Bertolucci's mitigated critique of their movie love differs from Godard's hectoring bedevilment of his characters' oblivious role-modeling. When Belmondo fashioned himself on Bogart in *Breathless*, to take the most obvious example, what we were supposed to see was the scarifying ease with which mass culture impresses itself on abject and unstable personalities, and the dangers of this potential. Though largely figments of the director's own cinephilia, Godard's characters are not, for the most part, cinephiles; Bertolucci's are, but they hunger for the movies not with the unthinking reflexiveness of Godard's lively ciphers, but with the impetuous self-reflexivity of a band of post-structuralists *avant la lettre*. They never doubt that their cinephilia is a form of political commitment – and that, for Bertolucci, may be just the problem.

May '68 put a decisive end to the tide of cinephilia that produced the French New Wave. For the critics who became the filmmakers of that movement – Truffaut, Godard, Chabrol, Rohmer, Rivette – it had been an article of faith in the era after World War II that movies served as a legitimate vehicle for the revival of a viable cultural politics seeking restitution from the bourgeois status quo. Their espousal of the *politique des auteurs* was, among other things, a manner of projecting the values of their own modernism onto redemptive elements of the establishmentarian mass culture of Hollywood. In its European form the auteur theory was founded not on reverence for Hollywood but on contempt for it. The small handful of auteurs who flourished within the Hollywood system were celebrated for keeping alive a spirit of implicitly modernist resistance to the degraded commercialism and global imperialism of American cinema, and for the auteurists this resistance was all the more compelling insofar as it took place in the very midst of Hollywood.

It was in this light that these critics glorified the existentialist disillusionment of film noir, the quasi-modernist self-consciousness of a Hitchcock or Welles, the irascible brutalism of a Sam Fuller, the embittered social critique of a Nicholas Ray or Douglas Sirk, even the diffident myth-making of a Raoul Walsh or John Ford. And it was in this same spirit that these critics continued to pay homage to their idols once they began to make their own films. In the case of Godard alone, his first feature, *Breathless*, was dedicated to Monogram Pictures, a minor Hollywood studio known for producing primitivist B-movies; another, *Contempt* (1963), vents just that against the crassness of Hollywood filmmaking while honoring the Hollywood films of Fritz Lang, who appears in the movie as a chimerical misanthrope; Sam Fuller turns up in *Pierrot le fou*, a film that seems modeled in part on Nicholas Ray's *They Live by Night* (1949); and virtually all of Godard's films of the 1960s are brazen composites of Hollywood genres, rendered with derelict satire. Like many of the other filmmakers of the movement, Godard reveled in a makeshift freedom that enabled him to pursue the modernist project of the great auteurs to its logical conclusion; at times it seemed as if he were making the movies he thought the auteurs would have made, had they not been beholden to the constraints of the Hollywood system.

As *The Dreamers* chronicles, an inaugural line of protest in May '68 was precipitated by the firing of Langlois from his post as director of the French Cinémathèque. Bertolucci's film begins with footage of key figures of the New Wave objecting angrily to his dismissal, and the movie expresses a certain wistful awe that there should ever have been a time when film culture seemed so directly connected to the politics of culture more generally. As the movie also shows, that time was very near its end. Once the protests escalated to enraged dissent against the onset of neo-colonialism in Vietnam, the stakes must have seemed raised to a degree that made earlier notions of the contiguity of film culture and cultural politics seem to have been a complacent, naïve, and ineffectual delusion. After all, Langlois was reinstated to his post, while the interventions in Vietnam increased exponentially. How close a connection could there really have been between such events, if one ended in a pyrrhic victory and the other in a defeat so ignominious as to appear apocalyptic?

Godard, for one, after May '68, promptly repudiated any lingering allegiance to Hollywood on the grounds that it could only be seen, from that point, as an arm of the American power machine. By then, the great auteurs were mostly specters of the past anyway – finished off in part, ironically, by the modernising novelties of the New Wave that had rendered their work hopelessly rearguard – but what could their resistance have amounted to, in any case, if it had failed to fend off this disastrous expansion of American empire? Seemingly overnight Godard's artistic practice became overtly politicised in a new way, now looking back not to the bourgeois commonwealth of Hollywood but to precedents of Communist cinema, especially in the Soviet film of the 1920s. Forging a new mode of guerilla filmmaking, Godard by the early 1970s had formed a collective called the Dziga Vertov Group in honor of the Russian director of *Man with a Movie Camera* (1929), and in some of his subsequent films (notably *Letter to Jane* [1972] or sections of the video series *Histoire(s) du cinema* [1988–98]) the now-demoted auteurs are portrayed, however lovingly or regretfully, as having been little more than dupes of a dominant ideology.

In the year following May 1968 Godard denounced Bertolucci, his former disciple, for accepting money from a Hollywood studio to make *The Conformist*. He broke with Truffaut after delivering a scathing response to the latter's 1973 film *Day for Night* (titled in French with only half-hearted irony *La Nuit Américain*). Godard's lacerating indictment was built on the charge that Truffaut's whimsical comedy about the movie industry failed to expose the fraudulent mechanisms of filmmaking *tout court*, and especially Hollywood filmmaking:

> Probably no one else will call you a liar, so I will. It's no more an insult than 'fascist', it's a criticism, and it's the absence of criticism that I complain of in the films of Chabrol, Ferreri, Verneuil, Delannoy, Renoir, etc. You say: films are trains that pass in the night, but who takes the train, in what class, and who is driving it with an 'informer' from the management standing at his side? (1988: 383)

Truffaut replied furiously, at great length, in a letter that occupies seven tall octavo pages of his published correspondence, a blistering excoriation that stands as a bitter epitaph for the French New Wave. He begins by calling his former comrade 'a piece of shit on a pedestal' (1988: 387) , and goes on to chastise Godard for his own claims to political virtue:

> Between your interest in the masses and your own narcissism there's no room for anything or anyone else. After all, those who called you a genius, no matter what you did, all belonged to that famous trendy Left that runs the gamut from Susan Sontag to Bertolucci via Richard Roud … and even if you sought to appear impervious to flattery … you fostered the myth. (1988: 384)

Throughout the 1960s, the cinephiles of the New Wave may have loved the mythologies of movies as the expression of a hoped-for post-industrial romanticism, but from the start, they all hated the damaging political implications and real social consequences of those same mythologies. This contradiction was basic to the complexity of their responses to American movies, always inflected in nearly equal parts by love and hate, and the films of the movement committed themselves to debunking these mythologies as a practice of activism in the realm of cultural politics. Once that impulse to progressive iconoclasm devolved into just another kind of myth-making, as Truffaut suggests, there was no further to go. It was the end not just of the movement itself, but of the cinephilia that had bred and long supported it.

Bertolucci made *Last Tango in Paris* four years after May 1968 as if officially to mark the end of the New Wave. In its use of an American star (Marlon Brando) as an index of cultural sensibility, the film points back to the earliest tendencies of the movement (quite specifically, to the casting of Jean Seberg in *Breathless*). Yet the film combines a melancholy, elegiac mood with open derision of certain New Wave attitudes embodied in the figure of Jean-Pierre Léaud, cast for his associations with the movement and treated with tart satire – as if Bertolucci had come to praise the movement *and* to bury it.

In both *The Conformist* and *Last Tango in Paris*, Bertolucci broached a new internationalism of a type that was fairly incidental to the main currents of the movement, seen chiefly in such distinguished yet marginal items as Truffaut's *Fahrenheit 451* (1966), Jacques Demy's *The Young Girls of Rochefort* (1967), or Chabrol's *The Champagne Murders* (1967); for all its cosmopolitanism, and its errant trafficking with Hollywood, the New Wave remained a home-grown venture and a strikingly nationalist enterprise. Pursuing this ascendant internationalism incomparably further than the New Wave ever did, Bertolucci's subsequent career is far more representative than Truffaut's or Godard's of the next wave of the European art-film – in its abandonment of the quest for a viable political critique as well as in its intemperate and often exoticist border-crossings. Bertolucci's work of the following decades encompasses the terrains of Asia (in *The Last Emperor* [1987]), South Asia (in *Little Buddha* [1993]), Africa (in *Little Buddha* and *Besieged* [1998]), North Africa and the Middle East (in *The Sheltering Sky* [1990]).

Recent efforts to revive cinephilia, or to bring its enduring presence to light, have similarly appealed to a new globalism in film culture as a source of inspiration. The cinephiles of *The Dreamers* look back to a now-familiar canon, split between the films of Hollywood auteurs (*Scarface* [1932], *Blonde Venus* [1932], *Queen Christina* [1933], among others) and a handful of duly enshrined art films, particularly those of Godard (*Breathless* and *Band of Outsiders*). Especially from the vantage point of the present, what's most striking about this pantheon is its decidedly Euro-American bias; even its dual tracks reveal this mutual implication, the Hollywood films often bearing clear European associations (*Scarface* as proto-noir, *Blonde Venus* and *Queen Christina* directed by Europeans, Von Sternberg and Mamoulian) and the European ones showing Hollywood ties (via the influence of the American gangster film on Godard's movies). After the New Wave, French cinephilia turned toward an ascetic severity, represented by the devout high theory of *Cahiers du cinéma* in the 1970s; though these recon-structed cinephiles were as apt to scorn Hollywood as to celebrate it (see the *Cahiers* editors' essay on Ford's *Young Mr. Lincoln* [1939], widely reprinted), they operated from much the same canon. As represented in film, American cinephilia of the 1970s, only a pallid specter of that of the previous decade, migrated to the New Hollywood, which harked back to the New Wave in making its characters' film-watching habits a going concern. In that vein cinephilia functions to entomb a few dusty old Hollywood classics in the pale tributes of movies like *The Last Picture Show* (1971) or *Mean Streets* (1973). In its slightly more sophisticated versions, as in movies by Paul Mazursky or Woody Allen (growing out of a revived New York film culture surrounding the Bleecker Street Cinema and other inde-pendent art-houses), this cinephilia is still chiefly concerned with defining a canon that bridges a divide between 'high' and 'low' tastes. In Allen's films of the late 1970s, such as *Annie Hall* (1977) or *Manhattan* (1979), the pantheon runs from Ingmar Bergman and *The Sorrow and the Pity* (1969) to Groucho Marx and W. C. Fields – leaving the Euro-American axis squarely in place.

In *Movie Mutations: The Changing Face of World Cinephilia* (2003), edited by Jonathan Rosenbaum and Adrian Martin, a collective of contemporary critics and self-defined cinephiles attempt to track the evolution of cinephilia over the past decade or so. They conclude that the situation of the formerly most power-ful centers of production is dire indeed, but far from sounding the death knell, they find that this circumstance points to new directions in the development of film. In their view, cinephilia remains consolidated around ongoing projects of rediscovery and the constitution of an alternative canon that reflects an emerging (or already arrived) 'world' cinema. This pantheon includes, among others, a few holdovers from the New Wave and after, never quite given their due – Jacques Rivette, Jean Eustache, Chantal Akerman; a small number of contemporary Europeans, like the Hungarian Béla Tarr or the Portuguese Manoel de Oliveira; a few directors from Latin America, like the Chilean-born Raúl Ruiz; and a large number of filmmakers from Asia and South Asia, including Abbas Kiarostami and Jafar Panahi (from Iran), Wong Kar-wai (from Hong Kong), Edward Yang and Hou Hsiao-hsien (from Taiwan), and Yasuzo Masumura (from Japan).

Heartening as the greater pluralism of this list may be, the new cinephilia still conducts itself in a manner much in keeping with the old cinephilia. In large part, its project remains to discern the work of individual 'masters' (a category that remains very male) – only now they're Abel Ferrara and Olivier Assayas instead of Sam Fuller and Jean-Pierre Melville. What's more, the value of the work most admired is typically attributable to the extent to which it echoes the past products of a mainline auteurism, reverberations detected in the unlikeliest places. Panahi's *The Circle* (2000), for example, may be an incisive account of the politics of gender in contemporary Iran, but according to Jonathan Rosenbaum (among the key film critics of our time and an editor of *Movie Mutations*), one of its salient features is its resemblance to 'a punchy Warners proletarian-protest quickie of the '30s'. Masumura's work is treated over four lengthy sections of the book, meanwhile, less for its cultural specificity in a Japanese context than for its extensive parallels to the films of Howard Hawks.

As noted earlier, the cinephiles of the New Wave were sometimes accused of projecting their own cultural biases toward a modified Euro-modernism onto a very different sociocultural context, that of Hollywood, which they insufficiently understood – how else to explain their love of Jerry Lewis, went the programmatic complaint. Despite the global range of reference one finds in *Movie Mutations*, it is difficult to escape the impression that the real cultural differences it encompasses collapse, in the end, into a rather cozy universalism. This impression is fostered, for instance, when the Iranian master Kiarostami mouths ancient clichés about film as 'a universal language', though he above all should be cognizant of the stifling homogeneity such pieties have frequently generated when they have been put into practice.

What the new cinephiles have most in common with the old cinephiles, in fact, is their status as a quite delimited interpretive community, in which shared tastes and collective references define the terms of the discourse. *Movie Mutations* consists largely of exchanges of emails and letters conveying the correspondents' sense of themselves as an international cabal – they use the word themselves – and the 'personal' nature of these interactions is redolent of a self-styled movement in the making: They refer to one another, affectionately, as 'the mutants'. They represent a range of countries – the United States (Rosenbaum), Australia (Adrian Martin), Canada (Mark Peranson), France (Nicole Brenez), and even Argentina (Edouardo Antin), but though they are, of course, incomparably more international as a group than the *Cahiers du cinema* writers and New Wave directors, they still reflect among their number very little of the diversity of the multinational cinema they so admirably promote. To their credit, the contributors note this very aspect of their enterprise in a long concluding dialogue, but it is still worth asking to what extent this new cinephilia recasts its newly global pantheon in the vestigial terms of a lingering Euro-modernist auteurism.

Perhaps most striking about *Movie Mutations* is the commitment to intellectual rigor it sustains, at least rhetorically, even at its most personal. (In this these writers look back to the attitudes of 1970s' *Cahiers du cinéma* or *Screen* more than to the French cinephilia of the 1950s or 1960s.) The reconciliation these writers seek with the academy, for instance, despite their frequent hostility to it, may be what most palpably distinguishes this new cinephilia, because it is so much at odds with the belligerent intellectual rebelliousness of the New Wave cinephiles. The contributors to *Movie Mutations* speak from time to time of a longing for 'a cinema of the body', but they seem to be referring to the body as a figural presence rather than a carnal object. Though the work of the new masters they enshrine may be highly sensory in technical terms, with lovely visual textures and beautifully layered sound designs, its most typical samples are characterised by some form of asceticism, often an extreme one – as in the cases of de Oliveira or Kiarostami. In their advancement of cinema as cross-cultural communication, the lingua franca of the global age, these writers also turn away from the model of cinephilia as proprietary desire. By contrast to that ardent impulse of the earlier generation, these writers love the movies they love not so much because they apprehend them as somehow immediately theirs, but because they open up some access to spaces of 'otherness' which might thereby, in a sense, be duly repatriated.

For these reasons, and despite the parallels, the new cinephilia – if that's really what it is – is of a very different kind from its earlier counterparts. In fact, it is not really proper to speak, as above, of 'longing' on the part of these writers, for they appear to have repudiated a model of cinephilia as yearning intoxication, desirous and driven by appetites. Especially by comparison to their predecessors, they espouse a love of movies that is meticulous and sober – a cinephilia for grown-ups. Theirs is a cinephilia that is, in its way, *post*-voyeuristic, therefore blessedly free of the boorishness that often emerged from the hothouse boys' club of the New Wave. It no longer upholds the cinema as a simmering cauldron from which new identities might be promiscuously culled, even if it still cherishes the hope that film might have something urgent to do with the politics of culture, might even intervene crucially in the world's shifting geopolitical order. If Bertolucci's film memorialises cinephilia as a manifestation of youth that must be put aside in the onset of a longed-for but impossible maturity, then the cinephilia of *Movie Mutations* may be the best realisation of what can remain in that wake. A cinephile of the old school with affinities for the new dispensation, Peter Wollen recently defined cinephilia as 'a symptom of a desire to remain within a child's view of the world, always outside' (2002: 5). For better or worse, adulthood may be where cinephilia goes when it does *not* die.

But if cinephilia *is* dead, it may be because finally, in an odd way, it triumphed. What is left of film culture in the United States, after all, bears the legacy of a free-wheeling, film-generation-style cinephilia, not the influence of Stanley Kauffmann's wary, cautionary cavils. Though even his moment seems already to have passed, Quentin Tarantino – with his convulsive referentiality, his passive-aggressive framing of stylised sex and violence as the essence of movie love – is the quintessential director of a debased cinephilia, the ultimate video-store auteur. Young audiences don't typically get the references, but they know they're there, so the allusions function as a gauge of the movies' hipness. Like so much on the recent film scene, Tarantino's movies are designed for audiences wanting to be flattered for their knowingness, and DVDs decked out with directors' commentaries and a host of 'special features' similarly appeal to a consumerist desire to know – and the kids in *The Dreamers*, in their basic mannerisms and emotional styles, seem like the products of this atmosphere of self-satisfied knowingness more than they ever do of the culture of May '68. Cinephilia may have craved knowledge of the beloved, but this longing was, in part, conditioned on the unattainability of its object, an elusiveness that was what gave movies some of their mystic allure.

The proliferation in the last decades of so many new media through which films may be channeled – cable or satellite TV, the ceaseless diorama of the Internet, the winking Maxwell's Demon of the TiVo, ungainly cassettes or lithe, shimmering discs – would seem to have realised all the cinephile's proprietary dreams, but in fact it puts an end to fantasies of film as a dimension of nymphean love, and maybe for that reason to cinephilia itself. To the extent that these new media make more movies more available to more people than ever before, they surely foment cinephilia on a mass scale; but to the extent that they function to process and package movies, they are just another stage in the advanced commodity fetishism of the digital era. The age of mechanical reproduction was supposed to have already robbed art of its aura, but it took these new avenues of access, diminishing that faint nimbus to the vanishing point once and for all, to prove how much there had really been still to be stripped away. Converting the obsession with movies into a worldwide racket, a network of global trade, they reduced the cultism of cinephilia to a plebeian ware in a multinational marketplace. It is clear in retrospect that the *aura* of movies was exactly what cinephiles had cherished, and though their love was certainly a form of fetishism, what they wanted was to possess the movies – not to own them.

REFERENCES

Godard, Jean-Luc (1988 [1973]) 'Jean-Luc Godard to François Truffaut' in *François Truffaut Letters*. Eds. Gilles Jacob and Claude de Givay; Trans. and Ed. of English edition Gilbert Adair. London: Faber and Faber, 383–4.

Rosenbaum, Jonathan and Adrian Martin (eds) (2003) *Movie Mutations: The Changing Face of World Cinephilia*. London: British Film Institute.

Sontag, Susan (1996) 'The Decay of Cinema', *New York Times Magazine*, 25 February, 60–1.

Truffaut, François (1988 [1973]) 'To Jean-Luc Godard', in *François Truffaut Letters*. Eds. Gilles Jacob and Claude de Givay; Trans. and Ed. of English edition Gilbert Adair. London: Faber and Faber, 385–91.

Wollen, Peter (2002) *Paris Hollywood: Writings on Film*. London: Verso.

CHAPTER TWO

THE VIRTUAL SPACES OF CIVIL RIGHTS
Steve Spence

As Lev Manovich observes in his groundbreaking volume *The Language of New Media*, our various digital devices continue to shape experience long after they have been powered off: 'As we work with software and use the operations embedded within it, these operations become part of how we understand ourselves, others, and the world. Strategies of working with computer data become our general cognitive strategies' (2002: 118). To test that thesis, in the following pages I examine our changing relationships with the pre-digital past, focusing on examples drawn from the archive of the US civil rights movement – the miraculous struggle, between about 1954 and 1968, that reshaped the social order of the United States and much of the world.[1] Here I concentrate on genres and venues that are rarely considered by digital media scholars: an HBO film, an animated television special, three existing heritage museums, and one proposed but never realised museum. Although few of my examples make overt use of digital technologies, together they offer insight into the ways that digitisation transcodes our archives and transforms our historical experience. All the examples attempt to reanimate memories of the civil rights movement, and all thus demonstrate a common yearning to bring the past and present together. All work to create these virtual meeting points in ways revealing a changing relationship to historical knowledge. And, finally, all enact formal strategies that tell us a great deal about what is 'new' about new media.

Any attempt to represent the civil rights movement today is complicated by the fact that it was the first revolution to be televised. The movement was born simultaneously with the television industry that covered it, and numerous accounts have chronicled their complex and interdependent development.[2] As Sasha Torres summarises:

> Telejournalism, obviously, needed vivid pictures and clear-cut stories; less obviously, it also sought political and cultural *gravitas*. For its part, the civil rights movement staked the moral authority of Christian nonviolence and the rhetoric of American democracy to make a new national culture; to succeed, it needed to have its picture taken and its stories told. (2003: 15)

Figure 1: The March on Washington for Jobs and Freedom, 28 August 1963.
Photograph by U.S. Information Agency.

But even in the crush of history as it happened, observers recognised that television communicated more than simply an aggregation of pictures and stories. Shortly after more than 200,000 peaceful protestors gathered around the Lincoln

Memorial in Washington, DC, for example, *New York Times* correspondent Jack Gould noted:

> The medium of television is proving an indispensable force in the Negro's pursuit of human rights. Through the home screen the Washington drama of mass protest was brought to life in virtually every household in the nation, a social phenomenon inconceivable before the age of electronics. And the unforgettable stroll of 200,000 persons down Constitution Avenue, welded together in relaxed determination, was something that had to be seen to be felt. The gentle entrance and exit of so much petitioning humanity was an editorial in movement. Its eloquence could not be the same in only frozen word or stilled picture. (1963: X15)

Something new was at work in this encounter between mass audience and mass movement, and, as this passage suggests, its proper analysis requires an approach like phenomenology. Working in concert, hundreds of thousands created an animate, corporeal rhetoric, and this 'editorial in movement' found expression only through the engaged perceptions of an audience tuned in to screens dispersed throughout millions of households. The insight captures an essential facet of the movement's strategy of mediated, nonviolent resistance, which has been imprecisely called 'nonviolent theater'.[3] It also dovetails with the phenomenological description of television offered by media critic Derrick de Kerchhove, who argues that televisual perception is a tactile, haptic experience: 'We understand moving spectacular experiences through submuscular integration … we see that which we observe *with our whole body*, and not only with our eyes' (quoted in Hansen 2004: 231–2; emphasis added). Mark Hansen's gloss develops the point: 'The affective body does not so much see as *feel* the space of the film; it feels it, moreover, as an energized, haptic spatiality within itself' (2004: 232). To be sure, these undifferentiated descriptions of 'television' and 'film' risk a flattening abstraction. Different kinds of motion pictures engage different kinds of viewers in multiple and different ways.[4] Nonetheless, given the intensity of the passions aroused by the movement's mediated appeals – ranging from spiritual revelation to homicidal mania to visceral revulsion – no analysis of its immediate effects or subsequent representations can neglect their affective, bodily dimensions. Certainly this is true of any attempt to grasp the extraordinary powers of the movement's most eloquent spokesperson, Martin Luther King Jr, and the complex legacies of the textual, audio, and video archive within which these powers are inscribed.

Like most geniuses, King's talents are easy to recognise but hard to define. Perhaps the best description of his ineffable powers appears in an interview with Rufus Lewis of the Montgomery Improvement Association, the organisation that transformed King from freshman minister into movement leader:

> It's very hard for an ordinary person to describe Reverend King's speaking ability … He could make you feel what he was saying as well as hearing what he was saying. He was sincere and dedicated, and he could lift you out your seat. You couldn't just be quiet. It was such a stirring thing that it would affect you. It would just go right through you. (Hampton 2006)

The affective and synaesthetic effects described here link King to a long ministerial tradition. As Cornel West has argued, King was an organic intellectual – the son and grandson of preachers, he was immersed from birth in the centuries old traditions of the African American church (1988: 3–21). It was this crucible, clearly, that most deeply shaped King's mastery of the ancient arts of oratory and rhetoric. But it is one thing to electrify a Sunday-morning congregation in Montgomery, Alabama, and another to evoke outpourings of emotion – and concrete action – from a global television audience numbered in the millions (see Spence 2011). While King's special genius lay in his ability to do both, identifying the wellsprings of this ability requires a shift away from hagiography. As Robert Parris Moses has observed, King was a wave within the ocean that was the movement: 'Let us shift our attention from the wave to the ocean, because the wave is not the ocean. Even it it's a tidal wave, it has no meaning apart from the ocean … That's what has to be studied to get a deeper understanding about who and what Dr. King was' (1990: 73).

Contrary to popular remembrance, King often followed the civil rights movement rather than led it. As biographer Taylor Branch notes, in 1960 and 1961 King watched while the vanguard of the movement took enormous personal risks and endured vicious assaults, at a time when King occupied himself with speaker's tours and church politics (2006: 249–51). This vanguard – mostly college students, many of whom later formed the core of the Student Nonviolent Coordinating Committee (SNCC) – pioneered sit-ins and freedom rides, strategies that depended on the provocation and endurance of unmerited suffering.[5] 'And although he was honest enough to praise the students' courage King repeatedly declined the drumbeat summons – "Where is your body?" – by which they made the first test of leadership not statements or seniority but a stark, primitive surrender to public witness' (Branch 2006: 25). As Branch also notes, by the end of 1961 King's physical detachment ended. He launched himself into campaigns of civil disobedience, repeatedly putting his body on the line alongside rank-and-file activists. By the end of his life, King defined the very engine of historical progress, a power he called 'soul force', as the energy created 'when people of goodwill put their bodies and their souls in motion' (1998: 219). In short, King embraced the tenet implicit in the SNCC summons: that bodies and souls could not be separated, and that bodily experience was an inescapable part of movement toward social justice.

Like King's broader intellectual life, the key concept of soul force is multi-layered, drawing from disparate traditions that include Mohandas Gandhi's philosophy of *Satyagraha* as well as the richly textured meanings of 'soul' within African-American religious and secular culture. In all its many valences, however, soul force offers a fundamental critique of two dualisms that dominated the ideology of King's time and place: the Cartesian elevation of mind over body and the Liberal primacy of individual over community. From the African Baptist tradition, King drew on the examples of generations of preachers, sustainers and reformers, who nourished and challenged their flocks to make whole lives even within the midst of appalling brutality (see Lischer 1995: 28–37). From these traditions King drew an understanding of human society – indeed, of all God's creation – that set him apart from the liberal intellectuals that he otherwise admired.[6] For King, the congregation, rather than the individual, was the agent of God at work within history, and it was in the pews and in the streets that the Word of God became flesh (see Lischer 1995: 219).

This understanding of historical agency as both incarnate and communitarian led King to embrace the sustenance offered by the movement's participatory, performative rituals – freedom song, mass meetings, mass marches, and the 'jail – no bail' ethos of bodily witness. It also enabled him to recognise, far sooner than most, that the televisual mediation of these rituals also carried transformative power. In short, the nation's emerging televisual infrastructure opened channels into its sensorium, and it put bodies and souls in motion. Although it is an overstatement to claim (as Marshall McLuhan did) that television created the movement, its audio-visual archive today offers more than simply a record of events long past. Instead, the archive contains a *vital* part of the movement, in both key senses of that term. While popular historiography often promises unmediated encounters with the material and the carnate – promising viewers and visitors a return to history's presence – the texts analyzed below all struggle to reflect the fact that the movement's archive itself carries an animating power and that this power is central to the stories they wish to tell.

In the HBO film *Boycott* (2001) this problem expresses itself through a kind of stylistic exuberance. In many ways a straightforward biopic, *Boycott* presents the story of the 1956 bus boycott in Montgomery, Alabama, and its narrative centers on the development of the 26-year-old King from novice minister to movement icon. On the DVD commentary, director Clark Johnson describes *Boycott* as simply 'a love letter to Martin and Coretta', and the film depends primarily on the conventions of cinematic realism: actors playing historical characters re-enact historical events. Stylistically, however, *Boycott* also manifests a self-reflexive effort to bring contemporary sensibilities to this fifty-year-old story. The film's texture is variegated, mixing feature-film-style footage, archival documentary footage, staged documentary footage, staged 8mm home movies, anachronistic inserts, and composites of different perspectival and subjective spaces within single frames. Manovich usefully designates such heterogeneous mixtures 'stylistic montage'; as he notes, similar approaches stretch back to the painterly collage of the 1920s (2002: 159). Indeed, most of *Boycott*'s visual effects could have been achieved before the advent of digital editing in the 1990s. However, as Manovich also notes, only in the 1990s did stylistic montage become a common language among new media objects. *Boycott*'s innovation is to use this emerging language to stage new kinds of encounters with and experiences of the movement's audio-visual archive. As detailed below, this archive's influences are felt even within *Boycott*'s conventionally staged and scripted scenes. Valerie Smith has noted that the film's complex form prompts viewers 'to consider the role of the imagination in (re)constructing history' (2005: 536). I would add that *Boycott*'s stylistic complexity also prompts consideration of media's role in constructing and reconstructing the movement.

These tensions are condensed within a key moment in *Boycott*, when King's emotional response to the bombing of his home breaks the film's fourth wall. The events building up to this moment are conveyed through two inter-cut scenes, each carrying distinct stylistic markers: Martin King attends an evening meeting, lit flatly and shot with a shaky, handheld camera that repeatedly zooms, re-frames, and blurs focus; Coretta King, at home, is bathed in cinematic light and followed by fluid tracking shots. When the bomb explodes, Coretta runs in slow motion toward their daughter's nursery, and a messenger breaks into the mass meeting to carry the news to Martin. The camera operator follows the messenger as he rushes toward King, and the camera then attempts to frame King in close-up, evoking a journalist's or documentarian's effort to capture news as it happens. The shot is thwarted by King, played by Jeffrey Wright, who grabs the lens and pushes the camera out of his way as he strides past it.

The sequence constructs a contrast between public and private space, as well as between a public and private King. As movement leader, King encourages media coverage; as a husband and father whose family is at risk, he stiff-arms it. But *Boycott*'s corporeal encounter between actor and camera suggests more than this simple opposition. The camera acts also as the viewer's perceptival surrogate,[7] and King's gesture give this surrogate a physicality that is rigorously excluded from traditional Hollywood style. In other words, the character's physical repudiation of the camera, paradoxically, makes both it and the audience all the more present within the profilmic space. This sense of physical presence is reinforced in the following scene, which takes place in front of King's house. An angry crowd has formed, and they threaten to retaliate violently against the bombers. As the camera weaves through the crowd, they and it acknowledge one another. The camera responds to threats and gestures from the crowd – zooming, re-framing, re-focusing, and shifting positions – seemingly without a predetermined plan. Members of the crowd hide weapons when they find themselves within the camera's range, and, when it tries to follow King into his house, a police officer first blocks the way bodily and then blocks the lens with his hand. A cut then takes us into the warmly-lit and conventionally-shot interior of the Kings' home, but we soon return to the vertiginous, chaotic space of the crowd. And soon the film shifts again into a direct address soliloquy offered by one of the police officers on the scene, shot with a static camera and in grainy black-and-white. Similar soliloquies appear multiple times in *Boycott*; in style they echo the first-person interviews that formed a staple of television documentaries like NBC's 'Sit In' (prod. Robert Young 1960) and CBS's 'Who Speaks for Birmingham?' (prod. David Lowe 1961).

Repeatedly, *Boycott* borrows tropes from nonfiction filmmaking and, more specifically, from the movement's audio-visual archive, using them to locate viewers within an ambiguous space that telescopes past and present. These efforts are *Boycott*'s most characteristic gesture since the film often does so by miming the movement's archival record. In other cases, however, *Boycott* mobilises habits of body and mind that have been more directly inculcated by digital media.

The most telling example of this appears at the film's end. In the penultimate scene, King elects to remain behind as the other leaders take a celebratory ride in the front seats of a city bus. A shot of King through the bus's back window dissolves into the final scene of the film, which depicts the historical King walking down a street in twenty-first century, downtown Atlanta. The scene does not rely on special effects or aggressive editing, and its camerawork is straightforward. Nevertheless, its smooth blending of 1950s Montgomery and contemporary urban space creates a moment of temporal and spatial complexity. The scene's unstable, ambiguous space begins with its establishing shot – a slow tilt down the mirrored glass windows of a multi-story office building. The scene was staged in downtown Atlanta, between the Fulton County Courthouse and a historic church located across the street. This set-up isolates the church's reflection in the courthouse's mirrored glass, and the disorientation that results is twofold. As the shot dissolves into view, the audience first recognises the gothic stone façade as a church. We then resolve the grid of window frames, and only then do we understand that what we are seeing is actually a reflection. This spatial reorientation creates a temporal conflict, since an office building of this size and architectural style does not fit into the world of 1950s Montgomery within which we have been immersed. Viewers are thus called upon to actively process a complex series of spatial and temporal shifts, reorienting ourselves within a very different world – one in which Martin Luther King walks the streets of a contemporary city.

Bringing King bodily into our present suggests many things, including the profound debt that we owe to him and the movement as a whole, which created the world that we see in this final scene. King's sudden reappearance also evokes a sense of loss, grief for the activist who was murdered when he was just 39 years old, and also, I think, a sense of durable hope. This composite of past and present suggests that King continues to have a place in contemporary life – continues to have something to tell us and teach us – a fact that today is often disputed both within the African-American community and in American culture at large.[8]

To create these affects, the film builds a formal structure that also tells us something about contemporary perception. *Boycott*'s spatial merger of church and office building, and its temporal merger of 1956 and 2001, can best be described as a live-action composite. The description highlights the scene's similarities with digital compositing in the broader sense. Digital compositing, of course, is the computer operation that blends two or more discrete digital objects. Yet compositing is more than just one of the fundamental operations of new media. As we become accustomed to copy-and-paste operations in computer-based work and leisure, we learn new ways of thinking and new ways of interacting with the world outside the computer screen. The fluid space-time of *Boycott* suggests an emerging re-visioning of history, one that reveals the effects of compositing – and digital media more generally – on bodily experience. In other words, the choice to locate the historic, corporeal King in the streets of a contemporary city reflects a new flexibility in our felt relationships with space and time. The film mobilises this new experience to trigger an affective response to make Martin Luther King real for us.

It also recalls, inevitably, director Robert Zemeckis's *Forrest Gump* (1994), the Hollywood film that popularised similar blendings of 1960s past and digital present. Famously, the film used digital compositing to locate its A-list star, Tom Hanks, within the scenes and spaces of iconic figures from the 1960s, including John Lennon, three US presidents, and Alabama governor George Wallace. As Katherine Kinney has noted, the film works diligently to stitch together these temporal impossibilities, using careful crosscutting in the Wallace scene, for example, to fuse 1963 Tuscaloosa and 1994 Hollywood into a single continuous time and space, 'in the most literal minded representation of historical continuity imaginable' (2003: 381). The archival footage documents Wallace fulfilling his pledge 'to stand in the schoolhouse door' in order to block the entrance of black students into the University of Alabama. The governor's attempt at political theater is stagy and awkward, and the filmmakers selected this ham-handed moment, I believe, precisely because it would appear ridiculous to most contemporary audiences. The incongruous appearance of Hanks's famous face underscores the moment's silly artificiality, and the audience is in on the joke. Kinney and others have emphasised the politically regressive vocation evident throughout *Forrest Gump*'s re-editing of the 1960s, including its symptomatic exclusion of King from its roll call of assassinated leaders (see Byers 1996; Gabilondo 2000).

These critiques are persuasive, but it is also worth noting that all of Hanks's digital teleportations locate him within media events with already ambiguous relationships to reality. Hanks's appearances lampoon D. W. Griffith's *Birth of a Nation*'s (1915) claims to historical fidelity as well as Wallace's clumsy stagecraft, and his character's good-natured bumbling likewise disrupts three presidential photo-ops. His final insertion is an appearance on the *Dick Cavitt Show*, a literally made-for-TV moment. In this context, the filmmakers' decision to film, and then cut, Forrest Gump's encounter with Martin Luther King reveals something both about the movement's televisual strategies and also about the subsequent career of its archive.

A two-disc DVD released in 2001 includes the incomplete fragments of Hanks's digital encounter with King and other leaders of the Southern Christian Leadership Conference (SCLC), during what Forrest delightedly misidentifies as 'a parade'. The archival footage chosen as the scene's raw material documents a street confrontation between these leaders and Birmingham Police Commissioner Eugene 'Bull' Connor. This, too, was a made-for-TV moment: the SCLC labeled the final phase of the Birmingham campaign 'Project C', for confrontation, and during and after this campaign the organisation devised a number of 'innovative publicity techniques that placed the press, and particularly television, at the center of the organization's planning and strategies' (Torres 2003: 30). Like most of *Forrest Gump*'s other digital interventions, the title character enters this historical space and good-naturedly mucks thing up. When loosed police dogs charge the marchers, Forrest rushes into the scene, calls the dogs, plays rambunctiously with them, and then throws a stick that they follow off screen. The resulting deflation of tensions is played for a joke – or would have been, if the scene had made the final cut. The fact that it did not, I believe, reflects an inassimilable kernel carried within the movement's archive.

In the decades that followed, both King and the movement in general have been recuperated as figures of peaceful, loving reconciliation. The price of this popularity has been a widespread submersion of the challenges still posed by nonviolent resistance. Largely overlooked today, also, is the breadth of the movement's historical opposition. When SCLC ministers sent children as young as six into the streets to face police dogs and fire hoses, when militant pacifists absorbed savage beatings and then proclaimed from their hospital beds that they would die rather than stop, when the movement worked tirelessly to stage spectacles of violence for the national and international media – its claims to moral authority drew outraged refutations not just from the Ku Klux Klan, but also from the *New York Times* editorial board, the Nation of Islam, and the Kennedy administration. In the midst of the Birmingham campaign, for example, Bobby Kennedy issued a not-so-veiled threat: 'School children participating in street demonstrations is a dangerous business. An injured, maimed, or dead child is a price that none of us can afford to pay' (quoted in Branch 2006: 762). The movement, of course, persevered, and its moral authority is now as widely acknowledged as it is imperfectly understood. Forrest Gump's intervention in Birmingham did not work as entertainment because it raised an uncomfortable fact about the movement: the character's guileless deflation of this mediated confrontation undermined the combative, provocative strategy of nonviolent resistance.

Nevertheless, despite the challenges that the movement offers to core American ideologies like individualism and rational self-interest, its artifacts continue to exert a strong bodily attraction, evident in the ontological montage short-circuited in *Forrest Gump* and successfully enacted in *Boycott*.[9] Five years after *Forrest Gump* dropped King from its version of the 1960s, an animated television special tried again, this time turning ontological montage to the purposes of 'edutainment'. *Our Friend Martin* (1999), directed by Rob Smiley and Vincenzo Trippetti, is intended to introduce children to King's life and teachings. Through the conceit of a magical baseball glove, contemporary children travel into the past, and King himself visits present-day Atlanta. Like *Boycott*, *Our Friend Martin* montages fictional scenes and archival footage and, like both *Boycott* and *Forrest Gump*, it depends on the pleasures of ontological montage. For example, when the children return from their time-traveling journey to the streets of Birmingham, they participate in a classroom discussion about civil rights. They, and we, then watch a video presentation of the historic news footage, but with a twist: the animated children are composited into the live-action footage. Although *Our Friend Martin* is not a particularly successful example of the genre, there are real pleasures to be found in such multimodal experiences, similar to those offered by the theme park attractions tied to Hollywood franchise films. And, in fact, *Our Friend Martin* represents one component of a plan to create similarly diverse experiences of King's life and legacy. In 1994 King's youngest son, Dexter, unveiled a proposal for a $50million, multi-building complex modeled on Disney-MGM Studios in Florida. The incoming CEO of the King Center in Atlanta, Dexter King called this the 'Martin Luther King, Jr. Time Machine and Interactive Museum' and announced that it would use holographic projections and virtual reality games to immerse museum-goers within the key moments and spaces of his father's life (see Pousner 1994: C1). King's proposals included the children's program that became *Our Friend Martin* and, as the 'time machine' in the museum's title suggests, he saw both projects as part of a broader effort to brand, leverage, and cross-promote his family's intellectual property. Much as they now go to theme parks to 'ride the movies', King imagined that children who saw *Our Friend Martin* would come to Atlanta primed to 'ride the movement' – to immerse themselves within an interactive, digital environment.

Unfortunately for the plan's realisation, by 1995 Dexter King had become a lightning rod for criticism of the family's stewardship (see Sack 1997; Fears

2002). Critics dismissed the museum as one more attempt to commercialise the elder King's legacy. Atlanta newspaper columnist Cynthia Tucker labeled the proposal 'I Have a Dreamland', and the family's plan was shelved in favor of a more conventional visitor's center (1997: G4). Nevertheless, Dexter King's proposal demonstrates that he is an avid student of contemporary culture and media.[10] However fantastic, the 'Time Machine and Interactive Museum' reflects new engagements that link bodily experience and the media archive. These forces are also evident in the facility that replaced the family's vision for the site, the visitor's center for the King National Historic district in Atlanta, completed by the US Parks Service in 1996.

The center was designed by Ralph Applebaum Associates of New York, a firm that specialises in the creation of interpretive museums. Their portfolio includes the US Holocaust Memorial Museum in Washington and the American Natural History Museum in New York. The King Visitors Center is small by Applebaum standards; it consists of six multimedia kiosks that are arranged around a central installation. The six kiosks each incorporate video, audio, photographs, historical artifacts, built, low-relief simulations – King's jail cell in Birmingham, for example – and text. In a roughly chronological sequence, they sketch the milieu and major events of King's life, culminating with the 1968 march of striking garbage workers in Memphis, which was led by Coretta Scott King in the days after her husband was murdered.

Notably absent in this celebration of King's life and legacy is a life-sized figure of King himself.[11] Instead, the six kiosks surround a 30ft-long installation called 'Freedom Road'. The installation's base is sloped and painted to resemble blacktop, and a yellow striped line is painted down its center. On this road are life-sized mannequins representing eight marchers. Their features resemble those of actual participants in the movement, but the figures are rendered in monochrome shades of beige and brown and, within the installation, they remain unnamed. Visitors are invited to mount the platform and walk among the figures, joining the marchers on Freedom Road.

Although few would call it new media, 'Freedom Road' shares important similarities with many common applications of digital media, which are often described as immersive and interactive. In contrast to traditional memorial statuary, the installation does not elevate the figure of an iconic Great Man above the lived spaces of ordinary people; it is installed at ground level and celebrates the everyday people who served as the movement's foot soldiers. Visitors are encouraged to enter the field of the human figures, with the experience unfolding as they move among them. The installation reflects the inverse of the strategy pursued by *Boycott*. Rather than inserting King bodily into our twenty-first-century reality, 'Freedom Road' instead invites us to enter the space of history. And like both *Boycott* and Dexter King's time machine, the installation evokes the past through the creation of a virtual space (an impossible space), which it nevertheless invites to us to enter into and experience.

The built environments in the National Civil Rights Museum (NCRM) in Memphis reveal similar and even more ambitious efforts to create amalgams of mediated past and embodied present.[12] This can best be seen in the gallery depicting the 1963 campaign to end segregation in the shopping districts of Birmingham, one of the movement's most significant victories,[13] and, not coincidentally, the source of some of its most compelling images.

The narrow, L-shaped gallery is dominated by a built simulation of a storefront, complete with plate-glass windows and canvas awnings. A narrow sidewalk runs along the storefront, and the rest of the room's flooring has been treated to resemble asphalt. A newspaper machine, fireplug, and streetlight are positioned along the sidewalk, and a puddle of simulated water surrounds the hydrant. Visitors enter the gallery facing the store and exit around its corner.

While in the gallery, we are immersed within some of the movement's most recognizable images. The storefront's frosted glass 'windows' in fact serve as video screens. A projector runs continuously behind the glass, illuminating the windows with footage from the street confrontations between Bull Connor's police dogs, water canons, and the young protestors of May 1963. Audio effects add diegetic sound, including crowd and traffic noise, water, sirens, and movement song, some serving as background noise and some synched to particular images (for example dogs barking, car doors slamming shut). Unlike the quiet, orderly spaces encountered in other galleries, the 'Project C' room's frenetic sounds and images, combined with careful design choices, envelop visitors within the chaotic spaces depicted in the audio-visual archive.

Key to this effect is a simple addition to the wall opposite the store's window/screens. This wall wraps around the L-shaped storefront and displays objects similar to those offered in other galleries: newspaper facsimiles, photographs, and small artifacts. Unlike other galleries, however, the 'Project C' wall is composed of large, mirrored panels. As visitors examine the various items on these walls, we simultaneously experience the reflections of our own bodies in the mirrors. At the same time, we are positioned between the projection screen and *its* mirrored reflections, and are thereby situated within the continuously running footage. A composite is created of bodily image, built simulation, and archival footage – and the result is both unexpected and riveting. As we experience the reflected image of ourselves in the 'street' outside the 'store', we are also simultaneously both within and without the scenes depicted in the footage. Important to their effect, for most visitors these black-and-white images will feel familiar. Bull Connor's rumpled suit and snarling police dogs, children knocked off their feet by blasts of water, and others frolicking in the spray – these are part of a collective, visual memory. And yet now they flow before and behind us, juxtaposed with our own mirrored image, and unmoored from the rectilinear screen that bounded their previous appearance.

These images belong to history. We have encountered them, perhaps have been moved by them, and have then stored them away within mental frameworks marked by past-ness and distance. Their return, here, creates an uncanny space – both familiar and strange, carrying the charge of both reality and dream. In a perceptive reading of a similar video installation, Bruce Brasell investigates its effects on the experience of the incorporated footage:

> The display operates on a purely visceral level, transforming the mass media image into an 'art' object, thereby offering an aesthetic experience. Yet this aestheticization does not weaken these images but rather transforms their power from a cognitive one with informational reverberations to an affective one with emotional resonance. (2004: 3)

Surely our viscera are at work, both within the installation that Brasell reads and the one described above. I do not believe, however, that the distinctions between mass media and art, between information and emotion, are as neat as Brasell's passage suggests. When they appeared on television screens in 1963, these images carried the charge of the real.[14] They moved bodies and souls, minds and guts. The happy effect of these installations is to return to us some sense of this historical experience.

All the projects that appear as examples here – all efforts to bodily engage the movement – continue a process identified by Walter Benjamin in his famous 'Work of Art in the Age of Mechanical Reproduction', which is founded on the insight that human sense perception is shaped by historical circumstances as well as by natural ones. The avid response of mass audiences to the photographic media of his time, Benjamin argues, reflects a changing sensibility, marking the advent of a perception 'whose "sense of the universal equality of things" has increased to such a degree that it extracts it even from a unique object by means of reproduction' (1968: 223). This is most visible in the changing status of traditional art objects, which lose their quasi-religious aura – a sense of distance that cannot be overcome – and instead enter into the ongoing process of 'adjustment of reality to the masses and of the masses to reality' (ibid.). This decline of aura, Benjamin suggests, is manifest in the desires of contemporary audiences to bring the objects of perception into close, bodily proximity. Benjamin's insight bears directly on the movement's attempts to create televisual affect, as well as contemporary efforts to locate audiences within the spaces of its historical experience. In bringing Benjamin to bear on the mediation of the US civil rights movement, however, I wish to emphasise a facet of the 'artwork essay' that is often neglected. Benjamin wrote as a committed (if unconventional) Marxist, and he saw nothing inherently progressive in the historical processes that he describes. For Benjamin, the new desires of mass audiences mark a *potentially* emancipatory moment within the otherwise corrosive effects of capitalist commodification. These desires can also be turned to other accounts, and other recent representations of the civil rights movement underscore this unhappy fact.

In 2001, for example, television audiences were offered a new image of the March on Washington, one that transformed the familiar two-dimensional archive into an uncanny, three-dimensional space. Created by the Hollywood special-effects house Industrial Light and Magic (ILM), the black-and-white footage opens with a shot of King standing at a podium on the steps of the Lincoln Memorial. Unlike the iconic footage, however, here King stands alone; the dozens of fellow speakers and leaders who shared the platform in 1963 have been digitally excised. The (virtual) camera then tracks around King, using 3D modeling to take viewers into a new, and impossible, proximity to King's body. This camera move disturbs on several levels, but overwhelmingly because it reveals that King now speaks to nobody – the hundreds of thousands who converged on the Mall that day have disappeared. This re-visioning of the movement has an unlikely motivation. It was commissioned by the telecommunications company Alcatel, and used in a commercial that introduced US consumers to the company's brand of networking appliances. Like King, the voiceover explains, Alcatel 'connects'. Here, then, is an effort quite literally to commodify the movement. The commercial collapses the March on Washington into a fetishistic celebration of the heroic individual and then aligns its shrink-wrapped wares with this leader's ability to 'touch', 'inspire', and 'connect'. The 200,000 or so who actually embodied the march have been evacuated from the scene, their three-dimensional fullness collapsed into a hypertrophied image of the great man.

The commercial's appropriation of King's legacy provoked public controversy, and it was probably meant to do just that. Asked to respond to widespread criticism of the campaign, an Alcatel vice president told reporters, 'We began the campaign with almost no awareness. Now we're water cooler talk … From a branding perspective, we couldn't be more pleased' (quoted in McCarthy 2001). In other words, the exploitation of King's image helped Alcatel break through the advertising white noise that surrounds US consumers. Whatever its motivations, however, ILM's re-visioning of the March on Washington did prove fascinating to contemporary audiences. Like the other examples cited above, the commercial reflects a widespread bodily desire to return to the spaces of the movement. My final example enacts a similar desire to enter the March on Washington, and it demonstrates a more progressive effort to take up the movement's legacies.

The Birmingham Civil Rights Institute (BCRI), opened in 1992, sits adjacent to Kelley Ingram Park and the 16th Street Baptist Church, ground zero for the great traumas endured and triumphs achieved by the movement in 1963.[15] Like the NCRM in Memphis, the institute serves, in part, as a tourist attraction. Its permanent exhibition – combining artifacts, built installations, and multimedia presentations – chronicles the movement's pre-history, its key events, and its international legacies. The galleries devoted to the movement itself are punctuated by four 'mini-theatres', each built around a single- or multi-channel video installation. These installations recount the Freedom Rides, voter registration drives, the 'Project C' Birmingham campaign, and the March on Washington. Each installation incorporates archival news footage from the movement's 'feet in the street' campaigns: picket lines, sit-ins, demonstrations, and marches.

The final mini-theater, called 'The March', is built around a single-channel video presentation of footage from the March on Washington. The March's status as a media event is emphasised: viewers pass a two-story, illuminated facsimile of a *Washington Post* front page to enter a room painted with murals created from news photographs. The space is organised around a large video screen set into one of the walls, which plays a video compilation of excerpts from King's closing address, remembered today as the 'I Have a Dream' speech. This final mini-theater functions as a kind of endpoint for the exhibition as a whole, and the video's content reinforces this sense of closure. Viewers are thereby encouraged to interpret King's famous speech as a kind of culmination, both of the historical movement and of the exhibition itself. The effect is reinforced when visitors leave the mini-theater: we enter a large, open room with windows, a change in the built environment that signals the end of the self-contained immersive spaces of the exhibition. Visitors soon shift focus to the here and now, either moving to the windows to look outside, following signs to the building's exit, or continuing on to a separate exhibition devoted to human rights movements in other times and places.

However, as we first enter this open, windowed room, visitors encounter one final installation which complicates this sense of closure, creating a liminal space that blends the archival footage in 'The March' with the corporeal existence of museum-goers. The effect begins with the end of the mini-theater's video. Immediately following its climactic ending, a *dénouement* presents footage shot in the March's aftermath – demonstrators are seen breaking down chairs, saying goodbyes, and walking singly and in groups away from the site. We leave the mini-theater with these images fresh in our minds, and we turn the corner to find ourselves on a path shared by eight life-size mannequins, rendered in monochrome grey. Dubbed 'The Processional' by the exhibition's designers, the figures depict a diverse array of people, varied in age, race, clothing, gender, and physical ability.[16] Most face outward, toward the windows; some turn toward their fellow marchers, offering gestures of support and encouragement. The marchers seen in the video's *dénouement*, then, are suddenly incarnate in three dimensions, and oriented so that visitors walk with them as we leave the exhibition. We are

Figure 2: 'The Processional'. Photograph courtesy of the Birmingham Civil Rights Institute.

thus encouraged to blend our mediated experience of the March on Washington with our immediate experience of the exhibition, carrying the inspiration of these encounters with the movement into the rest of our lives.

NOTES

1   Dating the movement is itself a tendentious act. Martin Luther King, Jr's dominance within both popular and scholarly histories results in the familiar 'Montgomery to Memphis' narrative stretching from 1955 to 1968. This neglects the organised activism of the US Communist Party in the 1930s and the NAACP in the 1940s and 1950s, and it also overstates the split between the movement's southern phases and the northern, as well as Black Power movements that remained vibrant well into the 1970s. Scholarship on the movement is voluminous, but among comprehensive accounts Taylor Branch's epic, three-volume series remains influential, if not definitive. For scholarly assessments of its strengths and limitations, see 'AHR Forum' (2009). Among King's many scholarly biographers, Garrow (1986) and Fairclough (1987) are probably the most frequently cited.

2   Notable scholarly accounts of the movement/television nexus include Torres (2003), Hunt (2005), Acham (2005), and chapter one of Donovan and Scherer (1992). A list of memoirs by early television workers is available in Torres (2003: 112; n.5). Relevant

studies that take up the movement's relations to journalistic media more generally include Lentz (1990), Johnson (2007), Murphree (2003), Hon (1997), and Ward (2001). This last includes an important essay by Julian Bond, Student Nonviolent Coordinating Committee (SNCC) communication director.

3   The phrase was coined by Adam Fairclough who used it to characterise the particular tactics and strategies developed by one arm of the movement, the Southern Christian Leadership Conference (SCLC). The phrase is apt in that 'theater' emphasises the enacted, bodily dramas that SCLC sought to create through its campaigns of nonviolent resistance. It misses, however, both the performative nature of performance and the fluid blendings of these dramas with their technological reproduction. The work of dancer, performance artist, and theorist Susan Kozel is relevant here. On performance, Kozel cites Rosalyn Diprose: 'Identity is actualised as is it performed, rather than being caused by an inner essence identity is open to disruption' (2007: 73). And on technology, Kozel cites avant-garde theater director Tim Etchells: 'What I am saying is that you have to think about technology, you have to use it, because in the end it is in your blood. Technology will move in and speak through you, like it or not. Best not to ignore' (2007: 67)

4   Vivian Sobchack, for example, distinguishes among the different effects of photography, cinema, and electronic media on the sensory coordinates that shape human experience: 'Each technology not only differently mediates our figurations of bodily existence but also constitutes them. That is, each offers our lived bodies radically different ways of "being-in-the-world"' (2004: 136). Among scholars of digital media, phenomenological approaches are a vibrant subdiscipline, including Hansen (2004), Kozel (2007), and Munster (2006).

5   The tensions between the Freedom Riders and King are detailed in Arsenault (2006: 249–51).

6   Lischer (1995: 51–64) offers an illuminating discussion of the encounters between King's theological insights, rooted in the African Baptist tradition, and the liberal Protestantism that he studied while a graduate student at Crozer Theological Seminary and Boston University. Erskine (1994) is a comparative study locating King's thought among liberal, Black liberation, and womanist theologies.

7   The most influential articulation of this camera/spectator relationship in cinema is Sobchack (1991).

8   Boyd (2003) makes perhaps the most provocative argument for the movement's contemporary irrelevance.

9   Manovich defines ontological montage as 'the coexistence of ontologically incompatible elements within the same time and space' (2002: 159).

10 Before acceding to his mother's request to take over leadership of the King Center, Dexter pursued a career in entertainment media. In a 1997 magazine interview, he contrasted his approach with that of his father: 'His media was marching. We are substituting the means of today – CD-ROMs, the Internet, books – to get the message out'

(quoted in Plotz 1997).

11 A donated, bronze statue of Mahatma Gandhi is installed outside the visitor's center.

12 Like the King Historic District's visitors' center, the NCRM's exhibition is the work of Ralph Applebaum Associates.

13 The first two volumes of Branch's history of the movement, for example, pivot on Birmingham. Invaluable histories of the campaign's local contexts are Eskew (1997) and Manis (1999).

14 I borrow the phrase 'charge of the real' from Sobchack (2004: 258–85).

15 The institute's long journey from proposal to realisation is detailed in Eskew (2006: 28–66).

16 A printed exhibition guide notes that the figures 'symbolize the countless individuals from all walks of life who participated in the Civil Rights Movement' (Cooper 2002: n.p.).

REFERENCES

'AHR Forum' (2009) *American Historical Review*, 114, 4, 978–1016.

Acham, Christine (2005) *Revolution Televised: Prime Time and the Struggle for Black Power*. Minneapolis: University Minnesota Press.

Arsenault, Raymond (2006) *Freedom Riders: 1961 and the Struggle for Racial Justice*. New York: Oxford University Press.

Benjamin, Walter (1968 [1936]) 'The Work of Art in the Age of Mechanical Reproduction', trans. Harry Zohn, in Hannah Arendt (ed.) *Illuminations*. New York: Schocken, 217–51.

Boyd, Todd (2003) *The New H.N.I.C.: The Death of Civil Rights and the Reign of Hip Hop*. New York: New York University Press.

Branch, Taylor (1989) *Parting the Waters: America in the King Years 1954–63*. New York: Simon and Schuster.

_____ (1999) *Pillar of Fire: America in the King Years 1963–65* New York: Simon and Schuster.

_____ (2006) *At Canaan's Edge: America in the King Years, 1965–68*. New York: Simon and Schuster.

Brasell, R. Bruce (2004) 'From Evidentiary Presentation to Artful Re-Presentation: Media Images, Civil Rights Documentaries, and the Audiovisual Writing of History', *Journal of Film and Video*, 56, 1, 3–16.

Byers, Thomas B. (1996) 'History Re-Membered: *Forrest Gump*, Postfeminist Masculinity, and the Burial of the Counterculture', *Modern Fiction Studies*, 42, 2, 419–44.

Cooper, Priscilla Hancock (2002) *The Birmingham Civil Rights Institute: A Living Institution*. Pamphlet. Birmingham: Birmingham Civil Rights Institute.

Donovan, Robert J. and Ray Scherer (1992) *Unsilent Revolution: Television News and*

American Public Life, 1948–1991. New York: Oxford University Press.

Erskine, Noel Leo (1994) *King Among the Theologians*. Cleveland, OH: Pilgrim Press.

Eskew, Glenn T. (1997) *But for Birmingham*. Chapel Hill: University of North Carolina Press.

_____ (2006) 'The Birmingham Civil Rights Institute and the New Ideology of Tolerance', in Renee C. Romano and Leigh Raiford (ed.) *The Civil Rights Movement in American Memory*. Athens, Georgia: University of Georgia Press, 28-66.

Fairclough, Adam (1987) *To Redeem the Soul of America: The Southern Christian Leadership Conference and Martin Luther King, Jr*. Athens: University of Georgia Press.

Fears, Darryl (2002) 'Entrepreneurship or Profiteering?; Critics Say King's Family Is Dishonoring His Legacy', *Washington Post*, 8 April, sec. A, p. 1.

Gabilondo, Joseba (2000) 'Morphing Saint Sebastian: Masochism and Masculinity in *Forrest Gump*', in Vivian Sobchack (ed.) *Meta-Morphing: Visual Transformation and the Culture of Quick-Change*. Minneapolis: University of Minnesota Press, 183–207.

Garrow, David J. (1986) *Bearing the Cross: Martin Luther King, Jr. and The Southern Christian Leadership Conference*. New York: Harper Perennial.

Gould, Jack (1963) 'Television and Civil Rights', *New York Times*, 8 Sept., sec. X, p. 15.

Hampton, Henry (prod.) (2006) 'Awakenings', *Eyes on the Prize*. DVD. Boston: Blackside.

Hansen, Mark B. N. (2004) *New Philosophy for New Media*. Cambridge, MA: MIT Press.

Hon, Linda Childers (1997) '"To Redeem the Soul of America": Public Relations and the Civil Rights Movement', *Journal of Public Relations Research*, 9, 3, 163–212.

Hunt, Darnell M. (ed.) (2005) *Channeling Blackness: Studies on Television and Race in America*. New York: Oxford University Press.

Johnson, Clark, dir. (2001) 'Director's Commentary' in *Boycott*. DVD. HBO Films.

Johnson, David (2007) 'Martin Luther King Jr's 1963 Birmingham Campaign as Image Event', *Rhetoric & Public Affairs*, 10, 1, 1–25.

King, Martin Luther (1998 [1968]) 'Remaining Awake through a Great Revolution', in Clayborne Carson and Peter Holloran (eds) *A Knock at Midnight: Inspiration from the Great Sermons of Reverend Martin Luther King, Jr*. New York: Warner Books, 205–24.

Kinney, Katherine (2003) 'Hanoi Jane and Other Treasons: Women and the Editing of the 1960s', *Women's Studies*, 32, 4, 371–92.

Kozel, Susan (2007) *Closer: Performance, Technologies, Phenomenology*. Cambridge, MA: MIT Press.

Lentz, Richard (1990) *Symbols, the News Magazines, and Martin Luther King*. Baton Rouge: Louisiana State University Press.

Lischer, Richard (1995) *The Preacher King: Martin Luther King Jr. and the Word That Moved America*. New York: Oxford University Press.

Manis, Andrew (1999) *A Fire You Can't Put Out: The Civil Rights Life of Birmingham's Reverend Fred Shuttlesworth*. Tuscaloosa: University of Alabama Press.

Manovich, Lev (2002) *The Language of New Media*. Cambridge, Massachusetts: MIT

Press.

McCarthy, Michael (2001) 'Alcatel gets static from "dead" ad campaign', *USA Today* (29 May), http://www.usatoday.com/money/advertising/adtrack/2001-05-29-ad-track-alcatel.htm#more

Moses, Robert Parris (1990) 'Commentary', in Peter J. Albert and Ronald Hoffman (ed.) *We Shall Overcome: Martin Luther King, Jr. and the Black Freedom Struggle*. New York: De Capo Press, 69–76.

Munster, Anna (2006) *Materializing New Media: Embodiment in Information Aesthetics*. Lebanon, NH: University Press of New England.

Murphree, Vanessa D. (2003) 'The Selling of Civil Rights: The Communication Section of the Student Nonviolent Coordinating Committee', *Journalism History*, 29, 1, 13–32.

Plotz, David (1997) 'Content is King: Dexter King is a King for the '90s.', *Slate*, http://www.slate.com/id/1816/

Pousner, Howard (1994) 'King Family Plans Disney-like Park', *Atlanta Journal*, 11 August, sec. C, p. 1.

Sack, Kevin (1997) 'Sheen of the King Legacy Dims on New, More Profitable Path', *New York Times*, 19 April, http://www.nytimes.com/1997/08/19/us/sheen-of-the-king-legacy-dims-on-new-more-profitable-path.html

Smith, Valerie (2005) 'Meditation on Memory: Clark Johnson's Boycott', *American Literary History*, 17, 3, 530–41. [XXX main text has Vivien not Valerie?]

Sobchack, Vivian (1991) *The Address of the Eye: A Phenomenology of Film Experience*. Princeton: Princeton University Press.

_____ (2004) *Carnal Thoughts: Embodiment and Moving Image Culture*. Berkeley: University of California Press.

Spence, Steve (2011) "Cultural Globalization and the US Civil Rights Movement", *Public Culture* 23, 3, 551–72.

Torres, Sasha (2003) *Black, White, and in Color: Television and Black Civil Rights*. Princeton: Princeton University Press.

Tucker, Cynthia (1994) 'A Dream Gone Astray', *Atlanta Journal Constitution*, December 18, sec. G, p. 7.

Ward, Brian (ed.) (2001) *Media, Culture, and the Modern African American Freedom Struggle*. Gainesville: University Press of Florida.

West, Cornel (1998) *Prophetic Fragments: Illuminations of the Crisis in American Religion and Culture*. Grand Rapids, MI: Eerdmans.

Zemeckis, Robert, dir. (2001) *Forrest Gump Special Collector's Edition DVD*. Paramount Home Entertainment.

CHAPTER THREE

STAG FILMS, VINTAGE PORN, AND THE MARKETING OF CINECROPHILIA
David Church

Whether appearing under adjectives like 'classic', 'retro', or predominantly, 'vintage', a growing niche market for pornography made between roughly the 1890s and early 1980s has appeared on pornographic websites and in video retail catalogues. Encompassing almost a century's worth of photographed sex acts, 'vintage porn' is most often compiled and marketed as a distinct fetish category, either ensconced within niche-specific websites (such as *Retro Porn Archive*, *Vintage Cuties*, and *Vintage Taboo*) or listed as one of many subcategories on large porn metasites broken down by niche (e.g. by specific body parts, performer types, sexual practices, fetish objects). While the proliferation of such niches seemingly suggests user-oriented fantasies of sexual freedom and plenitude, Zabet Patterson argues that, 'in reality, what cyberporn tends to offer – especially with a rapidly consolidating market – is an environment in which desire and subject position are produced as "truths" of the self through a discourse of categorisation and classification' (2004: 106).

What does it mean that pastness has become eroticised as a sexual fetish for today's viewers? How are archaic images of explicit sexual representation, originating at a historical remove from our supposedly 'liberated' era, discursively framed for contemporary consumption? And how does cinematic memory animate desire for this particular kind of historical, pornographic moving image? Unlike more porous, potentially overlapping niche categories (e.g. 'breasts', 'close-ups', and 'cumshots' commonly factor to some degree into the standard heterosexual hardcore scene), the existence of a niche market for vintage porn suggests the discursive creation of a specific audience and set of viewing expectations built around the apparent age and appearance of these artifacts. This phenomenon invites a number of questions which I hope will not only point toward the workings of a particular proclivity, but also reveal larger implications for our understanding of cinephilia. While accounting for the variety and uses of vintage pornography is beyond the limited scope of this chapter, I will restrict my focus to the contemporary reception of stag films (i.e. those stags commercially available at the time of this writing), which, because of their privileged status as authentic moving images of hardcore sexual practices, crystallise many of the broader dynamics of vintage porn consumption.

Vintage porn sites typically offer both photographs and video clips, each consisting of softcore (glamour, burlesque, striptease, non-penetrative sex) and hardcore (genital penetration) variants. Often serving as the centerpiece of vintage porn sites, stag films are traditionally (but not always) of the latter type, valued for the relative rarity and historically scandalous nature of the explicit hardcore acts they show. That said, not all vintage porn sites span the same time periods; while some provide content stretching from the development of early photographic technology through to the 'Golden Age' of 'porno chic' in the 1970s and early 1980s, others delimit their product to a tighter range of years. (Even porn as recent as several decades old can be considered 'vintage' due to the relatively short careers of even its well-known performers.) The bulk of these websites, however, agree that the 'vintage' era stretches until at least the mid-to-late 1960s – not coincidentally the period widely viewed as the beginning of a national loss of sexual innocence in the United States. Because this transformative period also marked the decline of the stag film, as hardcore pornography began to increasingly surface from the shadows of obscenity into public visibility, it suggests how central the stag film is to contemporary notions of what constitutes 'vintage'. Since stags are commonly associated with a prelapsarian sexual past, they are also sometimes released under the banner of 'erotica' today, finding distributors not only within the porn industry, but also with more 'legitimate', niche distributors of art and cult films. To more fully explain the reasons for this use, we must first backtrack to what stag films are, and how they were initially used during their period of production. I will then return to their present-day consumption, which I believe maps a conflicted sexual politics onto the past, all the while activating necrophilic desires rooted in cultural memories of cinema history.

THE FORM AND HISTORICAL FUNCTION OF STAG FILMS

Stags are silent, black-and-white, pornographic films no more than one reel long (approximately twelve-to-fifteen minutes or less). According to Joseph W. Slade (2006: 32–3), they probably first appeared around 1905–06, several years after the introduction of longer film reels and the development of the close-up. In their history of stags, Al Di Lauro and Gerald Rabkin note that most titles were produced in the United States, France, Germany, Italy, Latin America, and Japan, with only French and Mexican films successfully imported to the US; often existing as single prints, most stags were produced and exhibited in a given locality, restricting their regional and global reach (1976: 52). The films were usually untitled, with filmmakers and performers either uncredited or appearing under pseudonyms; while the male performers were typically amateurs (sometimes hiding their identities behind ridiculous fake mustaches and other disguises), the female performers were more likely professional prostitutes, according to Thomas Waugh (2001: 285).

Many stags (especially the earlier extant films, I would emphasise) are centered on a bawdy comic incident, usually involving sexual excitation 'by visual means' (e.g. voyeurism), which swiftly culminates in heterosexual intercourse (see Di Lauro & Rabkin 1976: 48, 51), though later stags are typically more amateurish, consisting of mere copulation with very little (if any) narrative pretense. Displaying a 'limited degree of [causal] narrative technique', the stag film's simple plot eventually falls apart into close-ups of genital penetration, which Linda Williams argues are addressed directly to the (male) viewer, displayed with a frontal presentationality as self-sufficient spectacle; the viewer is reminded of his place as a spectator, making difficult any identification with the onscreen male performer that could suture the viewer into the stag's diegetic space (1999: 65, 67). Complicating the Mulveyan notion of visual pleasure in voyeuristic mastery of the objectified female, this performative aesthetic provided a pleasurable oscillation 'between the impossible direct relation between a spectator and the exhibitionist object he watches in close-up, and the ideal voyeurism of a spectator who observes a sexual event in which a surrogate male acts for him'; in other words, there is 'the pleasure of the collective male group expressing its heterosexual desire for the bodies of women on display', alternating with 'moving toward, but never fully achieving, identification with a male protagonist who performs sexual acts with the female body that shows itself to the viewer' (1999: 80).[1] Williams and Slade both observe that stags retained this primitive aesthetic (which recalls the 'cinema of attractions' described by Tom Gunning [1990]) for decades, long after narrative films had grown more technically sophisticated, because the awkward and amateurish qualities of the films and the performers therein served as markers of authenticity (1999: 77–8; 2006: 30). In addition to the results of economic constraints, Slade goes on to speculate that stags' devotion to anachronistic primitivism and technical roughness may have enhanced their illicit appearance, their appeal to blue-collar tastes, and their role as an unchanging rite of passage for young men (2006: 39–40).

As implied by the name 'stag', these films were semi-publicly screened to exclusively male, 'upper-lower to lower-middle-class' audiences (Waugh 2001: 284), often in fraternal organisations and men's social clubs; the name 'smoker' was also a common label for such films, derived from men's 'smoking parties', as was the name 'blue movies'. An itinerant 16mm projectionist, who was often also the filmmaker, would be hired for an evening's entertainment, in which the men filled the silence with sexualised heckling, boasts, and jokes about the screened material. While Williams claims that 'the primary pleasure [of stag viewing] seems to involve forming a gender-based bond with other male spectators', in which 'the woman's body mediates the achievement of masculine identity' (1999: 73, 80), Waugh observes that the homosociality of the all-male stag viewing triggered anxiety and embarrassment for heterosexual men who tempered their arousal around other men by resorting to compulsory displays of aggressive masculinity and class-inflected misogyny (2001: 280, 285).[2] Owing to this exhibition context, Williams observes that stags seem intended 'to arouse and then precisely *not* to satisfy a spectator', making masturbation unto orgasm far less expected than for more solitary viewers of later, feature-length pornography exhibiting greater sexual numbers during the course of a narrative; in Europe, for example, stags were most often screened in brothels to turn on (male) customers while they waited to be serviced in the flesh (1999: 74). This viewing situation, she argues, is also why stags sometimes end with penetration shots themselves, not always the close-ups of external male ejaculation (or 'cum shots') conventionalised in more contemporary porn (1999: 72).

If early stags, however primitive, seem more technically proficient and narrative driven than later stags, Di Lauro and Rabkin speculate that the prohibitive cost of filmmaking equipment kept the means of stag production out of most amateur pornographers' reach during the first several decades of the twentieth century. The price of 8mm and 16mm cameras and projectors made the technologies more accessible for home use by the 1950s, allowing stags to not only be more cheaply made, but also exhibited in the privacy of one's own home; as a result, semi-public stag screenings became rarer, replaced by mail-order sales of stag reels (1976: 55–9). Meanwhile, the fraternal organisations at which stags were originally shown 'started to fade from everyday life, sometime around the late 1960s' (Thompson 2007: 4), lessening men's opportunities to view stags in a social setting. During the 1960s, stags could still be viewed surreptitiously in the storefront peepshow arcades and adult bookstores found in large urban centers, where they evolved into 8mm single-reel hardcore loops, which eschewed narrative altogether because they were shown in several-minute fragments on coin-operated machines (the film starting up where the last fragment left off). By the mid-1960s, these machines were placed behind curtains in booths to give viewers some small measure of privacy for solitary masturbation (2007: 201).[3]

This move from semi-public, group viewing to private, individualistic viewing of stags roughly coincided with decreasing legal restrictions on the public exhibition of other forms of filmed pornography. Eric Schaefer has traced the industrial and technological basis for the gradual progression from the illicit hardcore imagery of 8mm and 16mm stags and the softcore narratives of licit 35mm sexploitation features toward the open theatrical exhibition of 35mm hardcore features. He dates the end of the stag era at 1967, when advertisements first appeared for public showings of 16mm 'beaver films' (short, silent striptease reels focusing on female genitals), shortly followed by 16mm 'simulation films' (films simulating intercourse but not showing penetration), and finally *Mona* (1970), the first 35mm hardcore narrative feature (2002: 4, 7, 17). Around this time, suggest Di Lauro and Rabkin, 'classic' stags were pushed off the market by newer hardcore loops shot in color, featuring higher production values, a wider array of sexual practices, and, with the swift rise of 1970s porno chic, known performers. Writing in 1976, during the theatrical hardcore boom, they nostalgically lament that 'the faded black-and-white images of the past are losing their erotic power', becoming 'an endangered species' (1976: 112). Yet, one of the earliest feature-length hardcore films to play theatrically was Alex de Renzy's *A History of the Blue Movie* (1970), a compilation documentary containing both excerpts and full versions of stag films dating from as early as 1915. Like de Renzy's *Pornography in Denmark: A New Approach* (1970), the documentary form provided a legitimating cover for depicting actual sex acts onscreen (as would be the case with *Polissons et galipettes* (*The Good Old Naughty Days*, 2002), a more recent compilation documentary), paving the way for fictional porn features like *Deep Throat* (1972) and *Behind the Green Door* (1972).[4] The appeal of stag films as late as 1970 thus provided a major impetus for opening the door to the more 'modern' forms of pornography that quickly replaced them, suggesting that the erotic power of stags had not diminished in itself, but was merely supplanted by the eroticism of newer products, increasing the apparent pastness of the former. Of course, this is not to say that stag films or any other forms of pornography are inherently erotic to any audience in any historical period, but merely that a continuity exists between porn's earlier and later incarnations. Indeed, the appeal of pornography, like any filmic genre, cannot be divorced from its historicity – especially in lieu of the cultural discourses that mark it as illicit in a given period. However, as I will now explain, the afterlife of stag films has proven far more complicated with the resurrection of stags in the video and internet age, making the historical distance represented by these films a source of eroticism in itself and a site of problematic sexual politics.

THE CONTEMPORARY RECEPTION OF STAG FILMS

Stag films were compiled on home video during the VHS porn explosion of the 1980s, but the rise of the internet has arguably created a more focused niche through the hypertextuality of metasites and search engines that categorise diverse sexual proclivities into easily marketable commodities. Due to their short length and already substandard visual quality, stag films would seem particularly amenable to online use, even if the vintage porn niche may have become more fully developed by the time better connectivity and streaming video technologies improved the visual quality of online video in general in the early 2000s. These technological factors aside, I am proceeding from the premise that erotic desire is, in large part, discursively constructed, so the ways these films are framed through promotion and advertising may tell us how viewers' expectations about the films are shaped – and, in effect, how viewers are taught how to desire. As Williams argues, following Michel Foucault, the physical effects (such as arousal) created by viewing body genres like pornography 'may seem like reflexes, but they are all culturally mediated', produced through a historically constructed fetishisation of the female body as a moving object about which knowledge (whether correct or not) is pleasurably gained by the (male) spectator (1999: 5, 45).

Unfortunately, fan discourses surrounding stag films are difficult to find and even harder to interpret with any degree of generalisability, especially because the untitled, anonymous status of many stags is not as conducive to fannish appreciation of specific performers or films, at least in comparison with the fan activity surrounding more recent porn. When specific performers are mentioned, they tend to have been active in only the most recent decades to be considered 'vintage' (e.g. the 1970s and 1980s) – that is, decades after the stag film had already given way to more contemporary forms of porn. On websites like *Vintage Erotica Forums*, there are discussion threads devoted to specific pin-up models and burlesque dancers, but very few of these women crossed over into working in stags – with a few notable exceptions, like Candy Barr, a burlesque dancer who starred in *Smart Alec* (1951), one of the most widely distributed stags of the 1950s. Instead, fan discourse tends to focus around the availability of stags, such as providing information about where to obtain them, or posting links to groups of films uploaded to file-sharing servers, which are often treated as largely undifferentiated clusters of content. Even if individual stags are seldom archived in meticulous or accurate ways, the very collectability of, and knowledge about, these rare objects confers a sense of subcultural capital upon the collector, because, as Barbara Klinger observes, 'offerings that fall outside of the exhibition mainstream help to constitute the uncommon, sought-after media object, suggesting that the collector's trade has found a way to construct the categories of authenticity and rarity for mass-produced film artifacts,' spurring 'the competitive gamesmanship and "sport" characteristic of this enterprise in general' (2006: 67).

The discourses about stag films and vintage porn that are most visible and commonly available include those self-promotional discourses displayed prominently on the front pages of websites and the covers of videos themselves, as well as a considerable number of website reviews. Many of the latter are posted on review metasites like *Porn Inspector* and *Vintage Porn Review*, which profile and review multiple porn websites as a service to prospective membership buyers. These review websites are often closely affiliated with the websites they review – a fact enhanced by the sample photo galleries and video clips they offer viewers – so even if some of these generally generous reviews are more mixed than others (at least outwardly suggesting the work of impartial critics), it is reasonable to treat them as an extension of the websites' self-promotion. In addition, the modifiers 'classic', 'retro', and 'vintage' are not treated as mutually exclusive on vintage porn websites more generally, and there are no commonly accepted differences between the connotations of each.

To explore the marketing discourses around stag films and vintage porn through a few representative examples, we can first turn to one of the oldest and most notable vintage websites, *RetroRaunch*, which began operating in 1997 with the stated purpose of 'bringing the tasty, nasty, wild, wacky, outrageous, shocking, beautiful, erotic and utterly special soft and hardcore porn from the past into the high-tech present of the internet' (Anon. 1998b). This contrast between the past and the present is the most prominent discourse surrounding vintage porn, whether figured in terms of technology, performers' bodies, or cultural taste.

Weaving fantasies about a time with less complicated sexual politics, the past is nostalgically idealised as a lost sexual wonderland, more authentic and natural than the world of hardcore pornography today, but potentially no less explicit. (One vintage website is even named *Nostalgia Porn*.) From the perspective of the supposedly more sophisticated, sex-saturated present day, this nostalgia for the then-newness (now-pastness) of explicit sexual representation rests upon imagining the pre-1960s past not as an innocent time, but as a time in which sex was still illicit and obscene; the notion of a sexually innocent past is mobilised only insofar as to charge these images with a lingering, retrospectively framed air of the taboo. Whereas mainstream Hollywood films of the era sublimated their eroticism into kisses and implied-but-elided love scenes (see Williams 2008: 25–42), contemporary discourses imply that stags enacted the onscreen sexuality that less prudish viewers may have secretly wished to see, but were not adventurous enough to seek out – allowing today's viewers to retrospectively occupy that exploratory role. For example, daring and originality are often credited to stag performers (and stag filmmakers as well), as in Dave Thompson's comments that 'the girls who made cheap stag films in the 1920s were no less actresses than those who perform in the big-budget erotic movies today, and no less deserving of the viewer's admiration and respect. In fact, they may have even merited more, for today's stars are essentially rumpling sheets that have been rolled on for close to a century. The actresses of the 1910s and 1920s were looking at a freshly made bed' (2007: 43). In the Frequently Asked Questions section of *RetroRaunch*, one of the questions asks if the site will ever run out of 'fresh material', with the answer 'someday we certainly will, there's only so much in existence. But considering that there's an awful lot of it out there, *RetroRaunch* will be able to provide our members with thousands of fresh, never-before-seen-on-the-net … images for well into the foreseeable future' (Anon. 1998a). The past is thus figured as a period of historical plenitude, slowly revealing its lurid secrets for collectors to pour over, and yet, the limited quantity of these historical documents necessitates their almost museum-like archiving in modern digital formats like DVD and online video files – albeit more for profit than posterity. As another site says, 'Of course vintage porn can't boast with [sic] millions of pics as the modern adult industry can but that's what makes our repro [sic] porn collection so unique. We did a really great job to collect these 40K vintage photos and 300+ videos. We really handpicked them sure that you deserve only the best' (Anon. 2004).[5]

According to this quasi-preservationist logic, vintage porn can serve an almost pedagogical function by revealing that the prelapsarian past was far less innocent than we supposedly think it today. These discourses are perhaps most clearly enunciated in the *RetroRaunch* site tour, in which each page contains a photo of a 'prim and proper', 1950s-attired woman who gradually removes layers of clothing as one clicks through several pages of website description and sample photos. As this imaginary tour guide explains:

> Being a history teacher, it's perfectly natural for me to want to teach you about the history of sex and erotica. Of course, education is best accomplished with visual aides. People seem to think that nothing interesting happened in the world of sex until after the sexual revolution of the 1960's. Well, excuse me if I have a good giggle about that! Every single wild act, fetish, obsession, and nasty thought or deed that people indulge in today was indulged in by their parents and grandparents going all the way back. (Anon. 1998c)

Because vintage porn celebrates sexual images temporally distant from us today, pornographic films made prior to the 1960s 'sexual revolution' are privileged as novelties for showing a range of explicit sex acts not often associated with the pre-revolution past. As Schaefer points out, the 16mm film gauge became associated with theatrical hardcore films around the time that the late-1960s counterculture adopted it for underground and avant-garde films, reinforcing 'the association among 16mm film, alternatives to mainstream practice, and freer sexual expression and cultural change' (2002: 14). It is therefore the sex acts themselves that transcend the pre- and post-lapsarian eras, allowing 8mm stag films to become exoticised artifacts of a seemingly ahistorical sexuality. For example, taking a similar marketing strategy to *RetroRaunch*, a 'male' tour guide (personified only through text, not photos, thus retaining the same anonymity as the male performers in stag films) at the website *Good Old XXX* describes his sexual adventures across periods of changing sexual mores, with each page of the tour devoted to a decade from the 1940s to 1970s – suggesting the fantasy of being an eternally youthful, eternally potent, male time traveler, with sex acts providing the historical continuity between each period (Anon. 2006).[6] 'Don't be mistaken looking at old little ladies walking calmly with their respectable gentlemen – they know more about sex than you can imagine', says another website (Anon. 2001), while a DVD box claims that 'You kids can wallow in all kinds of bathroom hijinks with guys and gals in masks doing things you can *still* get arrested for in some states'.[7] Therefore, in so intently fetishising the pastness of these historical documents, vintage porn discourses paradoxically de-historicise the actual sex acts portrayed, naturalising the films' address to male heterosexual viewers. Following Foucault, we can say that the perverse implantation of desire for vintage porn rests upon the misleading assumption that the prelapsarian past was more sexually repressed (1990: 47–9); in actual fact, however, our supposedly 'liberated' contemporary era finds digital technologies of power proliferating the categorisation of fetishes (as with pornographic niches), which, in the case of vintage porn, reinforces the supposed historical transcendence of (male) heteronormative desire.

Ancestral connections are often cited as another means of temporal continuity between past and present. Stag films and vintage porn are frequently portrayed as discoveries from a father or grandfather's secret porn stash, things found hidden in attics and basements; this image suggests that stags were originally meant for private, solitary viewing, not the semi-public, collective viewing context in which most of them were actually shown. 'Just imagine – your Dad or maybe even your Grandfather was crazy about these pin up girls and their "next door" girlfriends', says one vintage website (Anon. 2004), while others jokingly hint that one's ancestors may even be the performers in the films, constituting a recovered cinematic primal scene.[8] These Oedipal connotations of patriarchal lineage suggest that sexual desires are congenitally inherited, not discursively constructed, but this paradoxically ahistorical universalising of male desire also extends to female stag performers. Explaining differences between modern and vintage porn, the *RetroRaunch* tour guide says:

> In the old days the women looked like REAL women … you know, the kind you can actually meet and get to know. The kind who never heard of silicone. The kind who knew what some really nice underthings could do for a gentleman's urges. The other difference is that the pictures weren't staged and fake looking. They were pictures of real people having a really good time, and it shows! (Anon. 1998c)[9]

The apparent authenticity of 'real women' accessible to the viewer is constituted through their difference from the stereotyped image of the heavily modified, heavily mediated, modern porn star. A *Porn Inspector* review of *Vintage Cuties*, for example, states that:

No photography tricks to highlight their hair, or an airbrush stroke to remove a scar, these ladies (and men) inhabit this content in their every day true form. [...] And the best part of this site is it goes much further back in time, when rounded, ample bodied women were considered the epiphany [sic] of sexual desire. So what if their hips were a bit more full, that also meant their breasts were larger which made most nostalgic men lick their lips and ready to bed these beauties. (Missy 2008b)[10]

Whatever body-positive sentiment is read into these seemingly archaic signifiers of 'naturalness' is severely tempered by the essentialisation of femininity as a historically transcendent ideal for women, to be consumed by men: 'Elegant hats and silk stockings make these wonderful vintage ladies look so feminine and very much desired. No wonder men can hardly wait to probe their greedy holes!' (Anon. 2004).[11] Even though stag films are sometimes praised for the diverse range of sexual practices they depict (e.g. lesbianism, BDSM, threesomes, etc.), those practices do not markedly complicate the essentialisation of femininity because, like more recent porn, they remain primarily framed for the pleasure of their originally intended audience: heterosexual male spectators.[12] Thus, as Williams observes, 'any nostalgia for these films must also partake of a nostalgia for an age when male spectators of pornography could take their pleasure in investigating the woman without having to worry much about *her* pleasure' (1999: 92; emphasis in original).

This is not to say, however, that the vintage market is solely male and heterosexual oriented today, for some 'vintage' iconography has also found admirers among women and become adopted for a variety of desires. For example, the apparent contradiction between historical plenitude and the limited quantity of surviving documents may be part of the impetus behind what *Vintage Porn Review* terms 'modern re-creation' websites (Anon. n.d.) – including *Martha's Girls*, *Angela Ryan*, and *Vintage Queens* – which feature largely softcore images of contemporary models simulating 'vintage' pastness through their dress, hairstyles, poses, and props; some of these websites, such as *Martha's Girls*, even digitally manipulate the photos to more closely resemble Victorian-era nude postcards, 1940s pin-up spreads, etc. As Despina Kakoudaki notes, 'soft-core images such as the pin-up have a wide range of cultural uses because of their ability to both "pass" for mainstream images and to retain the excitement and explicit sexuality of their pornographic component' (2004: 344). The discursive address of these re-creation websites is generally more gender-neutral, not solely presuming a male, heterosexual viewer. Indeed, as Maria Elena Buszek observes, vintage erotic imagery has been previously appropriated for such diverse purposes as the sadomasochistic photography (aimed at both men and women) in *Bizarre* magazine; Kate Millett's 1970s faux-stereoscopic photos of female genitalia;

campy, pin-up-inspired imagery in the lesbian sex magazine *On Our Backs*; and fanzines in the 1990s 'riot grrrl' movement (2006: 244, 282, 321, 345). As Buszek explains, members of the latter embraced recycled, mass-culture, 'girlie' signifiers with a mix of criticism and affection endemic to third-wave feminism: 'while recognising the inadequacy of the pin-up to effectively represent women's complex experiences and vast potential, they also recognise and admit the appeal of the very sexualised imagery that they seek to upend' (2006: 345).[13]

A related, if more problematically post-feminist sentiment can be found in the recent growth of 'alt-porn' (or 'alternative porn') websites like *Suicide Girls* and *Burning Angel*, which feature female models visually associated with rock music subcultures (punk, goth, emo) but sometimes drawing upon the iconography of 1940s and 1950s pin-up icons like Bettie Page.[14] Yet, while the pin-up-inspired, but primarily rock-modeled performers on alt-porn sites like *Burning Angel* may go hardcore, modern re-creation websites seem reluctant to recreate the sort of hardcore imagery associated with stags, suggesting that even vintage hardcore (which presumes a male, heterosexual viewer) is too overcoded with patriarchal connotations for easy appropriation by ostensibly post-feminist media. Although stags depict male and female sexual pleasure as identical – which would seem conducive to post-feminism's de-politicisation of collective female identity through a rejection of what is seen as a stereotypically 'feminist' sense of political correctness – they also 'represent the female body as a pure object of pleasure with no significant will or desire of its own' (Williams 1999: 176). While vintage porn essentialises femininity as a historically transcendent ideal that contemporary women can engage with some ironic distance, hints of a gender-neutral address in vintage porn may actually encourage post-feminist female viewers of stag films to 'distance themselves from the negative associations of femininity' by (sub)culturally becoming "one of the boys"' (Hollows 2003: 39). Even if women now have access to stags, proscribing the traditionally male, homosocial bonding of stag viewing (see Williams 1999: 76, 305), I would argue that the films' remediation into the temporally distinct, 'vintage' niche echoes stags' move into more private viewing contexts since the 1980s, encouraging their subcultural adoption by removing them from the cultural visibility loosely associated with the supposedly 'feminising' effects of mass culture – including the 'mainstream' contemporary pornography from which stags are so often differentiated.[15]

This cultural distinction between the seemingly mundane aspects of mainstream porn and the more selective connotations of vintage porn can occur because stag films are consumed not solely as culturally 'low' pornography, but also as art and cult objects. Because they are fetishised as historical artifacts that must be collected and preserved, they are sometimes aestheticised as artistically pleasing for the connoisseur, despite the cheapness and crudity of their actual form. For example, many vintage websites and DVD box covers use art deco fonts and visual design, emphasising the international origins of many films (especially French stags), and proclaiming that the films are restored and remastered to a higher quality.[16] The collectability of such mobile archives thus recalls a general tendency in contemporary film collecting that 'involves a complex interplay of nostalgia and presentism that glories in the past and its acquisition only if the past has been renovated through the newest technological standards' (Klinger 2006: 87). Several vintage sites even include sections of erotic art; membership in *Erotic Past*, for example, includes online access to 'Modern Art Galleries [that] feature some of the most prominent artists of the time including Klimt, Rodin, Picasso, Gauguin, and more'.[17] Such appeals to artworthiness and high technology imply a viewer with higher cultural capital than the average porn consumer. For instance, *RetroRaunch* bills itself as 'the thinking person's adult site' (Anon. 1998b), while *Delta of Venus* (named after Anaïs Nin's collection of erotic stories) prides itself as 'an alternative to the vast sea of unimaginative porn out there. Sex is a (the?) central focus of our lives, but I don't think endless photos of professional models getting screwed in every possible position really reflect what it's all about. Some people are happy with that, but this site is designed for folks who love sex, erotica, and obscenity but also want something literate & enlightening' (Anon. 2002b).

This sense of a more 'literate', active viewership is enhanced by how the poor quality prints and amateurish filmmaking techniques of stag films negatively affect the 'maximum visibility' sought by hardcore pornography; viewers must literally pay closer attention and gaze harder to see all the naughty bits.[18] One reviewer even compares vintage porn to spending hours watching unscrambled satellite TV channels for 'taboo' bits of nudity: 'That's the way I feel going through this site, these are the type of pictures and material that in no way were eyes suppose [sic] to really behold!' (Missy 2008a). As Joan Hawkins says of bootleg paracinema tapes, poor image quality becomes a mark of 'outlaw status and a guarantor of its authenticity', spurring the high reader participation endemic to subcultural appreciation (2000: 47–9).[19] Perhaps it should be no surprise, then, that cult film distributors are a major source for stag films – as with Something Weird Video's *Grandpa Bucky*'s series or the Cult Epics series of decade-specific *Vintage Erotica* DVDs – with the cult subculture standing in as a semi-public, male-oriented, homosocial viewing context providing collective pleasures for solitary viewers. While collecting may be 'bound up not merely with acts of consumption but also with the powerful sense the collector has of being the source, the origin of the objects purchased and organised into a system' (Klinger 2006: 88), these individualistic pleasures are supported in the cult context through the feeling of being part of a niche audience with shared, non-normative tastes.

Whether consumed as art or cult objects, the application of high cultural reading strategies raises stags from their lower socioeconomic roots, but this process can also gloss over their potentially misogynistic appeal – most commonly by associating them with 'erotica' over 'pornography'. This recoding would also seemingly enhance their appeal to women, if we recall the argument advanced by many anti-pornography feminists that 'erotica' is politically acceptable for women while 'pornography' is not. Erotica supposedly 'takes the viewer to the frontier of legitimate culture, allowing the viewer to be aroused but containing that arousal within the "purified, contemplative mode of high culture"' (Williams 1999: 285).[20] Branding vintage material as 'erotica' instead of just 'porn' ensures a wider market, and also allows a greater range of (softcore) material to fall under that label (e.g. pin-up, bondage, burlesque, and striptease photos and films). The banner of 'erotica' encourages stags to be seen as cute curiosities, charmingly perverse anachronisms representing a 'happier, more polymorphous era of sexual play'; for example, such remediated stags often have 'tinkling piano accompaniment, as if the films were the equivalent of Harold Lloyd or Charlie Chaplin comedies, run[ning] the risk of a bogus nostalgia associated with mainstream silent films' (Williams 2005: 129). Williams identifies this approach in the French compilation documentary *The Good Old Naughty Days* (2002), which enjoyed an arthouse release after playing at Cannes. For example, in a quaintly adolescent tone, the intertitles between individual stags romanticise their role in initiating French boys into manhood, inviting us to occupy that viewing position: 'Imagine the young men's astonishment while watching the secrets of a woman's body unveiled to them for the very first time, revealing at long last their box of tricks, their curlies, their butcher's window or even their little boy in the boat'. The aesthetic distance afforded by high cultural reading strategies (and enhanced by the films' presentational aesthetic of attractions) allows the apparent cuteness and innocence of stags to be held in tension with their depictions of acts as explicit as contemporary porn. While still primarily directed at male viewers today, this mode of address can also implicitly acknowledge a female audience who projects onto the historical past a more 'feminine' desire for the sexual intimacy not often associated with contemporary heterosexual porn.

While stag viewing may have originally involved a snickering 'adolescent male bonding at the expense of female difference', especially centered around the humor in seeing respectable women (who were 'presumed to be more chaste than men') performing sex in the first place (Williams 1999: 233; 2005: 118), the potential humor in stag viewing today seems somewhat different, particularly now that women are potential viewers. The quaintly adolescent humor of their bawdy narratives may continue to amuse (at least in the case of stags that do have narratives), but the once-novel existence of sexually adventurous women may now be campily obvious to both male and female viewers, even as explicit photographic evidence of them remains posited as a curiosity. Indeed, in her list of examples of the camp aesthetic, Susan Sontag notably includes 'stag movies seen without lust' (2008: 43). Although Waugh suggests a queer charge while viewing stags in the company of heterosexual men, which could help facilitate a camp reading, I would argue that the private consumption of stags today more likely leads to the depoliticised, mainstreamed readings of straight camp – which, following Williams, may be linked to our contemporary reactions to the campiness of mainstream silent films. Nevertheless, the existence of a *porn* market for stags, lucrative enough to enable the existence of a growing number of online paysites, suggests that the fetishisation of these films is not simply reducible to the distanced contemplation of 'erotica' or the ironic ribbing of camp; contra Sontag, for some (male) viewers, stags are indeed still seen 'with lust', despite the almost prerequisite aesthetic distance entailed in their consumption.

CINEPHILIA AND NECRO-EROTIC DESIRE IN STAG FILM SPECTATORSHIP

Because stag films are no longer categorised as depicting 'normal' sex, but instead classified as fetish objects by virtue of their archaism, I finally turn to a fuller consideration of the spectatorial pleasures afforded by these films today. This is not to posit a universal spectator, nor to circumscribe all other possible forms of sexual pleasure provided by these films, but to hypothesise one major mode of cathexis: a broadly necrophilic eroticisation of filmic decay. As a *Porn Inspector* review of *Vintage Taboo* says, 'You can almost smell the mildew type of aroma that will waft from yellowed pages in an old photo album, touching with great care so the film paper doesn't crackle and crumble under your touch. [...] Some of the material is so extremely aged on this site that it doesn't show with the clarity (far from it) that we are use [sic] to in today's digital age. But, in my opinion, *that's what enhances the erotic side of it*' (Missy 2008b; emphasis added). Yet I would argue that this necro-erotic desire notably overlaps with cinephilia in general, generating what we might term a 'cinecrophilia' that allows stag films to activate viewing pleasures not often associated with hardcore porn today.

Theoretical comparisons between cinephilia and necrophilia are certainly not without precedent. For Paul Willemen, cinephilia has 'overtones of necrophilia, of relating to something that is dead, past, but alive in memory' (1994: 227); while Susan Felleman observes that the process of mechanical reproduction overcomes death by 'preserving dead objects of desire' in the cinematographic image, so that necrophilia serves as cinephilia's 'mirror image' (2006: 47–8, 55). Meanwhile, Thomas Elsaesser describes:

> the love that never lies (cinephilia as the love of the original, of authenticity, of the indexicality of time, where each film performance is a unique event) [which] now competes with the love that never dies, where cinephilia feeds on nostalgia and

repetition, is revived by fandom and cult classics, and demands the video copy and now the DVD or the download. [...] The new cinephilia is turning the unlimited archive of our media memory, including the unloved bits and pieces, the long forgotten films or programs into potentially desirable and much valued clips, extras, and bonuses, which proves that cinephilia is not only an anxious love, but can always turn itself into a happy perversion. (2005: 41; emphasis in original)

This perverse 'love that never dies' allows stag films to be re-framed through the label 'vintage', reviving these archaic, otherwise forgotten sex films for the high-tech era. The crude amateurism of stags serves as a marker of authenticity, of a temporal anchoredness in a period seemingly distant from our own, yet made recognisable to us today through the explicit acts they depict and the mnemonic links they provide to contemporaneous Hollywood films. They are decayed vessels of cultural memory that are salvaged by filling them with affect through an eroticisation of their very pastness. No amount of remastering can make these prints look pristine and modern, so their scratches, grain, and outmoded mise-en-scènes are fetishised as material traces of prior use.

Because cinema is 'dead' in its response to our desires, unable to reciprocate, viewers can project their own memories (ego) onto it as an otherly container, much like the desire projected onto the necrophile's unresponsive partner. In this respect, cinephilia and necrophilia are both primarily narcissistic desires – which, in the case of stag films, translates (according to Williams 1999: 164) into a disregard for female pleasure, and explains why porn narratives often involve the sexual coercion of women (though necrophilia specifically involves a partner unable to consent). Lisa Downing theorises necrophilia as 'a radically narcissistic type of desire' that 'mobilises psychical energy in order to make a lost object return at will, but equally to enable a glimpse of self-loss in the perception of the other's death' by objectifying the corpse as a marker of 'radical absence' (2003: 52–4, 58). Necrophilia thus shares many parallels with Dennis Giles's psychoanalytic theory of heterosexual porn spectatorship, which is similarly based around the male spectator's intensely narcissistic projection of his ego's feminine aspects onto the empty, otherly space of the woman, allowing him to desire those parts of himself that he cannot openly acknowledge (1977: 56–7).[21] Like the corpse, the onscreen woman thereby serves as 'not so much a female "being" as a *lack* of being. [...] If the woman is nothing but a hole or series of holes, there is nothing and no one *there* to be loved' (1977: 60; emphasis in original). Giles even posits the woman's transition from everyday subjectivity to this state of pornographic non-being as 'a dying to the world'; symbolically speaking, 'insofar as the woman is *dead* – to lie with her is an act of necrophilia' (1977: 63–4; emphasis in original). As culturally 'lost objects', necro-erotic desire can be more easily projected onto stag films than contemporary films in circulation. Much as stags assumed that 'viewer "attraction" to these [onscreen] bodies will ultimately "rebound"... back toward the self because there is no [physically] *present* woman to touch' (Williams 1999: 294; emphasis added), necrophilia and cinephilia are similarly invested in lost objects of desire that may have a visceral affect upon the beholder, but which are not *temporally present* in a reciprocal sense. The corpse/film may be present as a kind of material trace, but the selves that once animated those forms have been lost to death and the ravages of time, leaving the desire projected onto them narcissistically circulating back to the beholder's self.

Yet, Dany Nobus observes that breaking social taboos about the sacralisation of death may be as important to the necrophile as the helplessness and uncon-sent of the dead partner (2002: 188). In this respect, the fetishisation of stag films projects desire onto female performers who are symbolically (and often quite literally) dead, but that projection excessively sexualises a medium today most often regarded for memorialising Hollywood performers from the same era. As the chief producer of moving images during the stag period, classical Hollywood cinema serves as a mnemonic reservoir for temporal reference points seen in stags – including hairstyles, fashions, décor, etc – that allow one to roughly esti-mate their decade of production. Due to the relatively high price of 8mm and 16mm filmmaking equipment during much of the classical Hollywood era and the shortage of distribution networks for non-professional material, amateur footage (such as home movies) from the pre-1950s period is far less familiar to us than 35mm Hollywood films, allowing the latter to occupy the cultural imagination of viewers too young to have personally experienced that era. This imaginary per-spective of history as seen through classical Hollywood allows stag films to gain a cinephilic dimension uncommon in contemporary hardcore porn films – espe-cially because vintage porn viewers, sometimes consuming the films as erotic art and cult objects, are perhaps more likely to have higher levels of cultural capi-tal, and therefore have more knowledge of classical Hollywood, than other porn viewers today. Writing as a stag film fan, for example, Thompson says:

> There is an almost unmistakable ambience to the best stags of the 1930s, an almost surreal sense of glamour that was as tangible as that which pervades Hol-lywood's best-loved efforts of the same period. [...] Hollywood portrayed life as a series of increasingly flamboyant fantasies. Stags reversed the equation, trans-forming fantasy into what was once (and, hopefully, would again become) real life. (2007: 100)

The apparent authenticity communicated by the amateurism of stags is thus complicated by the fantasy elements mnemonically associated with classical Hollywood. 'The collection seeks a form of self-enclosure which is possible because of its ahistoricism', says Susan Stewart of collecting; 'in the collection, time is not something to be restored to an origin; rather, all time is made simultaneous or synchronous within the collection's world' (1993: 151). In this regard, when collected and archived in digital formats today, the stag's specific historical origins are flattened into a broad notion of 'the past' by the very presentness of the collection, allowing the 'history'-via-Hollywood mnemonic to serve as a cinephilic fantasy rooted less in the actual historical past than in the eroticised distance from that imagined past, as seen from the present day. Consequently, because classical Hollywood films are typically perceived as relatively wholesome testaments to their deceased stars, the libidinal overinvestment in stag films providing numerous mnemonic links to old Hollywood product effectively violates the former's cultural sanctity in necrophilic ways, turning the nostalgia inherent in cinephilia into a means of 'desecrating' the sacralised classical Hollywood fantasy. Indeed, today's stag viewer is likely struck by the almost surreal sense of incongruity elicited by hardcore moving images taking place during the same time period as beloved Hollywood classics which seem all the more sexually staid by comparison.

Yet such sexualised fantasies about stags and classical Hollywood were even reinforced during the classical era through rumors that certain stars began their careers as stag performers. There were persistent whispers about youthful onscreen indiscretions by actors like Greta Garbo, Joan Crawford, Marilyn Monroe, and Ronald Reagan, though none of these rumors has been validated; for example, Jean Harlow and Clark Gable were even alleged to have filmed hardcore inserts for South American prints of *Red Dust* (1932) at the time they were already stars (see Thompson 2007: 166–75).[22] According to Slade, such rumors 'reflect a cultural propensity to debunk celebrities, but also a willingness to believe that stag films were commonly made in Hollywood' (2006: 47; n. 82). A widely seen stag from 1924 called *The Casting Couch* (in later years, rumored to feature Crawford) enhanced this suspicion, advancing the now-predictable premise of a movie producer propositioning a young starlet in exchange for a juicy part. The stag era even roughly paralleled the rise and fall of classical Hollywood, although it was a series of legal changes in obscenity standards that initially allowed hardcore porn to emerge from the shadows, not legal challenges to the mainstream film industry itself.[23] The stag market fell into decline around the time of classical Hollywood's demise in the 1950s and 1960s – yet this period also saw the rise of repertory theaters reviving classic films, which Mark Jancovich (2002: 315–17) observes also spawned the cult film subculture that would rediscover paracinema (and eventually stags). This gradual transition from stags and classical Hollywood as contemporaneous entities to stags and classical Hollywood as retrospectively marketable commodities arguably set the stage for the unearthing of stags as vintage porn in later years.

Of course, the mnemonic links between stags and Hollywood operate in the other direction as well, with Hollywood looking back to historically distant, vintage-era porn as subject matter for imagining a more innocent, idealised sexual past in films like *The Notorious Bettie Page* (2005) and *Boogie Nights* (1997) – a marked contrast from Hollywood's tendency to demonise contemporaneous pornography in films like *Hardcore* (1979) and *8MM* (1999). In mobilising memories of filmic possibility through the recycling and memorialising of past cinematic signifiers, the former often draw upon what Elena Gorfinkel terms the 'film-historical imaginary', using cinephilic aesthetics that 'capitalise on the visibility of anachronism as a means of highlighting the pathos of historical difference' (2005: 153). *Boogie Nights*, for example, 'possesses an overwhelming fixation with the "dated" status of 1970s porn; it is its very outmoded quality that imbues the film with bittersweet melancholia and wistful tragedy, as the obsolescence of porn on film becomes an allegory for various characters' mistakes, delusions, and frailties' (2005: 160). That Hollywood would capitalise on some of the more regressive sexual politics entailed in vintage porn discourses is perhaps of little surprise, but it points toward the marketability of a necro-erotic fascination that is, in its most explicit forms, confined to a pornographic niche, and yet is curiously attractive to wider audiences through the more common, seemingly innocuous workings of cinephilia. As perhaps the epitome of vintage porn, stag films may remain an acquired taste in their repurposed forms, but the discursively constructed desire for these archaic, decayed artifacts is a taste that cannot be easily relegated to the depths of low culture.

AUTHOR'S NOTE

Thanks to Joan Hawkins for her generous comments on this essay, and to the Kinsey Institute for Research in Sex, Gender, and Reproduction, Inc.

NOTES

1 Lacking the identification with male onscreen surrogates that later, feature-length porn narratives would provide, the male stag audience was left 'not "gazing" – the sense of omnipotent mastery, but "looking" – in the sense of a vulnerable fascination' (Williams 1999: 294–5).

2 Waugh cites 'this element of populist male blame that channels the stresses of masculinity awakened by the stag film setting, this social scapegoating attached to the

attractive/repulsive lumpen femme fatale' as an expression of 'the familiar hypocritical class-centric contempt for the working girl, since the female performers were undoubtedly assumed by the audience to be sex workers' (2001: 285). The 'threat' of homoeroticism is also blamed for the disproportionate focus on female genitals (and female nudity in general) over that of their onscreen male partners (2001: 276).

3   Of course, arcade booths were never solely used for solitary sexual pursuits, often providing a location for homosexual encounters between customers.

4   Chuck Kleinhans (2007) discusses the deployment of documentary tropes to seemingly mitigate (with mixed success) the sleazy portrayal of sexual subject matter.

5   Webmasters for many vintage porn sites specifically include contact information so that newly discovered content from private collections can be sold or traded to the websites.

6   For example, the tour guide explains that 'Society might have been a little slow at adopting fun sexual attitudes, but they were slowly getting there. We still have a few decades before people really get the sticks out of their asses, so I had to be a little bit discrete during the 40s. There was something about this sexual repression that really drove the ladies mad with desire though. Maybe it was a way for them to forget World War II, but these lonely housewives and ladies let out their frustrations by getting in front of the camera and fucking it all away' (Anon. 2006).

7   *Grandpa Bucky's Naughty Triple XXX Stags, Loops, & Peeps, Volume 7*, Something Weird Video, DVD, 2006. In another example, the DVD back cover of Volume 13 of this series reads 'Though Presidents changed, wars were fought, aviation was conquered, man walked on the moon, and the atom was split, fucking and sucking sure remained the same!'

8   *RetroRaunch*, for example, offers this tongue-in-cheek disclaimer concluding its site tour: 'RetroRaunch takes no responsibility for distress caused by seeing naked pictures of your grandmother' (Anon. 1998c); while the DVD box for Volume 14 of the *Grandpa Bucky's* series asks 'And just which of these copulating couples were your grandparents?'

9   As another site says, 'No stale screwing scenes, coked-up porn stars … or similar nonsense. One gets the impression that these folks are pretty fucking excited to be on camera and pretty excited to be, well, fucking on camera' (Anon. 2002a). As this latter quote implies, there is actually a high degree of presentationality in stags, with performers often appearing highly conscious of the camera.

10   In a different review, the reviewer 'liked knowing the fuller figured ladies were respected, revered, and appreciated in this time frame', but then goes on to celebrate the women's 'full bosom area, and you know it wasn't silicone then' (Woods 2010).

11   The desire to see 'natural', unmodified women is also arguably a major impetus behind the recent explosion of so-called 'amateur' porn – which is far from 'amateur' in its industrial organisation, and has spawned its own set of known star performers who look more like 'real' people.

12 For example, according to Dennis Harvey of the *San Francisco Bay Guardian*, 'What's really surprising about them is that while the scenarios are predictable fantasy ones … the sex acts are a lot more diverse than they would have been in standard American porn, then and now' (quoted on back cover of *The Good Old Naughty Days* DVD, Strand Releasing, 2003). Male-on-male sex is very rare in stag films, owing to the need to avoid homoeroticism in the homosocial viewing contexts they were originally meant for. There are, however, several gay porn websites, such as *Lavender Lounge* and *Athletic Model Guild*, with subsections dedicated to the licit physique photos and films that served as erotica for the gay community from roughly the 1950s to 1960s, before hardcore gay porn gained greater visibility (see Waugh 2001: 286–88). On the history of vintage gay erotica/porn, also see Waugh (1996).

13 On the related resurgence of interest in burlesque as a potential means of female empowerment, see Ferreday (2008).

14 As Buszek says, Page was groundbreaking in her over-the-top poses and lighthearted approach to the sadomasochistic content of her most famous photo sessions. Going from 'top' to 'bottom' with apparent glee, her performative approach to modeling destabilised the binary sex roles underlying 1950s erotic photography, exposing it as a potential medium for women's expression (2006: 247). On the taste politics of alt-porn, see Attwood (2007).

15 As Williams notes, the 'move back to more private viewing venues – the home equipped with VCR and computer; the booth of the arcade – is thus not a return to the true exclusivity and homogeneity of the era of the ob/scene, even if it is a return to more private viewing situations' (1999: 313). Some contemporary sources for stag films, such as Something Weird Video's *Grandpa Bucky*'s series, make no distinction between pre-1960s stags and the later 8mm peepshow/arcade loops that replaced them.

16 In its compilation of French stags, the box-cover text on the *Vintage Erotica: Anno 1930* DVD (Cult Epics, 2000) begins: 'Artists have explored the erotic image since the beginning of time', citing Hindu temples, cave paintings, and ancient scrolls as other examples. This is not to say that all stag collections archive their films in very meticulous ways; the *Grandpa Bucky*'s series, for example, features both whole films and fragments of stags, mostly lacking titles and dates. 'Of course, I put this together the way I think lately, namely in no goddamn order', admits the box of Volume 14. 'Fortunately, the wonderful hairdos on display instantly peg what decade it was made in'.

17 The site tour continues: 'The French Revolution brought us a whole new perspective on sex. These paintings included sex with animals, orgies, and other sexual fantasies' (Anon. 1999).

18 Maximum visibility is the principle by which certain body parts, sexual positions, and generic conventions are privileged in porn, seemingly allowing the body to visibly 'confess' its pleasure (see Williams 1999: 48–9).

19 As Hawkins points out, paracinema fans describe such visual quality with references to

forbidden culture like pornography ('labial-pink'), and taped-over paracinema bootlegs sometimes contain 'bits and pieces of old porn flicks' (2000: 47).

20 Williams also reiterates the familiar saying that 'one person's pornography is another person's erotica', so these two categorisations cannot be easily separated (1999: 6).

21 Williams argues that Giles's theory more specifically fits stag films than later, more elaborate, feature-length hardcore films that allow 'other points of secondary, fictional identification beyond those merely of phallus or hole' (1999: 83).

22 Di Lauro and Rabkin claim there is evidence that hardcore inserts actually were filmed by unscrupulous local distributors, 'with look-alikes finishing what Harlow and Gable started' (1976: 73).

23 On these changing obscenity standards, see Williams (1999: 85–91).

REFERENCES

Anon. (n.d.) 'Browse by Niche', *Vintage Porn Review*, available at: http://www.vintageporn-review.com/Reviewbyniche1.htm (accessed 17 April 2011).

_____ (1998a) 'Frequently Asked Questions', *RetroRaunch*, available at: http://retroraunch.com/faq.htm (accessed 17 April 2011).

_____ (1998b) 'Main', *RetroRaunch*, available at: http://retroraunch.com/main.htm (accessed 17 April 2011).

_____ (1998c) 'Tour', *RetroRaunch*, available at: http://retroraunch.com/tour0.htm (accessed 17 April 2011).

_____ (1999) 'Erotic Art', *Erotic Past*, available at: http://www.eroticpast.com/art.html (accessed 14 April 2011).

_____ (2001) *Retro Lady: Sex From 1870 Till 1970*, available at: http://www.retrolady.com (accessed 17 April 2011).

_____ (2002a) 'The Films', *Delta of Venus*, available at: http://www.deltaofvenus.com/intro/tour3.php (accessed 17 April 2011).

_____ (2002b) 'An Introduction', *Delta of Venus*, available at: http://www.deltaofvenus.com/main.php (accessed 17 April 2011).

_____ (2004) *Retro Porn Archive*, available at: http://www.retropornarchive.com (accessed 14 November 2010).

_____ (2006) '1940's', *Good Old XXX*, available at: http://www.goodoldxxx.com/tour.php?nats=&section=13 (accessed 12 April 2011).

Attwood, Feona (2007) 'No Money Shot?: Commerce, Pornography, and New Sex Taste Cultures', *Sexualities*, 10, 4, 441–56.

Buszek, Maria Elena (2006) *Pin-Up Grrrls: Feminism, Sexuality, Popular Culture*. Durham, NC: Duke University Press.

Di Lauro, Al and Gerald Rabkin (1976) *Dirty Movies: An Illustrated History of the Stag Film*,

1915–1970. New York: Chelsea House.

Downing, Lisa (2003) *Desiring the Dead: Necrophilia and Nineteenth-Century French Literature*. Oxford: Legenda.

Elsaesser, Thomas (2005) 'Cinephilia or the Uses of Disenchantment', in Marijke de Valck and Malte Hagener (eds) *Cinephilia: Movies, Love, and Memory*. Amsterdam: Amsterdam University Press, 27–43.

Felleman, Susan (2006) *Art in the Cinematic Imagination*. Austin: University of Texas Press.

Ferreday, Debra (2008) '"Showing the Girl": The New Burlesque', *Feminist Theory*, 9, 1, 47–65.

Foucault, Michel (1990) *The History of Sexuality, Volume 1: An Introduction*, trans. Robert Hurley. New York: Vintage Books.

Giles, Dennis (1977) 'Pornographic Space: The Other Place', *The 1977 Film Studies Annual: Part 2*. Pleasantville, NY: Redgrave, 52-65.

Gorfinkel, Elena (2005) 'The Future of Anachronism: Todd Haynes and the Magnificent Andersons', in Marijke de Valck and Malte Hagener (eds.) *Cinephilia: Movies, Love, and Memory*. Amsterdam: Amsterdam University Press, 153–67.

Gunning, Tom (1990) 'The Cinema of Attractions: Early Film, its Spectator, and the Avant-Garde', in Thomas Elsaesser (ed.) *Early Cinema: Space, Frame, Narrative*. London: British Film Institute, 56–62.

Hawkins, Joan (2000) *Cutting Edge: Art-Horror and the Horrific Avant-Garde*. Minneapolis: University of Minnesota Press.

Hollows, Joanne (2003) 'The Masculinity of Cult', in Mark Jancovich, Antonio Lázaro Reboll, Julian Stringer, and Andy Willis (eds.) *Defining Cult Movies: The Cultural Politics of Oppositional Taste*. Manchester: Manchester University Press, 35–53.

Jancovich, Mark (2002) 'Cult Fictions: Cult Movies, Subcultural Capital, and the Production of Cultural Distinctions', *Cultural Studies*, 16, 2, 306–22.

Kakoudaki, Despina (2004) 'Pinup: The American Secret Weapon in World War II', in Linda Williams (ed.) *Porn Studies*. Durham, NC: Duke University Press.

Kleinhans, Chuck (2007) 'Pornography and Documentary: Narrating the Alibi', in Jeffrey Sconce (ed.) *Sleaze Artists: Cinema at the Margins of Taste, Style, and Politics*. Durham, NC: Duke University Press, 96–120.

Klinger, Barbara (2006) *Beyond the Multiplex: Cinema, New Technologies, and the Home*. Berkeley: University of California Press.

Missy (2008a) 'Good Old XXX Review', *Porn Inspector*, available at: http://www.porninspector.com/reviews/review/good-old-xxx/ (accessed 17 April 2011).

_____ (2008b) 'Vintage Cuties Review', *Porn Inspector*, available at: http://www.porninspector.com/reviews/review/vintage-cuties/ (accessed 17 April 2011).

Nobus, Dany (2002) 'Over My Dead Body: On the Histories and Cultures of Necrophilia', in Robin Goodwin and Duncan Cramer (eds.) *Inappropriate Relationships: The Unconventional, the Disapproved, and the Forbidden*. Mahwah, NJ: Lawrence Erlbaum

Associates, 173–92.

Patterson, Zabet (2004) 'Going On-Line: Consuming Pornography in the Digital Era', in Linda Williams (ed.) *Porn Studies*. Durham, NC: Duke University Press, 104–23.

Schaefer, Eric (2002) 'Gauging a Revolution: 16mm Film and the Rise of the Pornographic Feature', *Cinema Journal*, 41, 3, 3–26.

Slade, Joseph W. (2006) 'Eroticism and Technological Regression: The Stag Film', *History and Technology*, 22, 1, 27–52.

Sontag, Susan (2008 [1964]) 'Notes on "Camp"', in Ernest Mathijs and Xavier Mendik (eds.) *The Cult Film Reader*. Maidenhead: Open University Press/McGraw-Hill, 41–52.

Stewart, Susan (1993) *On Longing: Narratives of the Miniature, the Gigantic, the Souvenir, the Collection*. Durham, NC: Duke University Press.

Thompson, Dave (2007) *Black and White and Blue: Adult Cinema from the Victorian Age to the VCR*. Toronto: ECW Press.

Waugh, Thomas (1996) *Hard to Imagine: Gay Male Eroticism in Photography and Film from Their Beginnings to Stonewall*. New York: Columbia University Press.

_____ (2001) 'Homosociality in the Classical American Stag Film: Off-Screen, On-Screen', *Sexualities*, 4, 3, 275–91.

Willemen, Paul (1994) 'Through the Glass Darkly: Cinephilia Reconsidered', in *Looks and Frictions: Essays in Cultural Studies and Film Theory*. Bloomington: Indiana University Press, 223–57.

Williams, Linda (1999) *Hard Core: Power, Pleasure, and the 'Frenzy of the Visible'*. Berkeley: University of California Press.

_____ (2005) '"White Slavery" Versus the Ethnography of "Sexworkers": Women in Stag Films at the Kinsey Archive', *The Moving Image: The Journal of the Association of Moving Image Archivists* 5, 2, 106-35.

_____ (2008) *Screening Sex*. Durham, NC: Duke University Press.

Woods, Montey (2010) 'Vintage Taboo Review', *Porn Inspector*, available at: http://www.porninspector.com/reviews/review/vintage-taboo/ (accessed 17 April 2011).

CHAPTER FOUR

BE KIND ... REWIND/OR, THE A-Zs OF AN AMERICAN *OFF-MODERN CINEPHILIA*

Jason Sperb

Fig. 1: The *digital* disruption of an 'analog' video image – all caught on film. The awkward co-existence of different media in *Be Kind Rewind* articulates the film's larger ambivalence towards modernity, technological progress, urban space and even cinephilia.

'Yet this is how a utopia defines itself, at least for me: Its something that is not supposed to happen outside of your mind, like sleeping with a girl you are in love with. Sorry, that's not the subject. Besides, a utopia is an imaginary city. But ideas are like cities: Once they are started they keep on building on themselves, accumulating incongruous layers over the years to form a complex texture resembling organic matter'.

– Michel Gondry (2008: 8)

'In 2008, I ranked *Be Kind Rewind* as 3rd on my year-end movie list. The quirky humor, oddball story, and glorious mise-en-scéne were mesmerizing to me, and apparently me alone. It's been a year since then, I've watched the film again, and I stand by [my] decision. I still love this movie. It's weird, surreal, funny, and just plain attractive to me as a filmmaker. Mos Def is cool, Jack Black is Jack Black, and the ending pulls at my heartstrings. And yet, no one else can stand it. I accept there's nothing I can say to convince more people to like this movie, but regardless of how people feel, it's still dripping with Michel Gondry's signature style. I can take solace that, at some point in the future, it will be mentioned in scholarly texts. *Auteur theory for the win!*'

– anonymous blogger (2010)

Auteur – a film's 'author'. After several decades, after countless discussions about the sociality of production and the complexity of reception, it remains common to begin a cinephiliac essay by branding a beloved text with the mark of an auteur. It cannot simply be *Be Kind Rewind*; it must be Michel Gondry's *Be Kind Rewind* (2008). But why? Auteur theory remains engulfed in the politics of taste – we label something as the work of an author in order to justify its existence, and to validate its closer scrutiny.

Gondry's achievement represents one of the great American films of the last decade. I emphasise 'American' in the title and throughout this chapter not to arrogantly ignore others, but to make clear the *limited scope* of my project. While Gondry is of course French, the film seems to be most explicitly a product and reflection of many US issues. More specifically, I will explore how *Be Kind Rewind* skims gently and lovingly across a remarkable range of surfaces which have come to frame the history of twentieth-century American media – race, technology, ritualistic consumption, cinephilia, community, digital cinema, and geography. It is an elegy to the continuing, affectionate presence of a (mediated) century past.

As the above fan quote foregrounds, authorship is as much about critical validation as an accurate reflection of production histories. When the film is seen (in a scholarly text) as part of a larger, cohesive body of work, the logic goes, people will finally appreciate *Be Kind Rewind*. Of course, this is nothing new, or at least it shouldn't be. As cinephile *par excellence* Zach Campbell recently noted, 'Auteur-centered cinephilia was once a polemical defense of some popular as well as some unpopular cinema' (2009: 210). Ironically, both authorship and cinephilia have largely fallen out of favor with academics (and not without good reason), just as defending 'popular' (often American, often Hollywood) films have too often fallen on deaf ears amongst new breeds of cinephiles. And yet, through all that, the auteur endures in very real ways, albeit carrying very different connotations, for very different types of cinephiles, and used towards sometimes very different ends – but someone must be *responsible*, someone must own the film.

At the same time, however, one of the many rich themes underlining this remarkably underappreciated and ambivalent film is how – as Gondry himself insisted on, and instituted throughout its production – it is a movie both produced and received by, and within, a community. And it focuses on thematic and narrative contexts that both reject and embrace competing notions of 'ownership'. *Be Kind Rewind* is the story of an old VHS rental store that – through a rather fantastical narrative device – has its entire collection demagnetised, and thus completely worthless. To save the store, then, the clerks impulsively concoct a dim plan to recreate those movies with their own VHS camera and whatever junk they have lying around.

Here, the film is also partly a parable about resistance to changing technology, about the historical instability of media platforms, and the difficulty with holding onto the past, which relates as much to the (stagnant) community around the store as to its mostly implicit frustration with the advent of DVD. This too works on a meta-level as the film itself is remarkably old-fashioned about the in-camera tricks it uses to recreate scenes from old films. The plan works momentarily – not because anyone is fooled by the ruse, but because the ruse itself is so seductively entertaining in not just its awfulness but in its *creative* awfulness. These crude imitations, meanwhile, implicitly remind us of the re-emergence of the amateur short film in the age of internet video distribution. Moreover, they remind us of the home movies we made when we were younger, trying to recapture a particular title, or even just a specific genre, on film. Only now, we were the stars. The joy of these films was not in their uncanny relation to the original titles; it rested in seeing ourselves on 'film' (really, most often video), in the accomplishment of making a film, and in its glaring imperfections. The crudeness of the movie, its impossible relation to an auratic original, is contradictorily also its appeal. These 'sweded' films in *Be Kind Rewind* suggest that perfection is not what film lovers are chasing – we are chasing an ephemeral moment.

On a first pass, it is obvious enough that Gondry's *Be Kind Rewind* is a cinephiliac love letter to an era passed in the age of digital reproduction – depicting a truly old-fashioned moment of cinephilia, evocative of the old days where Susan Sontag and Peter Wollen romanticised movie theatres and film-going experiences now past. But the love of films themselves (particularly 1980s Hollywood films) and their recreation in *Be Kind Rewind* is really a bit of misdirection, a quick highway glance at a remarkably complicated and deep film. It is time to get off that critical highway, one which constantly moves forward to more films, more auteurs. On that route, one briefly noted the film peripherally then moved quickly on. I wish to instead explore the local traffic of *Be Kind Rewind*. Better yet, this chapter will wander through the numerous, sometimes intersecting and sometimes divergent, side streets which show us much about cinephilia in the age of media convergence, about movies and the history of American twentieth-century modernity, and about cinematic negotiations with racial difference and urban spaces.

Initially, *Be Kind Rewind* was quickly passed by. When the film originally premiered in the spring of 2008, it received generally mixed reviews. In even the most positive evaluations, critics generally reduced *Be Kind Rewind* to an uneven comedy about people making aesthetically poor but technically creative remakes of Hollywood films such as *Ghostbusters* (1984), *Rush Hour* (1998), and *The Lion King* (1994). In his *Chicago Sun-Times* review, Roger Ebert (2008) summarised his affective response: 'I felt positive and genial while watching it, but I didn't break out in paroxysms of laughter'. Meanwhile, in a generally upbeat review in the *New York Times*, A.O. Scott noted that *Be Kind Rewind*

> treats movies as found objects, as material to be messed around with, explored and reimagined. It connects the do-it-yourself aesthetic of YouTube and other digital diversions with the older, predigital impulse to put on a show in the backyard or play your favorite band's hits with your buddies in the garage. (2008: E1)

When I showed the film to students in my English Composition courses several times throughout late 2008 and 2009, the most disappointed often cite, among other criteria, the fact that only the middle-third of the film is dedicated to the funniest aspect of *Be Kind Rewind* – its narrativising of amateur film remakes, which are humorous in their simplistic, even at times crude, DIY aesthetic. In no small measure, this reflected many professional critical responses. While these imitations are often quite cleverly done, it's the silliness of the staging that at bests tends to amuse audiences the first time through. Like so many of the critics, a lot of students just didn't find it funny enough, or even at all, because they reduce *Be Kind Rewind* to a standard comedy that fails to achieve those genre obligations. Still other students didn't like it because of the ambiguous ending, which certainly offers very little closure or resolution.

While more clever than hilarious, the home movies by themselves offer just one of many interesting glimpses into the film's sense of cinephilia. In one of the first scholarly discussions of *Be Kind Rewind*, Chuck Tryon suggests 'the film is essentially a celebration of the amateur production cultures that make movies in basements and backyards, often just for a few close friends' (2009: 31). His assessment nicely captures the cinephiliac spirit of Gondry's film; yet I will argue in the following pages that issues underlying *Be Kind Rewind*'s love of film are often remarkably more complex, themes and ideas which the film's deceptively sweet and soft tone quietly masks. Moreover, I will argue that *Be Kind Rewind*'s complexity challenges many of the old assumptions underlying the phenomenon of 'cinephilia', a powerful, but elusive and even counterproductive, concept for many to define. Gondry's film is so distinctive, as a formalist text and as a cultural event, that in its most powerful moments, it points towards the possibilities of an *off-modern* cinephilia.

Be Kind Rewind's unique ambivalence about the passing of time, about technological progress, about the impacts on urban space, about the value of loving cinema, about the reassurances and trappings of nostalgia, about the cultural, historical and cinematic implications of utopia, suggest less a modern (or postmodern) preoccupation with film than an *off-modern* one. As Svetlana Boym argued in *The Future of Nostalgia*, this alternate aesthetic trajectory celebrates the zig-zags and gaps of cultural and aesthetic possibility, rather than the straight historical line of modernity; the off-modern project, writes Boym, is 'a history of nostalgia [that] might allow us to look back at modern history not solely searching for newness and technological progress but for unrealised possibilities, unpredictable turns and crossroads' (2001: xvi). This can be a model for the new type of cinephilia which Gondry's film suggests, but which existing cinephiliac narratives of artistic utopia and critical elitism cannot account. *Be Kind Rewind* is a cinephiliac look at the spaces modernity left behind, and the regenerative potential – partly through the medium of film and the culture of cinema – which remains to those who live literally and figuratively within those marginal worlds.

Somewhere across modernity's passage in the twentieth century from utopic future to nostalgic past, the medium of film too came and went. Film, like all great instruments of modernity (like trains, radio, highways, television), attempted to unite the world, for the better and often for the worse. Through the dreamlike experience of cinema, we could be anywhere, see anything. Filmgoing, at its most utopic, was always about a deep, genuine love for the medium's artistic, technological and cultural potential, and the bliss momentarily achieved during flashes of its half-realisation. Yet, as with all those other modernist vehicles, the evolution of Film's production and reception across the twentieth century left messy gaps in its wake – the pockets of images still unshown, the realities at times horribly distorted, the places untraveled, the ideas passed by, the other possibilities for both culture and technologies forgotten that people often left behind. In all, the rush towards a myth of total cinema, or of a truly democratic one, left many alternative trajectories unfulfilled, often times even unimagined.

The gently polemical impulse, the call, to 'rewind' in *Be Kind Rewind* represents of course the film's affection for the era of VHS and for patronising rental shops (themselves extinct in the era of internet distribution venues like Netflix and Hulu). It is a remarkably old-fashioned film only on the surface, with its love of home video, of trains, of black and white images, and of dilapidated old buildings. However, it also symbolises the film's larger 'reflective nostalgia' (Boym) and its insistence that people figuratively, and literally, *slow down* to take another look at pre-existing histories and cultures still to be explored . Not for nothing is the sign for the 'Be Kind Rewind' video and thrift store painted *under a highway* which also serves as the culmination of the film's establishing shot. At its core, *Be Kind Rewind* encompasses the (cinephiliac?) ambivalence of cinema itself – our fundamental desire to wander, to see more of the world, while also seeing ourselves; to see movies as vehicles into other places and other cultures, but with the hope we will also recognise ourselves there (here); to see Film everywhere and everywhere through Film; to celebrate the endurance of the ephemeral, rhizomatic communities that Film periodically creates (every cinema is a community, and every community is a cinema); to hold onto 'cinema' at a time when, as D. N. Rodowick, among others, has noted, 'film' has long since gone.

Cinephilia too was a modernist preoccupation, an old-fashioned, even nostalgic, fascination with a technically and symbolically dead medium. Cinephiles, for all their emphasis on marginalisation, have always been front and center in championing the medium's further expansion and consumption through theatres, festivals and private screenings. They also embraced the technological advancements which ensured the growth and ubiquity that cemented itself as the great visual medium of the twentieth century (the next one will be, I suspect, quite different, and *Be Kind Rewind* hints that it already is). Susan Sontag's famous melancholy at the end of twentieth century was also, it must be noted, a lament for the end of modernity. Her sad ambivalence about cinephilia – that it is *so hard to just love the cinema* – came a couple of decades after similar revelations by Roland Barthes and Christian Metz. If we think of Sontag's most-contested proclamation that a particular brand of cinephilia was dead from the standpoint of being a movie lover, it is merely annoying in its self-serving lament. But if we look at her perspective from a larger historical standpoint of twentieth century modernity's promises and ultimate failures, it is not only fair, it is positively devastating. But, in any case, life always goes on; the movies continue. And *Be Kind Rewind*, in its glorious ambivalence, asks us not to mourn, but merely to get off the highway, to wander, to take our time, and to look again.

Take another glance – the alphabetical structure of this chapter is intentionally rhizomatic. In a discursive tradition that includes the distinguished likes of Robert Ray, Peter Wollen and Christian Keathley, this study proposes to demonstrate what I will call an *off-modern cinephilia*, one which does not work towards a simplistic thesis statement, but which like Gondry's film wanders through the different side streets of Film's cultural, institutional, and technological histories. I don't feel cinephilia, through its presently contested meanings, can quite account for a film like *Be Kind Rewind*, unless we define 'cinephilia' in its crudest possible iteration – a love of watching movies. Of course, many cinephiles hate such a vague definition, and further resent how this conception of the term has gained a certain amount of traction in popular film criticism today – simply, and not inaccurately, because it's watered down the term to the point of being meaningless (not to mention, 'common'). Thus, since the film's conception of movie love begs the question, this chapter will be in large measure a critique in passing of older models of cinephilia, including ultimately my own. *Be Kind Rewind* – which *is* about a deep love of the affective, technological and communal possibilities of Film – points towards a type of cinephilia the cinephiles haven't yet uncovered. Of course, it may be that *Be Kind Rewind* is *not* a cinephiliac text; but if this film does not work for cinephilia, then 'cinephilia' itself does not work. If so, I will explore some possibilities that Gondry's *Be Kind Rewind* has left for us in the unrealised pockets of Film's, and perhaps of cinephilia's, wake.

B lu-Ray – As often happens with new films, we begin with possibilities for the future. Being a relatively recent release at the time, *Be Kind Rewind* was one of the first titles I bought on the new home video format after my wife and I invested in a high-definition widescreen television and Blu-Ray digital video player (we generally live a modest existence – we don't even have cable access – but my love of film, which is not to be confused with cinephilia, got the best of me here). Movies and books are my sole vices as a collector (whiskey, thankfully, does not take up that much room, nor linger for long). At the same time, though, the possibilities of Blu-Ray are another reminder of how difficult it is to 'own' a film – the perfect sound, the perfect image, the 'total' cinematic version of a film, feels increasingly out-of-reach with each new platform that proclaims the highest clarity and resolution yet ('owning' a film's ideas and themes, meanwhile, is another equally problematic matter). Indeed, one problem which haunts cinephilia (and which *Be Kind Rewind* both embraces and rejects on at least two levels) is the potentially self-destructive obsession with personal ownership.

There is no question that the advent of Blu-Ray and high-definition home theatres have changed what it means to be a cinephile. If we take cinephilia to be, to have always been, a certain kind of *technophilia* – a love of the medium's technical potential, which is inseparable from its artistic identity – then it's hard not to appreciate the stunning clarity of image which these two innovations provide to the attentive cinephile. It is not 'film', of course, but it is what Film was trying to be.

Even on my modest 37-inch widescreen at home, details emerge that I'd never seen in movies before. Theatrical images, even 70mm or IMAX footage, may have the greatest *potential* for clarity to the viewer, but that sharpness always seems lost in the old (generally mechanical) projection, even or possibly especially on the biggest possible screens. Honestly, watching a movie on Blu-Ray, or even just a high-definition 'live' broadcast of a movie on television, at home is generally-speaking a more satisfying image of clarity than the pictures I catch at the local multiplex, whose blurriness is counterbalanced only by its considerable size, the nostalgic ritual of old-fashioned theatre-going, and the ephemeral community that is a large movie audience.

Since I began watching movies on Blu-Ray three summers ago, my sense of cinematic perception has unquestionably been altered. For the first time, I see the blurry corners, edges and lines around objects and people in regular DVD movies presented on a BR player; its imperfectly reproduced image now maxed out. I can see the faint spots of compression in HD television shows and movies on a regular television, its visual potential unfullfilled; theatrical presentations, which of course I would never for the world give up, nonetheless now contain a certain fuzzy layer of smudge that frustrates my eyes. Of course, this is all relative in the larger histories of film and home technologies. I can remember having some of the same reactions to watching VHS in the late 1990s after a few months of compulsive DVD consumption. And perhaps in another decade, I will feel the same way about Blu-Ray. Yet I have also felt at times that certain films, on the new format, have come as close to ideal as they may achieve – that moment when the *imperfections* of the captured image, which stayed hidden on VHS, television, and DVD for so long, have now become as glaring and as haunting as the perfection.

Such high-definition cinephilia is perhaps the closest we've come to a *virtual* approximation of Christian Keathley's crucial theory for the cinephile: *panoramic perception*, 'the cinephile's defining mode of vision' (2006: 30). The eye wanders, glancing across the HD widescreen image, taking in all the small details of the frame suddenly drawn into being by the power of high definition digital imagery. This new technology intensifies the cinephile's 'fetishizing of fragments of a film, either individual shots or marginal (often unintentional) details in the image, especially those that appear only for a moment' (2006: 7). Blu-Ray embraces the whole frame, and may even, one can hope, usher in a new era of Bazinian patience after decades of an obsession with various forms of montage – to once again let reality come back to the camera. I am not criticising montage as an aesthetic choice, but Blu-Ray – with the right console – reminds the homegrown cinephile what the wide, wandering frame can still potentially reveal.

Blu-Ray makes the opening shot of *Be Kind Rewind* even more striking – a helicopter boom shot over Passiac, New Jersey, crossing over a neighborhood of closely-nestled houses and then to the highway which plowed right through it, before cutting completely seamlessly to a crane shot that hovers alongside the highway, then down and panning over to camera left. The end of the shot reveals the film's main characters, Mike (Mos Def) and Jerry (Jack Black), painting graffiti on the underpass promoting the 'Be Kind Rewind' video store and thrift shop. It is a remarkable piece of virtuoso filmmaking in a movie that otherwise largely privileges simple, even crude, filmmaking 'Do-It-Yourself' techniques as forms of cinephiliac expression. The graffiti on the highways anticipates the characters' desire throughout the film to take mass-produced objects and remake them as their own, to mark them with an idiosyncratic reminder of the surrounding area. Hence, it's also a powerful, but subtle, statement on *Be Kind Rewind*'s complex and contradictory sense of 'community', which is crucial to appreciating the entire film.

Community – Not 'cinephilia', but 'community,' which are two very different things. At best, the film's notions of community offer an alternate cinephilia

– one not centered on obsessive personal fixation, but rather on the communities, however rhizomatic and fleeting, that films can create. Among contemporary cinephiles, Campbell offers the more satisfying account of what cinephilia is, or can be, today. After criticising both cinephiles who are too quick to criticise 'low-culture' popular texts and still others who embrace commodification blindly (itself perhaps a false binary), Campbell quite rightly suggests a cinephile's obligation would be ideally

> to cultivate connections beyond pockets and subcultures of cinephilia – in terms of location in geographical space and in terms of convergence upon objects (e.g. fan communities, avant-garde circles, bootleg traders). For me the fundamental question here is not one of art polemics but of community. (I feel that I run in cinephile *circles*.) (2009: 212; emphasis in original)

These pockets and subcultures of cinephile communities, presumably, offer an alternative space from the extremes of elitism and mindless consumption. Indeed, for cinephilia to thrive, it must embrace a truly selfless, democratic sense of community – though, as I will discuss later, that seems to be at odds with both elitist, and with blissfully self-indulgent, strands of cinephilia movements today.

But there are many other rhizomatic 'communities' in *Be Kind Rewind*. There is the community of people who visit the video store. There is the community that comes together to make films – a community of filmmakers. There is also the community that *watches* the films – a community of filmgoers. And within those groups remains a spirit of sharing, which stands in opposition to the rigid, controlling selfishness of urban planners and intellectual property lawyers. But even at their most intense, perhaps because of it, these communities too are all ephemeral, momentary.

These powerful, if fleeting, makeshift communities in *Be Kind Rewind*, meanwhile, have larger histories behind them. The 'Rent Party' that the people of Passiac have to save Mr. Fletcher's (Danny Glover) building in the end is taken directly from the history of Fats Waller. Gondry's idea to use Fats as a metaphor for the 'Be Kind Rewind' video store and for the community's tribute film at the end came from Waller's own performances early on at NY rent parties – get-togethers designed to help raise funds for poor families to offset unfair rent prices in African-American communities. 'Fats Waller Was Born Here' is itself ultimately a 'rent party' to save the *Be Kind Rewind* video store, but it's a powerful reminder too of the larger history of various discriminatory civic practices that also motivates the city of Passiac's desire to bulldoze the video store for upper-class condominiums.

Democratic – For so many reasons, it would be problematic to say that *Be Kind Rewind* presents a more democratic form of cinephilia, or of anything, and yet that does seem to be another one of its utopic impulses. However, I resist here any insistence on even more utopic ideas of 'participatory culture', as presently defined. It is not so much 'new media' that empowers audiences in *Be Kind Rewind*, but rather a clever reuse of old technologies like video camcorders and VHS. Importantly, the film also reminds us that participatory culture, like cinephilia, too often drives right over the economic and educational questions of access. 'Videophilia', writes Lucas Hilderbrand, 'has become a lifeline for millions of people who don't belong' (2009b: 216), as well as the people who cannot, logistically or financially, belong even if they wanted to.

Some cinephiles seem to have forgotten not just the *Cahiers'* championing of Hollywood films, but more specifically one central aspect to the otherwise much cherished French theorist André Bazin's ideas on film – not the indexicality of the image, but the *cinema as a democratic medium*. While Bazin was certainly focused on the aesthetics of this once new medium, he was also acutely aware of its use-value. Cinema, Bazin understood, was made for an audience and not just for its own stylistic sake. In his famous essay, 'Adaptation, or the Cinema as Digest', he argued that popular Hollywood adaptations of well-known, and deeply respected, literary works may be aesthetically crude, or even insulting to the source material. But, Bazin argued, the adaptation was not made with total fidelity in mind; rather, it was about taking the essence of a popular literary work and using the medium of film to transmit those themes and ideas to a larger general audience. As a result of the essential ontological differences between two different media, rather than condescending oversimplification, the art of literature, he wrote, 'has been made more accessible through cinematic adaptation' (2000: 26). One could rightly note a certain elitist strand to Bazin's thinking – he saw film as distributing the high culture of literature to the 'masses' of regular folks. But Bazin also understood, and even embraced, that film was a commercial and populist medium first – something that cinephiles have perhaps increasingly lost sight of in the decades since, as they work to resist Hollywood and other 'popular' films in the search for more marginalised texts and auteurs. This is a valid critical project to be sure, but one whose consequences remain undefined.

If one has any illusions of film as, if not necessarily a truly democratic medium then at least a more ambivalent one, then it is perhaps easier to *not* be a cinephile. This is where I find myself personally today, dissatisfied equally with both prevalent notions of cinephilia – on both sides of the low/high culture divide – and with increasingly complicated attempts to define 'film' ontologically in a new age of remediation and convergence. And if the most prominent contemporary cinephiles, such as Australian critic Adrian Martin, choose to define cinephilia as unapologetically elitist (as I discuss later), how can it become anything but?

This nagging, persistent question of elitism, the curious obsession for some with separating out the mere fan, or even just the wrong kind of fan, also suggests to me that Campbell's admirable notion of a truly integrated cinephile 'community' is impossibly utopic.

Be Kind Rewind's love of Hollywood films, of the ability for *anyone* to express their cinephilia, and of the affective potential of these films to generate a sense of community, harkens back to Bazin's more democratic form of cinephilia. Of course, it would be foolish to say unproblematically that *Be Kind Rewind's* glorification of amateur filmmaking is a truly democratic possibility for cinephilia, in no small part since Gondry's movie and its distribution ultimately works, intended or otherwise, to serve further the interests of corporate Hollywood. However, Mike and Jerry's (and Gondry's) emphases on a do-it-yourself filmmaking mindset represent a form of genuine cinephiliac *production*, beyond just loving movies, and sparked by a deep love of film, one which older models of cinephilia allow for. To a point, there is a truly 'amateur' sense of cinephilia at work in *Be Kind Rewind* (I say to a point because it is all ultimately a largely utopic diegetic and, thus, imaginary depiction of amateur filmmaking).

Ephemerality – or, *'the vibe'*. In his book, Gondry recalled an instance in the making of the documentary, *Dave Chappelle's Block Party* (2006), where he was trying to 'document' the day-to-day goings-on in Chappelle's life. Since nothing was occurring late one night, he wondered why Dave and his crew didn't just go to bed in order to get up at a normal time. Gondry remembered Corey Smyth, Chappelle's music supervisor, telling him that 'You don't stop the vibe, Michel. You don't stop the vibe. That's why' (2008: 13). The concept completely baffled Gondry:

> Damn it, what is 'the vibe'? A collective mood? Intellectual exchange? Laughter? … Not much was said. I was trying to feel the vibe. I had all my technological equipment ready to detect any type of vibration that my five senses might miss. Nothing. Two hours later, like the Big Bang, it came from nothing, out of nowhere: an idea. An idea to do a comedy tour in jails all over the United States. […] That night I understood what Cory had meant by 'the vibe', and why I had never managed to make a hip-hop video: I was never there at the right time. (2008: 13)

The vibe is an unplanned moment when different factors – people, moods, settings, technologies – come together to create and capture a fleeting event that transcends just one person or time. And just as quickly it had passed. It is, in essence, the holy grail of documentary filmmaking. Early in the film, inside the 'Be Kind Rewind' video store, children improvise a story of Fats Waller (with the film's diegetic auteur, Mike, setting the stage with the record player), foreshadowing *the spirit of ephemeral performance* which haunts the film, and which makes it all the more bittersweet, all the more heartbreakingly tender, in the end. The sweded films are in part about this ephemeral vibe, about working together collectively and spontaneously to catch on film a creative *something* before it's gone for good.

When the 'cast' in and of *Be Kind Rewind* finally sits down to watch *Fats Waller Was Born Here* at the end, Gondry filmed their actual reactions to seeing the footage of themselves for the first time. *Be Kind Rewind*'s final moments are *not* staged, at least as much as one could expect given the circumstances. Everyone watches attentively; their faces peeking from the darkness, illuminated by the screen. The cast of *Be Kind Rewind* really did shoot a complete documentary for the film on video, and – just as importantly – Gondry photographed them watching their work. It was this raw footage that was included in the final cut of the film:

> I wanted to see them get taken in by the images; capturing their first unfiltered expression before the knee-jerk reaction to act kicked in. I think they didn't expect much from those scenes, considering how rushed they were, and perhaps had forgotten about them by the end of principal photography. So I got exactly what I was hoping for: an expression of genuine surprise, pride, and laughter, loads of laughter. (2008: 19)

The final sequence is a snapshot of people watching yet another snapshot of their lives. *Be Kind Rewind*, like all cinephiliac texts in that old indexical, Bazinian sort of way, is about capturing moments, about capturing them in the act of passing. This ephemera also speaks to the experience of watching films – it echoes Barthes' notion of bliss, of Willemen and Keathley's respective work on the *cinephiliac moment*. At its most intense, films provoke us with a momentary glimpse of a fragment of an image that instills within us indescribable joy. *But it is so joyous precisely because it is so fleeting.*

Film – The medium of film itself is, or precisely was, fleeting. Gondry's work is a love letter to film that highlights seemingly every audio and/or visual medium except film. One could say it's a story in part about how film, as movie-going ritual and as artistic automatism, haunts the age of media convergence. But strictly speaking, there is no 'film' in a movie whose primary focus is a love of film. Within the narrative and the promotional strategies of *Be Kind Rewind*, there are records, radios, videos, televisions, flashes of DVDs, internet filesharing, and even digital projectors – but there is no actual film, not 16mm, not 35mm, not Super 8. Moreover, the film understands that technological change brings with it a nostalgia for earlier eras, which always already co-exists with the present. That, since the days of Walter Benjamin, the more 'innovation' pulls us forward, the more melancholy tries to pull us back.

In *The Virtual Life of Film*, D. N. Rodowick highlights the persistence of film in the age of new media – an era where film was fundamentally absent as a technological medium in our current digital culture; 'Film is no longer a modern medium', he writes, 'it is completely historical' (2007: 93). In the old days of film, when light bounced off an object and burned its shadow onto celluloid, there was an indexical link between the image and the thing captured in the image – 'a unique record', writes Rodowick, 'of a single duration' (2007: 15). However, with the emergent ubiquity of digital media, all images are now just ones and zeroes, captured by a camera and translated into binary code, before being re-translated back into a series of ontologically distinct images. Through this computer processing of information, that old duration, that powerful indexicality, is lost in a seemingly perfect digital simulation. The era of film – of Barthes, Bazin, and Cavell – has thus passed. And yet, as in *Be Kind Rewind*, the idea of film haunts our culture as an 'automatism', something which structures how we see and interpret visual media – 'the idea of cinema persists in the term "digital cinema", as a way of easing the transition to a different (media) world' (Rodowick 2007: 177). As a mode of perception and of appearance, the memory of 'film' remains the model by which we perceive and interpret moving digital images.

In some sense, *Be Kind Rewind* is the perfect cinephiliac text in a post-cinema world, because it's a movie that's about film in spirit only. As such, there may be few contemporary movies that, ironically, are more in tune with 'film' at our current historical moment, as it places the passing of the film within a larger history of modernist transformations, from trains to highways, from radio to television, from film to video, from VHS to DVD, from celluloid to digital projection, from tape to internet circulation. The store's owner, Mr. Fletcher (Danny Grover), is introduced as a man who possesses the inability to move on from the past, as established in a poignant early moment. Fletcher tells the story of waiting too long to ask a girl to marry him, and then not being able to move on to anyone else after the loss. It is a perfect metaphor for his own life, his own business (running a thrift store and renting VHS tapes in an age of DVDs), his own building. However, importantly, it is also a perfect metaphor for 'film' in an age of media convergence. We cannot let go of the medium even when so much else has taken its place. *Not that we necessarily should*, as the urban and technological transformations within and around Mr. Fletcher's store also illustrates. On the wall inside is a poster for the film, *Blast From the Past* (1998). Since 'Be Kind Rewind' also serves as a thrift shop, we see a larger celebration of modern media's past, littered with camcorders, record players, radios, and televisions, sometimes even in the same shot.

Gentrification – Beyond technological questions of the digital and of film, at the heart of *Be Kind Rewind* rests a cultural critique of what modernity did to American urban spaces. The highway plowed over the neighborhood in which the video store sits; Mr. Fletcher's store, too, is the site for Passiac's desire to 'start over' and replace his home with new condos for (presumably white) upper-middle class commuter yuppies, while he is relocated to the projects. The building is to be demolished for the ironically-titled '*Olde* Passiac Gardens' – a simulacrum of urban pasts, a faux-trendy complex less interested in restoring Passiac's past than in bulldozing another chapter of it for good. Gentrification, like the highways, not only destroys communities, but stresses as its justification nothing more than the abstract utopic ideals of 'Progress' and 'Convenience' for their own sake, with little concern for whom it benefits.

Highways – There is a kindred spirit in *Be Kind Rewind*, as there was in the course of twentieth-century modernity, between films and highways. This is perhaps most explicitly symbolised when the lawyers use a bulldozer late in the film to pulverise the pirated tapes into the road. Like these older, low-income neighborhoods, illegal copies of movies only stand in the way of profit and progress. Moreover, this connection is crucial to understanding the film's cultural critique. The first shot of *Be Kind Rewind* is an DIY image of a map of New York and New Jersey, an establishing shot for both the film, and the 'film within a film', *Fats Waller Was Born Here* – a documentary which is less a story of Fats Waller and more a celebration of the people in Passiac who are connected with the video store. Within this deceptively simple first geographical shot, we see many of the film's central concerns: a love of (black and white) filmmaking past, a love of (improvised) filmmaking present, a deep sense of place, and an enduring affection for the old transportation of trains in a pre-highway age. The next shot in the film is of the train where Fats (as played by Def) passes away from pneumonia. Thus, trains exist throughout the narrative of *Be Kind Rewind* as a companion and counterpoint to film, another forgotten fragment of modernity.

The opening montage also reminds us that highways took the place of rail. In one of the film's more subtly brilliant images (mentioned earlier), a helicopter overhead shot of the highway cuts seamlessly into a crane shot. The privatisation of cars took over the more outdated, public form of transportation. *Be Kind Rewind* reminds us immediately that highways plowed over and divided urban neighborhoods to the benefit of white suburban spaces – highways, like film, separated cultures and spaces further even while in the process of supposedly uniting them. But *Be Kind Rewind* is less interested in polemically condemning white flight than in championing the possibilities which struggle to exist in its wake (though we mustn't ever overlook that Gondry's self-reflexive film is also very much a deconstructive critique of the suburbs and of white privilege as it was institutionalised in the second half of the twentieth century). The same crane shot angles down over and under the highway, and shows the audience that which exists literally and metaphorically under the highway, what life continues on there … indifferent to the speed and rush in which so much of American road and media culture mindlessly exists.

The film's gentle, soft-spoken style, I believe, is a direct critique of this senseless cultural rush that both highways and Hollywood narrative films often perpetuate in a mutually reassuring movement towards a notion of profit and progress that benefits only an increasingly dwindling few. In the underpass, Mike and Jerry embrace graffiti's potential to re-appropriate the generic surfaces of modernity to mark a distinctive community. Jerry, meanwhile, lives in an old, probably undrivable, Recreational Vehicle in his junkyard – two images which continue the film's motif of highways (and of the highway's forgotten relics), while also subtly foreshadowing what will later become explicit – Jerry's distinct feeling of placelessness in Passiac, of being between locations, but with no way to leave, which in turn explicitly reinforces the elusive theme of community.

I mitation – Cinephilia is always partly about imitation, mimicking other films and other writers. *Be Kind Rewind* playfully highlights how even the most creative innovations aren't exactly 'original'. They are rooted in the imitation of others, which by virtue of its similarity paradoxically internalises its difference from the original (this is, of course, just my imitation of Deleuzian film theory). More precisely, cinephilia is often about finding new ideas in the act of imitation. The diegetic filmmakers in *Be Kind Rewind* find joy in imitating the medium of film, complete with black and white lenses and string to simulate film scratches, as well as recreating beloved movies like *Boyz n the Hood* (1991) and *Robocop* (1987); a more focused fan might also notice that *Be Kind Rewind* itself subtly imitates shots from *Ghostbusters* when Mike and Jerry leave the library, and again at the end when they wave to the crowd upon exiting Mr. Fletcher's building.

An attentive cinephile, meanwhile, may also note that this project of mine is an imitation of other cinephiliac scholarship – namely, Robert Ray's initial work in *The Avant-garde Finds Andy Hardy* (1995) and then developed further in *The ABCs of Classic Hollywood* (2008) along with Peter Wollen's remarkable essay, 'An Alphabet of Cinema' (2001) (pre-eminent cinephile blogger Girish Shambu has also called attention to this format on his own website). Both Wollen and Ray's respective works use the method of an alphabet, and the explicit passion of cinephilia, to open up larger truths about film theory and history. They are both intentionally playful, reflecting their cinephiliac origins. They both intentionally wander, reflecting their off-modern sensibilities. Yet they are by no means simple to compose. Being forced to find words for some letters also forces one to rethink the text(s) in question from new perspectives, as my own imitation has uncovered. This tangential style also has precedent, of course, in the 'cinephiliac anecdotes' of Christian Keathley's influential *Cinephilia and History*. The 'A–Z's of *Be Kind Rewind* are intended to reflect the non-linear, zig-zag nature of an off-modern cinephilia – I am less interested in putting forth one straightforward argument than in exploring the side streets of the larger technological, aesthetic, cultural and historical issues raised by the film. The peculiar format of this chapter is consciously constructed as homage to, and a continuation of, cinephiliac writings of the past. There is, in short, a whole discursively undiscovered tradition of off-modern cinephilia in which the present study is also situated.

Jamais Vu – Speaking of imitation, in 2005, I started a blog (*Jamais Vu*) mainly because Steven Shaviro blogged. It was novel then, but now every academic has a blog. The blogging moment (which Scott and I tried to capture in *Cinephilia in the Age of Digital Reproduction: Film, Pleasure and Digital Culture, Vol. 1*) has, by virtue of its ubiquity, now passed. And yet as long as there are compulsive writers like me, something like blogs will always linger. Writing, and sharing that writing through various internet venues, is a crucial part of being a cinephile today. As a writer, including one who struggled for so long to get started on this very chapter, I can appreciate the creative touchiness of Gondry's 'vibe'. I used to struggle endlessly for ideas, even motivation, procrastinating with television, internet, videogames and food, before the 'right time' takes over – at which point I can write and write for several hours, with little concern for anything but the idea (this process has shifted, by necessity, since I recently became a father). And most frustratingly, whether it is late, or time for a bathroom break, it is very, very difficult to stop once I've started. Even if I wanted to. The vibe has taken over. I tell my wife that I need at least fifteen minutes to wind down when I plan to stop. I cannot just hit 'Ctrl+S' and end. I feel I need to drain every last random, incongruous idea down on my laptop screen before I can stop. Later on, I can figure out what it was I was trying to say, as I invariably have any number of half or badly misspelled sentences lingering about, unfinished from my constant jumping around as ideas hit me.

This is not irrelevant to cinephilia, by the way, as any affection for the cinema must find a way to manifest itself in production. And I do not consider this chapter mine alone – it emerged from a process of reading other people's work, of watching and rewatching films, of conversations on Facebook, of writing blog posts on the film. Invariably, I find myself re-reading what I already wrote, often without any recognition of what it was I originally tried to convey. In that sense, my process of writing involves conversations with myself, too – not only in that I often talk to myself while writing, but in that I use the written traces of my own forgotten work to compel me in a new direction. As Sean Connery said in *Indiana Jones and the Last Crusade* (1989), 'I wrote [ideas] down in my diary, so that I wouldn't *have* to remember' them. But that is a memory for another day – and appropriately one I needn't write down to remember.

On *Jamais Vu*, I blogged twice about *Be Kind Rewind*. Typically, Paul Thomas Anderson, James Bond and *Star Trek* are the only texts I tend to revisit on multiple occasions (and the first only because I keep planning to write a book about him, and will one of these days). The first entry was in the fall of 2008, after I first watched the film on DVD (an appropriate confession – I've never watched this film in a movie theatre). In that entry, I was trying to describe its ritualistic impulse, which seemed to speak to my initial fascination. The second time was about a year later, as I was trying more fully to work through the ideas that were slowly and awkwardly finding their way here. Both blog posts were incomplete as ideas alone, but also a vital aspect of this writing process. And that ultimately is the value of blogging about film – to build a community, perhaps (these communities do not really hold), but more often to work towards a deeper idea.

*K*ane – whether or not it is the greatest American film ever made (and my vote remains Hitchcock's *Vertigo* [1958], for those folks keeping score at home), Orson Welles' *Citizen Kane* (1941) is an impossible one for any cinephile to get around today. Like *Citizen Kane*, *Be Kind Rewind* begins at the end, with footage and flashbacks of *Fats Waller Was Born Here* that only make sense once one has seen the entire film and then gone back (that is, *Rewind*). In ways more subtle than his earlier masterpiece *Eternal Sunshine of the Spotless Mind* (2004), Gondry's more recent film also plays with time. But, in *Be Kind Rewind*, time does not so much jump back and forth as it does *stop*, leisurely holding co-existent pasts and presents together simultaneously (the thrift store is littered with clocks, including ones that fittingly do not work). In the scene where the whole community comes together to put the shooting schedule for *Fats Waller Was Born Here* in order, they too decide that this must also begin at the end, with the death of Fats on the train. And, in case we miss the cinephiliac connection, one character is there to remind us that *Citizen Kane*, that great cinephiliac text du jour, also began at the end.

*'L*et Us Watch Our Film' – A love of film, as *Be Kind Rewind* dramatises literally, is so often about *watching ourselves*. We watch films to watch our own experiences, our own feelings, our own thoughts, our own needs, symbolically played out on film. Although it is easy enough to dismiss the projection and fascination as all more complicated, there nonetheless remains a very real element of narrative wish-fulfillment in cinephiliac love. In the film's finale, the community comes together to watch *Fats Waller Was Born Here* in the first floor of Mr. Fletcher's building. Here, that wish-fulfillment becomes literal, as well as nostalgic. As Gondry recalled:

> Watching the sincere expressions of joy on their faces, I rediscovered what it was like to watch Super 8 home movies. As kids, my brothers and I would purposely wait some years before allowing ourselves to watch our home movies again. I remember studying each scratch on the image as a mark of a previous screening. In fact, I would remember the last screening event more than the actual moment captured on the film.

The 'cast' watched the movie shown from a digital projector, and yet the old school effect of cinema remains. And the reason the end of the film, the unresolved narrative ambiguity, has moved me to tears in the past is because it's not about plot resolution – it is about ephemeral joy, *let us watch our film and then we'll go*, about filmgoing as a momentary community, as fleeting as every other source of delight and connection in our lives. Passiac has come together to watch its film – it is not an illusory moment of happiness, it is not false in any way. And yet it is not permanent either. Nevertheless, their joy, their laughter is, dare I say, '*real*'. The film ends with irresolution, but also with a genuine display of cinephiliac community. And one realises, at the very end of *Be Kind Rewind*, that this whole time we have not been invited to a story of video stores, amateur filmmakers or forgotten communities – we have been invited to witness, in both form and content, the powerfully ritualistic affect of media.

M ine – The crucial narrative turn in the plot of *Be Kind Rewind* (if one can call it a plot) is when the evil studio lawyers show up to destroy all the sweded movies, claiming copyright violations. Casting Sigourney Weaver as one of the lawyers who wishes to destroy any illegal copies of *Ghostbusters*, among other titles, gives the film an added level of irony. Conversely, one of the film's most memorable lines is Mrs. Falewicz's (Mia Farrow) declaration shortly thereafter that 'our pasts belong to us; we can change it'. The idea is that the community can make any movie they want about Passiac, because she believes that in many ways the city's history belongs to the residents who live there. *Be Kind Rewind* then ends twenty minutes later with these two competing and unreconciled notions of 'ownership' – on the one hand, corporate control in a new era of horizontal integration and globalisation, an extension of twentieth century modernity and 'progress', and, on the other, the more personal insistence that our memories, our passions, our failures, our hopes, always already belong to us.

Something at the heart of cinephiliac passion, something which rarely is sufficiently foregrounded, is an obsession with *ownership*, we think we own a film just because we love it, just because we own certain memories attached to a particular moment of its consumption, and because we think that that film which makes us so happy must love us in return. One of my own disillusionments with cinephilia of late, among many, is the recognition that films don't exist for me

– this is hard, maybe impossible, for a cinephile to accept. I may momentarily wallow in its bliss, either alone or communally, but it is not mine. It may seem harmless to simply want to 'own' a beloved film, to arrogantly display my own cinephilia as a self-justifying reason to think films belong to me, but that becomes complicated where there are many different 'cinephilias', each with very different agendas, and each one often more self-important, ignorant, and even intolerant of other cinephilias, than the last.

As an off-modernist text, *Be Kind Rewind* and Gondry's community utopia initially suggested to me a form of 'amateur' cinephilia, a type of film consumption and production that was, mainly due to economics and institutional factors, resolutely outside the traditional and elitist channels of cinephile behavior. But this presents a problem for cinephilia. For example, it is particularly trendy for hardcore cinephiles to self-identify as an 'amateur' cinephile, as someone outside the professional venues of old-school, dead-tree film criticism, of the scholarly rigor of academia, of the challenges of teaching cinema, or the ambitions of professional filmmaking. This has been particularly enabled by the proliferation of film blogs, which seems on the surface to have democratised film criticism (though this is a valid topic for another debate). But one problem with *amateur* cinephilia, however, is that it isn't really 'amateur'. Most every dedicated cinephile mobilises her/his life around film. Even cinephiles who don't technically work with film as a full-time job nonetheless dedicate much of their energy into writing about film, sharing films, producing films, and – most importantly – in defining film, *defining cinephilia* for everyone. This commitment significantly blurs the line between professional and amateur cinephilia.

The idea of an *amateur* form of cinephilia, as it is typically used, seems ultimately just to be a way for aspiring film critics to deny ownership of ideas, or more precisely, to *avoid responsibility*. Typically, the notion of an 'amateur' is deployed rhetorically to deflect expertise and attention – 'I'm just an amateur, but this is what I think'. This can, in cinephiliac circles, come across as a passive/aggressive attempt to avoid commitment, to never have to claim authority, to never have to stand by what you've written. This is a 'have-it-both-ways' form of writing about movies – to aspire to the highest level of discourse about the cinema, to write the best that has ever been written, but also to have an 'out' at the end of the day. A claim to amateur status allows one to retain the option, if necessary, to never have to acknowledge what anyone else has already written, to never have to undergo close scrutiny for the ideas casually put forth, and to never have to claim, let alone prove, that one has said anything truly new (and this un-reflexive aspect is too often the biggest problem with so much of the *amateur* writing on cinephilia). A truly 'amateur cinephilia', if one can call it that, is exactly that form of movie consumption which so many cinephiles actively resist, and even criticise.

Being a cinephile today presumes a very specific base of pre-existing knowledge and of behaviors (one travels to the right festivals, worships at the right theatres, reads the right authors, visits the right blogs, discusses the right films), and thus is *elitist to the core*. It might be less frustrating, at the same time, if cinephiles were more self-critical about their own elitism, but that too often is not the case. Preminent cinephile Adrian Martin even suggests that cinephiles are only deluding themselves if they resist their own elitism. In a 2009 article entitled, 'Cinephilia as War Machine', Martin writes:

> It is sometimes said that cinephilia is elitist. Why, so what, and who cares? Actually, the thought or the charge of this elitism sometimes gets through to cinephiles; they start imagining they are, instead, absolutely *of* the people, more like the people than the people themselves, conveyers of the very spirit of popular/populist art. (2009: 224)

According to Martin, the temptation for other cinephiles can be to see the cinema as a democratic medium, and by politicising it, to convince themselves somehow that cinephiles, in their deliberately self-marginalised polemics, are fighting for the 'people'. On the contrary, Martin insists, cinephiles must distinguish themselves by being above other mere lovers of film by their tastes and by their ability to put thought into writing about the cinema. Earlier, Martin describes what he views as the distinction between a cinephile and a film lover, between being a true connoisseur of the medium and simply its mindless consumer:

> The cinephile, however, wants to be identified as someone different from the mere film fan or film nerd who, in their dreary, uninspired ways, love the cinema. Cinephiles are a band of outsiders, a band apart – or they are nothing. And that is what is galling in the contemporary climate, when every second website is calling itself cinephile-this and cinephile-that, when the books and conferences on cinephilia as a scholarly topic are multiplying: when, in short, the institutionalization, and thus the taming, of cinephilia, looms. (2009: 221)

Since everyone loves going to the movies, since films are always already an intricate part of everyday life, he argues, it is not enough to be considered a cinephile. The term is thus becoming dangerously close to being appropriated as such by thoughtless filmgoers, and in turn commodified by various media industries as the latest marketing niche for a particular form of consumer. However, Martin seems equally dissatisfied with most every other previous form of cinephilia that more careful thinkers have previously put forth:

> I do not believe, for instance, that cinephilia is essentially a solitary activity, a melancholic activity, a Christian activity, or a surrealist activity. I don't believe that it

necessarily equates with either left or right politics, or a total lack of politics either. I don't believe cinephilia proceeds in tidy generational waves. I don't believe there is a discernible canon of cinephile films. I don't believe that cinephilia is dependent on any particular type of technology, whether the old-fashioned movie theater or the new-fangled DVD player. I don't believe that cinephiles only truly care about fragments (or Benjaminian ruins) of films in a modernist or postmodernist flux. I don't believe that cinephilia is essentially a matter of nutty, obsessive viewing rituals (however much fun these might be), or what Noel King calls 'discursive regularities' in the way that cinephiles write or speak or teach about what they love. For there is no such regularity. (2009: 222)

There isn't much room left to breathe in Martin's polemic. By the end of the essay, he pretty much makes it impossible to actually *be* a cinephile (and I'm not sure I disagree with that part), other than within an under-defined space reserved for the lucky few – a social construction defined through its own use-value, as established by a largely unspoken agreement between a handful of people. Arbitrary, and self-justifying. Those folks, it seems, can own the term.

What can we *do* with cinephilia? Martin's solution for how to define cinephilia is to suggest that it is at best a momentary cinephiliac impulse, which leads to a larger process of thought and production, instead of 'just a load of nonsense about devising best-film lists and seeing six thousand movies' (2009: 222). On some levels, this vague compulsion to thought and to discourse just echoes Keathley's earlier notion of the 'cinephiliac anecdote', which previously argued that the fetishised fragments which the cinephile so privileges is wholly incomplete unless it opens up into a larger informative narrative about pockets of film history. Martin and Keathley's respective work attempts to negotiate, as other chapters in this volume explore, the lingering issue of cinephilia's use-value. More than anything, it is this, the 'so what?' question, that creates a division between cinephilia and academia more-or-less as wide as that between cinephilia and fan cultures.

As with all the other ephemeral components of *Be Kind Rewind*, it is so hard for me to hold on to my cinephilia, so much so that I feel much better just letting it go, leaving it to others to haggle over (often in circles). Yes, everything I have ever published about cinephilia up to this very moment is completely wrong, but thankfully no one ever read those articles either. But I prefer to think of this off-modern digression as my elegy to cinephilia. I love film, but I love a lot of things. I love writing, and I love writing about a lot of things (and one of the main reasons I love *Be Kind Rewind* is that it both embraces a very intelligent form of cinephilia, to a point, but also reminds me that there are a lot of other important things in life too). Between my earlier writings on cinephilia and this chapter, I wrote an entire dissertation and later a book about the racial and convergence histories of

Disney's notorious *Song of the South* (1946), a project that had nothing to do with cinephilia or even my own personal opinions about media texts. It was as 'objective' as one can write, and, upon my return to this rocky cinephiliac terrain, that complicated reception study (along with other developments) has permanently altered my perception of the ambivalent *cultures* of movie 'love'. Ultimately, I am more comfortable self-identifying as a reception studies scholar (that too is subject to change, but I suspect it will be ultimately more enduring). It is less painful to write about how *other* people feel.

Nostalgia – Cinephilia, even at this most polemical, at its most violent, always retains more than one nostalgic strand in its heart. There are many nostalgias at work in *Be Kind Rewind* – many of them, directly or indirectly, Gondry's. The opening anecdote of *You'll Like This Film Because You're In It* is of the filmmaker's nostalgic embrace of his own suburban childhood. Gondry's youth, following his hippie mother, was (like the opening boom shot over the highways in *Be Kind Rewind*) a *return* from white flight, when he, his brother and mother moved back to the city. 'In Paris', he writes, 'there were no water towers or malls in sight' (2008: 7). Yet, and this is important, for all his disdain for the suburbs ('a conservative town plagued by hordes of old families wearing the same green loden from generation to generation' [ibid.]), Gondry also cannot give up the deep affection for his childhood home:

> I still visit and rebuy that [childhood house] every night in my dreams. I generally call my brother (from the dream) to tell him the great news: 'Guess what? I just bought the Versailles house. Mom is there already. Come with us. We are getting the family back together'. I am childhood-traumatized. (Ibid.)

There is also, building directly from those experiences, nostalgia for 1980s American cinema – *Ghostbusters*, *Robocop*, *Driving Miss Daisy* (1989), Danny Glover, Mia Farrow, Sigourney Weaver, and so forth. For being a celebrated visual innovator of music videos and stylised cinematic editing, Gondry seems grounded in a simple affection for a 'cinematic' childhood not entirely unlike my own (white, formulaic, suburban, Bill Murray).

Nostalgia often has a notoriously conservative connotation, of course, as it's usually associated with an unhealthy obsession with returning to an illusory and idealised past. It is, even at its best, a longing for something that cannot ever be reached. And yet I believe that nostalgia remains impossible to get around when thinking about cinephilia – I'm sure some cinephiles would disagree, particularly young ones. But a love of film always co-exists with a love of film's/films past. And so many cinephiliac anecdotes that litter scholarship and other writings on film are rooted in a deep nostalgia for places and people past. Do we not hold on to some films, to try to 'own' them, so deeply precisely because it's a chance to hold onto the particular moment in which we discovered them? That's not to say the particular title in question is irrelevant, only that over time our affection for the film and our affection for the context is irreversibly entangled. But, at the same time, this is not to say that such impulses from (towards) the past must be always already reactionary.

For this reason, in *The Future of Nostalgia*, Boym distinguishes between restorative and reflective forms of nostalgia. The latter is similar to the type of nostalgia more commonly associated with conservative conceptions of the past as an ideal world that must be protected, and used to justify legal, civic and military actions under a cause of national identity. Reflective nostalgia, meanwhile, is not only more personal, but more incomplete and fluid, too. 'This type of nostalgic narrative', she writes, 'is ironic, inconclusive and fragmentary … the past opens up a multitude of potentialities, nonteleological possibilities of historical development' (2001: 50). It recognised how unstable and unreliable the past is, no matter how tightly one tried to hold onto it. Reflective nostalgia is also more potentially progressive, according to Boym, because the opportunities lost or unfulfilled in the imperfect past could set new goals looking towards the future.

There's no question that *Be Kind Rewind* is nostalgic, but for what? Possibly for earlier technologies, for earlier modes of transportation, maybe even for an earlier notion of 'community' seeming lost in the advances of modernity. Yet the film's relationship to (and conception of) the past is complicated. As the most glaring example, *Fats Waller Was Born Here* is a deliberate distortion of Passiac's past by its own residents. The documentary at heart of *Be Kind Rewind* is an ideally reflexive contradiction – both the most perfect realisation of nostalgia's darkest impulse (*the past will be what we say it was*) and the most utopic nostalgic liberation (*we can reject tradition, to which we are not bound forever*). In this, Gondry's film becomes the epitome of nostalgia's (and cinephilia's) fundamental temporal ambivalence, futures told through lost pasts:

> Nostalgics of the second order [reflective] are aware of the gap between identity and resemblance; the home is in ruins or, on the contrary, has just been renovated and gentrified beyond recognition. The defamiliarization and sense of distance drives them to tell their story, to narrate the relationship between past, present and future. (Boym 2001: 50)

This is film's ambivalence as well, as the recent fears over the loss of titles as movies migrate to DVD and now to Blu-Ray indicates, or giant multiplexes or video stores overrun by a hundred copies of the same movie, rather than one copy of a hundred different titles still to be explored. Is this not a question of access against a tide of development which the cinephile often fights? This notion of nostalgia, not one rooted in a stable lost past, represents for Boym a renewed opportunity – against the forward, linear pull of technological, historical and cultural 'progress' – to investigate past histories still waiting to be explored. 'Sometimes', she adds, 'nostalgia is not directed towards the past either, but rather sideways. The nostalgic feels stifled within the conventional confines of time and space' (2001: xiv). Like *Fats Waller Was Born Here*, nostalgia is rarely about the past, of course, but rather is much more often about our *present* relationship to it.

Off-Modernism – So what of my persistent claim to off-modernism? '*Off*-modern pulls us sideways – that is, it pulls us away from an obsessive fixation on working towards the new, on following the linear, on seeing the end-game. The use-value of such a thing might be precisely in its inability to be easily categorised. For example, *Be Kind Rewind* has no clear ending in the old Classic Hollywood sense of the word – it doesn't try to satisfy the loose narrative threads running throughout the film. It invites us instead to go back and look again. Off-Modernism, wrote Boym, was a (forever?) unfinished project of modernity, one 'based on an alternative understanding of temporality, not as a teleology of prog-ress or transcendence but as a superimposition and coexistence of heteroge-neous times' (2001: 30). The notion above of reflective nostalgia leads directly to her discussion of the 'Off-Modernists', various artists who incorporated the affec-tive hindsight of nostalgia, of the contradictions of personal and public history, to envision creative spaces that moved with, against, and alongside the straight line of modernity. Rather than constantly proclaim the perpetual anticipation and arrival of a perfect cultural and technological future, Boym writes, 'Off-Modern art and lifestyle explores the hybrids of past and present. […] In this version of modernity, affection and reflection are not mutually exclusive but reciprocally illuminating, even when the tension remains unresolved and longing incurable' (2001: 30). I feel this might be beneficial to understanding *Be Kind Rewind*'s atypical form of cinephilia – the film foregrounds cinephilia's peculiar form of reflective nostalgia (as mentioned above), its distinct hybrid of technological and cultural time periods, and its symbolic and *literal* emphasis on the 'sideshadows and back alleys rather than the straight road of progress' (Boym 2001: xvii).

The recent obsession with cinephilia as a scholarly topic in academia, and as a critical lens in the blogosphere, in many ways heightens its ambiguity. An off-modern cinephilia might dwell less on what is or is not properly defined 'cineph-ilia', on who is or is not a cinephile, and would perhaps instead explore openly the intellectual and communal tangents and lines of flight which a love of film contin-ually, and unexpectedly, generates. It would be informed perhaps by a rhizomatic hybrid of innovative newness and still unrealised past technological potential, of pre-existing critical traditions and self-reflexive nostalgias. Only perhaps, though.

To dwell too much on a definition of an off-modern American cinephilia would be to miss the moment, and get too far from what the film is trying to show us in the first place.

As an off-modern text, *Be Kind Rewind* does not invite us to the definitive definition of being a cinephile, or of anything else. There is no utopic narrative of triumph, metatextually or narratively – one where the people's voices are finally heard, where the evil corporations and intellectual property lawyers are finally defeated, or where real estate developers finally see the destructive arrogance of their ways. No, life is somewhat as it was before, though intensified by a momentary, communal cinephilia so powerful (to me) precisely because it is so narratively modest. Anyone who sees a greater overcoming in the film's final moments is not looking close enough, and anyone who tries hard to see it regardless is merely fooling themselves about the film and about the world it has ambivalently captured. Yet *Be Kind Rewind* is hardly dystopic either; it seeks instead an exploration, an understanding, of cultural and technological pasts and presents as they intersect with the people who have and will continue to negotiate them, to alternately resist and celebrate them, in the years to come.

'Participatory Culture' – So much of *Be Kind Rewind*'s unique cinephilia is enmeshed in its unique depiction of movie *audiences*. Tryon noted that the film not only celebrated amateur filmmaking, but encouraged its audience to do likewise. *Be Kind Rewind*'s 'depiction of characters lovingly recreating these older films was also meant to inspire fans of the film – or of web video in general – to produce their own sweded videos, inviting them into the feedback loop of promotion and participation' (Tryon 2009: 31). It is tempting to read *Be Kind Rewind* at least in part through the lens of Henry Jenkins' idea of 'participatory culture', the sense in which audiences maintain greater agency and control than ever before over the media they consume, a 'culture in which fans and other consumers are invited to actively participate in the creation and circulation of new content' (2006: 290). Cinephilia is just one type of participatory culture (or vice versa, depending on who's framing the discussion). Within media studies, this is currently the predominant paradigm for examining how various audiences appropriate media content to their own ends, such as fan fiction, websites, movies, and other amateur productions that work in dialogue with the intellectual property that inspires them. But in at least two crucial ways, this paradigm doesn't quite work for *Be Kind Rewind*. For one, the intellectual property lawyers in the film would seem to dampen participatory culture's utopic conception of fandom and audience behavior. If anything, *Be Kind Rewind*'s diegetic and paratextual[1] promotion of amateur filmmaking represents, as Tryon might also argue, a further commodification of audience behavior by major entertainment corporations. For another, Jenkins' concept, as he himself admits in *Convergence Culture*, doesn't account for the continuing question of 'access', the socio-economic issue that haunts (new) media studies (though scholars such as Lisa Nakamura (2008) remind us that there is no shortage of great work being done on race in the era of convergence). For this latter reason, I believe, the internet is curiously absent from the narrative of *Be Kind Rewind* (the *event* of the film's appearance, its promotion and circulation, as discussed below, is a very different matter).

Quotation – Neither audiences nor films exist in a vacuum, but rather in a mutually reinforcing relationship, just as 'Participatory Culture' is dependent upon citing pre-existing media texts. And yet quotation for the cinephile is rarely about direct imitation, even if the deviation is often times subtle. *We quote something to build on it*. Part of the creative productivity which defines cinephilia is the constant building on a love of the text, whether its fetishising particular parts in excess of the rest, writing extensively about a film's relation to something beyond the narrative, or making (remaking) another film in a homage that transcends imitation. As such, cinephiliac repetition and difference is a key to *Be Kind Rewind*'s conception of moviegoing. The funniest 'laugh out loud' moment to me personally in the film is Jerry's butchering of the *Ghostbusters*' theme song – more precisely, I laugh at his slow, vaguely naïve insistence that the lyrics are correct, despite Mike's accurate observation to the contrary. The blissful humor of the 'sweded' movies in *Be Kind Rewind* rests in that liminal space between recognising the quotation of earlier films and simultaneously identifying the amusing deviations from those texts – whether it's due to misremembering, or to the DIY production values. Jerry's mangled lyrics speak to how films linger for us affectively; he is singing from memory – it doesn't really matter if he's wrong or right. It's funnier to us, of course, because he's wrong, but this does not change the durability of his nostalgic, affective bond to *Ghostbusters*, or the new moment he's created through the (mis)quotation.

Ritualistic – So much of the film works affectively. One reason why I feel *Be Kind Rewind* can be a hard film to figure is because so little of what it is doing is right there on the surface, visually as well as narratively. Thus, it seems nearly impossible to understand the film without at least an intuited sense of the important distinction between Jim Carey's old communication models of 'ritual' and 'transmission'. According to Carey, 'transmission' models focus on what media represent on the surfaces, what ideologies and beliefs are directly *transmitted*. This is a 'media effects' understanding of film – movies are seen in relation to the messages they send and which audiences receive. 'Ritual', however, argues that what is represented or transmitted is secondary at best – and the real point of communication is not to communicate a message directly, but to instead foster ritualistic behaviors and acts that bring people and communities together.

Be Kind Rewind is less about cinephiliac love for those films they 'swede' (*Ghostbusters*, *Rush Hour 2*, etc) and more about their *cinephiliac affect* – the feelings they generate in individuals and in communities. Indeed, it is not about the individual film recreated but entirely about the *communities that media create*. Focusing on the terribly inadequate mimesis of the cheap imitations these films offer completely misses how *Be Kind Rewind* is focused on the affective memories of these texts and on the ritual of consumption. What better way to illustrate that point than crappy homemade remakes which brings a community together for one fleeting, but powerful, moment of affective bliss? That's why *Be Kind Rewind*'s final documentary on Fats Waller is so perfect – despite the fact it contains few historical accuracies. It is *not* about Fats Waller – it is about the *effect* that the memory of 'Fats' has on this community, on how happy it makes them, on how their collective history is what binds them together as a community. Fats Waller Was Born 'Here' – the idea of their community was born 'here'. This is why the documentary is literally built off the interviews of the people in town – 'our pasts belong to us'.

S weded – The verb for copying movies is to 'swede' them. The word is partially meaningless, but evokes echoes of 'suede', a cheaper imitation of leather. It is also technically a narrative reference to Sweden, of course. The movies 'come' from Sweden, are 'sweded', and therefore cost more to the customers in Passaic. No one in *Be Kind Rewind* points out the important connection, meanwhile, that Sweden was for a very long time the one European nation with notoriously (or commendably) relaxed copyright laws. The condition was so troubling for copyright holders and major entertainment corporations that it led directly to the passing of the Intellectual Property Rights Enforcement Directive (IPRED) by the Swedish government in 2009. The intent, as with other such measures worldwide, was to crack down on illegal downloading and file-sharing – the same sort of cinephiliac innovation and *community* dissemination that *Be Kind Rewind* champions. In this sense, 'sweded' is another utopic, and at this point too nostalgic, yearning for an imaginary space (embodied by a particular moment in Sweden) where corporate money and greed could not stifle creative impulses. And yet, the film is self-aware of the limitations of that utopia as well, as the late emergence of the intellectual property lawyers acknowledges.

T eaching – I will go a step further: I will say that one cannot be a cinephile if one does not *teach* film. This is a horribly self-serving academic thing to suggest, of course, and since I'm not definitionally-speaking a cinephile, it doesn't matter what I think. Nevertheless, being able to teach film is a crucial component to loving film. Even more so than writing, I really do not understand any concepts until I've had to teach them to a large, incongruous group of people with which I otherwise had little in common other than the fact we exist in the same pedagogical space for ten, twelve or sixteen weeks. Things always make perfect sense in your own head, and even lecturing about ideas is in some ways easy enough. But for them to actually *get* it is a very different matter (and the more cynical amongst my peers would say that some students just never get it, but I completely reject that convenient, pessimistic and narcissistic excuse). Think about the most complicated concept you feel you understand, and then try to efficiently summarise it for someone else verbally. Nine chances out of ten, if you've given it little thought before now, you'll quickly descend into muttering stream of consciousness nonsense. And the idea you thought you understood, suddenly becomes more complicated. There is so much about how ideas come together that we can often take for granted.

No doubt, I have given *Be Kind Rewind* so much thought over the last two or three years because I have spent so much time with it in relation to the classroom. Between 2008 and 2009, I taught *Be Kind Rewind* around five times in an English Composition I classroom – the introductory college-level writing class. For the 'evaluative research' essay, I typically select a recent major film so that students will be relatively interested and, just as importantly, can find the film easily on their own if need be. Of course, I have to pick a film that interests me, too, and that is sufficiently engaging so that I can lead discussion on it multiple times and read, literally, hundreds of papers on it. The assignment requires evaluating the film – whether or not they like it – and supporting that with clearly explained criteria. The assignment is not about analyzing Gondry's film *per se*; rather, the essay is a simple exercise in making clearly organised, well-supported arguments, and in using properly documented and integrated outside sources.

As noted earlier, most students hated *Be Kind Rewind* because they found it boring, unfunny and disorganised. Some students genuinely loved it; others most likely faked liking it because they thought that that was what I wanted to hear or read. It wasn't – I'm just as intrigued by people who can make intelligent arguments *against* a film I love. Such thoughtful resistance has never threatened my own personal feelings and, at best, may even force me to think more carefully about why I think and feel what I do. In fact, every time I teach this assignment, regardless of the film, I try to resist stating too much of my own opinion precisely to avoid too much influence. A well-written condemnation of *Be Kind Rewind* will always get an 'A' on this assignment; a sloppy, disorganised celebration of the film will always fare considerably worse. In the classroom itself, I always prefer spirited discussion of the film, regardless of how positive or negative the responses. The only low point comes when students have nothing to say – their quiet, distracted indifference sinks the class that week (this happened the last time I showed *Be Kind Rewind*). Of course, as this implies, teaching a cinephiliac text is so risky because you expose yourself to such disappointment, and students' response to a film always reflects on the person who chose to show that one instead of a different title. I don't stop liking the film just because my students don't appreciate it, but I still take the collective disappointment personally because, ideally, I wanted them to.

Teaching a personally beloved film in the classroom, sharing that passion with students, is perhaps the closest the university remains to cinephilia. Although, as the above anecdote indicates, even that passion is inevitably tampered into ambivalence for even the most hardened cinephile through the weekly rigors of lesson plans, readings, syllabi and lectures. It is hard, institutionally, to remain a cinephile as an academic. I don't know how *actively* hostile academia is to cinephilia. Some of the more self-important are indeed deeply hostile, but they are the exception and not the norm amongst film and media scholars. Ironically, it tends to be younger 'media' scholars, and not the entrenched old-timers, who are the most stubbornly hostile to cinephilia – ironic because the ambitious newcomers can sometimes be as rigidly dogmatic, and at times close-minded, as the last generation's school of thought that they are now trying to challenge. Nevertheless, I wouldn't say there is a widespread personal opposition to cinephilia among academics (everybody loves movies!).

However – and this is the key issue – there is a strong *institutional* resistance to cinephilia, seen at work in the ways in which universities and departments design their curriculum. Film appreciation for its own sake has been waning for years, for a variety of reasons, and even offerings of 'Introduction to Film' (not quite the same thing) is increasingly dissipating or even morphing into a different class. At my doctorate alma mater of Indiana University, 'Introduction to Film' was retitled a few years back as 'Introduction to Media', and half the film material on the syllabus was gutted to make room for television and new media studies. This was partly the result of new ideologies taking over the curriculum, but also a very real institutional matter. The department could not afford to start offering intro classes for just television and so forth; so the only way to incorporate it into the curriculum was to cram it into existing courses. In that sense, Film Studies is getting a taste of its own medicine, after decades of weaseling its way into literature departments. As a recovering academic cinephile, film critic Jonathan Rosenbaum describes his experience of leaving the university:

> What finally drove me out of academic film studies and back into journalism in the late '80s was no less grim: the realization that I couldn't expect to parlay my knowledge or love of film into a livelihood that would have been granted to me, in any case, by film teachers who got along just fine without much of either. (2009: 182)

I probably wouldn't phrase it so harshly, though I do understand the position. Most scholars know several 'film teachers' – or, more precisely, people assigned to teach a film class – who don't have much 'knowledge or love of film'. Yet even this is relative. During three semesters at Indiana University, I had to teach Public Speaking, despite at least initially containing no personal 'knowledge or love' of the subject myself. This is sometimes just how departments are set up, and in an increasingly volatile economic age, people have to multitask, and teach subjects they aren't necessarily interested in, or even fully qualified to teach. However, overall, I nonetheless find the spirit of Rosenbaum's description of being a cinephile in academia to be heartbreakingly true, though I hope to not have to leave it as well.

U topia – At the heart of cinephilia, at the heart of modernity, at the heart of nostalgia, and certainly at the heart of Gondry's conception of *Be Kind Rewind*, rests the nagging question of 'utopia', the endlessly deferred ideal to which we aspire, and which by its own definition ('no place') cannot exist. Gondry himself wrote repeatedly about utopia in his book on the film's production, but notes that 'it's something that is not supposed to happen outside of your mind, like sleeping with a girl you are in love with'. *Be Kind Rewind* reinforces this. Indeed, utopia is the film's core *ambivalence*. It is too easy to dismiss the film as only 'utopic', as part of the film's frustration for some people is that *Be Kind Rewind* never gets there – the store is never saved, the sweded movies are never recovered. A particular sense of 'community' for Passiac is momentarily celebrated, but the forces of gentrification, commodification and globalisation move endlessly forward. There are utopic *moments* – making the sweded films, talking fondly in diners about films, watching films. But it never lasts, except in memory, except in the mind – the reason I weep at the end of *Be Kind Rewind* is not because the film's conception of utopia has been finally achieved. It's because I can feel in that joyous ambiguity that this is not a moment which will last.

V HS – *Be Kind Rewind*'s use of the now-largely marginalised medium of VHS is more complicated than it might first appear. On the one hand, VHS exists in *Be Kind Rewind* primarily for the plot device of Jerry's accidental demagnetising of the movies in the video store, something logistically simpler than with other technologies. On the other, the medium of VHS also makes it easier for Mike and Jerry to record new movies, without the financial resources, logistical demands and hands-on training needed to work digital video capabilities. There is something potentially more accessible about VHS in its production and distribution; moreover, its presence as a sight of cinephiliac re-appropriation in the film reminds the careful viewer that the industry of home video itself was created by various forms of audience behavior. 'Video, as a reproductive technology, was introduced for making recordings', writes Hilderbrand, 'and film buffs from the very beginning were bootleggers' (2009b: 215). While major studios rightly feared the loss of control over movies' circulation which the new age of home viewing would bring, he adds, instead 'it was [movie] buffs who made their own recordings and small business owners who developed the video store industry'(2009: 215). Is *Be Kind Rewind* in part about an attempt to hold onto cinephilia's pirated past?

Be Kind Rewind is a nostalgic love letter to an era when cinephiles defined their interests, tastes, and access, as much by the now defunct format of VHS as by the theatrical presentation of 35mm celluloid. 'The distinctly homemade quality of the sweded videos', writes Tryon, 'also articulates a larger nostalgia for VHS itself as the format becomes increasingly obsolete' (2009: 31). Does the sweded version of *Ghostbusters* in the film register more with me person-ally because I have more childhood memories of watching an awful copy of it, recorded off a late night HBO screening in the mid-1980s, rather than of watch-ing it in a Madison, Wisconsin multiplex? Like most die-hard movies buffs of my generation, I grew up on television. I grew up not on projected films, but on tele-vised ones (and on hastily recorded copies of televised ones), and VHS copies represented an ownership of the films I loved and thus, along with the intimacy of living room and bedroom viewings, a closer sense of an emotional bond to the movies in question.

VHS resonates in the movie for how the medium – like film only less subtly – haunts the digital image that is the *Be Kind Rewind* movie itself, and for how VHS co-exists closely alongside film in the larger history of media. In the crucial narrative scene early on, Jerry (now magnetised by a failed attempt to destroy the power plant) walks around the video store, unknowingly demagnetising all the titles. At a couple of moments when Jerry walks too close to the camera, the digital film image is deliberately altered to create the effect of an analog tape being warped by the magnetic field, mimicking a dysfunctional VHS analog image as the electronic pulses begin to fluctuate. It is a nod to the figurative ways in which, as Rodowick and Nicholas Rombes (2009) have argued, older media coexist with newer media. This disconcerting, deliberate imperfection is a perfect metaphor for how VHS literally and symbolically haunts the digital image in Gondry's film.

There is also, of course, a political element to this medium. As Hilderbrand notes in a superb discussion of 'videophilia', 'the politics of video have, from the beginning, been a politics of access' (2009a: 14). Fletcher's resistance to DVD is partly a reflection of his larger resistance to change, touched upon in different ways throughout the film. However, it is also a commentary on two crucial aspects of cinephilia in the age of digital reproduction – both related to the politics of access. One is the economics of the situation, the idea that older businesses and/or those struggling to survive in low income areas simply cannot afford to switch over their entire library of titles to a new format. Second, and this is related to the first point, newer platforms for watching movies necessarily contain fewer old titles. Older movies (specifically those not deemed as high-profit titles by studios) fall increasingly by the wayside as films migrate from newer format to newer format. This fear haunts my earlier celebration of Blu-Ray, of course, as this newest iteration of home viewing technology necessarily brings with it a smaller catalogue of titles. Film critic Dave Kehr notes that, 'for bringing the latest Hollywood blockbusters into homes, Blu-Ray is without parallel. But it is less friendly to older films, foreign films and films made with antiquated technologies (like 16 millimeter and analog video)' (2009). In *Be Kind Rewind*, Fletcher observes that the newer all-DVD rental store, West Coast Video, may have a 'larger' selection, but it mostly compromises of twenty to thirty copies of the same film, rather than a truly diverse and eclectic collection of movies. Holding on to VHS becomes one way to (try to) literally hold onto film's past.

Whiteness – *Be Kind Rewind* is very much a narrative of 'whiteness', of how white people cinematically frame a predominately African-American community. Of course, this is, to a point, par for the course with Hollywood. Since the earliest ethnographic work and travelogues, white Westerners have used a colonialist medium to explore the world, capture it on film, and return it back to the comfort of cafés, living rooms and auditoriums. In this way, film worked to mark the (non-white) 'Other' as other, which not only objectified newly discovered cultures and races, but masked the underlying whiteness behind the camera. Critical race theorists' relationships with various media formations over the course of the twentieth century have been in several ways an attempt to deconstruct this lens.

But part of the beauty of Gondry's film is how ambivalently aware it is of this racial lens. When he was originally approached by Chappelle to do the documentary, the French filmmaker's initial response was: 'why was he asking me, a white French guy, coming from a white nondescript French suburb, to direct a tribute to his musical community?' (2008: 9). Implicitly noting his own place as a white suburbanite, Gondry repeatedly remarks throughout his autobiographical account of *Be Kind Rewind*'s production on how foreign the idea of 'community' was to him, how he always felt – like Jerry, the film's only prominent white character – slightly out-of-place.

The film's critique of the US's legacy of institutional racism is remarkably powerful for how sweet and gentle the surface of the film is – but part of the impact is how unpolemical *Be Kind Rewind* remains. This may partly result from Gondry's own ambivalence and from his initial documentary impulse in *Block Party* – the desire to capture something Gondry doesn't claim to 'know' and thus is resistant to arrogantly defining. Of course, this may ultimately be a self-serving cop-out, another form of *amateur* insistence. And, if so, Gondry's excuse is also, of course, my own, as a white film scholar, from the American suburbs originally, who often writes explicitly about race in the media, but who is more comfortable with directly or indirectly criticising his own generic whiteness (and not without good reason) than with trying to define 'blackness'.

In his amusing coffee-table best-seller, *Stuff White People Like*, Christian Lander satirically mocks the trends and preferences of a particular brand of graduate-school educated, upper-middle-class 'white' people (I put white in quotation marks because it is – like all forms of whiteness – a partially arbitrary social construction, as not everyone the book playfully criticises is of Anglo descent, and Lander's target demographic is as much educational and economic as it is racial). Like my own work on media, and like the best work on whiteness (the two are mutually exclusive, by the way), *Stuff White People Like* is endlessly *self*-critical. It mercilessly mocks everything from sushi to coffee, from nonprofit organisations to dinner parties, from San Francisco to Portland, OR, from High School English Teachers to 'Having Black Friends':

> The most important role that black friends can play in white culture is that they can be used as physical evidence that white people are not racist … Black friends can be used to confirm that a white person is knowledgeable about African-American culture. Many white people are constantly striving to be recognized as experts, and many consider it a life achievement to be befriended and acknowledged by a black person. (2008: 15)

Later, Lander notes that 'all white people fantasise about being brought to an authentic "African-American" experience such as a Baptist Church or a barbecue restaurant in a neighborhood that they are afraid of' (ibid.). This brings us back to *Be Kind Rewind* – as a cinematic text, Gondry's vision of Passaic seems to be partially motivated as a fulfillment of this secret fantasy. However, even more appropriate to *Be Kind Rewind* is that both 'Michel Gondry' and 'Mos Def' appear in separate, but back-to-back, entries in *Stuff White People Like* as staples of white culture (without any direct references to *Be Kind Rewind*). As an actor, rapper and celebrity, Def is

> everything that white people dream about: authentic ('He's from Brooklyn!'), funny ('He was on Chappelle's show!'), artistic ('Have you heard "Black on Both Sides"?'), an actor ('He's in the new Gondry film!'), and not white ('I don't see race'). (2008: 87)

Lander's satirical work is easy to question as something short of a serious scholarly account of race in America, yet there is clearly a sense in which he's captured a particular demographic – a particular kind of whiteness not defined by earlier forms of evasive or reactionary forms of whiteness. Moreover, *Be Kind Rewind* as a film text situates itself perhaps most comfortably within this narrow economic and educational demographic. While ostensibly a narrative about a love of film amidst a minority community in an urban environment, *Be Kind Rewind* appeals to a certain form of (implicitly cinephiliac) whiteness. This is not a reactionary, evasive whiteness, but a more self-aware, self-congratulatory one which embraces film's potential to reveal often cinematically-marginalised racial spaces, and to deconstruct the racial utopia Hollywood often perpetuates when it does show racial difference (*Be Kind Rewind* directly criticises the racial politics of blackface, and of a problematic 'condescending' film like *Driving Miss Daisy*, even at the same moment it concedes the positive affective impact it made on Mrs. Falewicz).

X-Rated – When Mike and Jerry break into the West Coast Video store late in the film to steal the projector, they discover that the manager (played by August Darnell, aka the musician 'Kid Creole') is sleeping in the hardcore pornography room in the back corner of the store because he's homeless. It anticipates his own need for community, for his own need to belong, when he later loans the projector for the film's final screening – however, this narrative turn also highlights the *pornographic impulse* which always hides in the margins of cinephilia. In *Signatures of the Visible*, Fredric Jameson once famously wrote that the 'visible [medium] is essentially pornographic' (1992: 1). In purely theoretical terms, the self-indulgent passions of cinephilia are even more so inherently pornographic – celebrating, exploiting to excess, our endless ability to watch at a safe distance our secret or not so secret desires unfold on the screen, anything, anywhere, anytime.

Yet on a more material and logistical level, too, pornography is never far removed from cinephilia. Illegal pornographic films, often on 16mm, helped give rise in the first half of the twentieth century to what today we would call the 'home theatre', back when one could not literally watch such films in public. Later, as Hilderbrand argued in *Inherent Vice*, the same impulses benefited from, and helped to solidify, the home VHS market, where the porn industry supported VHS over Betamax.[2] With first video, and later the internet, there has always been a fine line, if any, between 'accessibility' for cinephiles and for pornography collectors. Likewise, even in the last few years, Blu-Ray won the high-definition home video war with HD-DVD in no small part because the former was the technology embraced by pornographic distributors and filmmakers. Our socially constructed notions of technophilia – embracing one medium over another – have often been shaped, knowingly or otherwise, by the preferences of the various porn industries that existed throughout the twentieth century.

YouTube – *Be Kind Rewind* is not explicitly about the internet's role in the circulation and production of cinephiliac new media texts – written or audio-visual. Yet its emphasis on humorously amateur re-enactments of beloved movies evokes one aspect to the popularity of video-sharing sites like YouTube. Moreover, this aspect of the internet itself was a central platform for the film's promotion (whether or not it was a successful promotion is a very different, but crucial, matter). The advertising team behind *Be Kind Rewind* set up a special page on YouTube just for people to post their own 'sweded' versions of movies, with the tagline 'If you love it, Swede it'. In this sense, the promotion of cinephilia (in promotion of the film itself) was pretty explicit. 'While the practice of making movie parodies and placing them on the web was hardly new', writes Tryon, 'Gondry's film sought to confer a degree of whimsical nobility on the practice, a sentiment that was actively circulated in the film' (2009: 31). Although the internet is not a part of the film's narrative, its renewed emphasis on the art of the short subject film perhaps better than anything explains the sweded movies' potential appeal.

Zelig (1983) doesn't really work here. Then again, maybe it does. Woody Allen's postmodern pastiche, which also featured *Be Kind Rewind* co-star Mia Farrow, is a cinephiliac relic from the 1980s that, as with *Fats Waller Was Born Here*, self-reflexively comments on how the history of the twentieth century was told through images, and about how those histories could be *re*-told, and altered, through that same visual medium. It is, after all, Farrow's character – in arguably her most crucial narrative moment – who reminds everyone else in the film that 'our pasts belong [cinematically] to us; we can change them' through the image. Her very presence in *Be Kind Rewind*, the persona she carries with, meanwhile, is a reminder of another era of cinephilia and of cinematic nostalgia. In that sense, Zelig represents *Be Kind Rewind*'s more overt, more cynical predecessor – a previous generation's similar commentary on film's mediated relationship to a historic past.

Yet, while *Zelig*, like all the great postmodernist texts, remains trapped in cinematic surfaces, in a slightly nihilistic, self-referential cycle, *Be Kind Rewind* reminds us that much was/is left in cinema's wake. Perhaps, then, Gondry's film is really more akin to Allen and Farrow's other great 1980s cinephiliac contribution to postmodern cinema – *The Purple Rose of Cairo* (1984). Like this latter film, *Be Kind Rewind* is not only about how cinema mediates our relationship with the world, with other people, with our pasts, even with ourselves. Gondry's film is also about the forgotten spaces, about the pockets of marginalised audiences, which remain forever just beyond the screen.

Over the course of the twentieth century, cinema missed more than it captured – but if we cannot rewind and go back, than perhaps we can at least go sideways. In the end, *The Purple Rose of Cairo* and *Be Kind Rewind*'s respective bittersweet ambivalence towards the power, influence and limits of film is also my own; their ephemeral embrace of cinephilia, along with their awareness of the medium's deep sense of loss, is likewise mine. Like Paul Willemen, I still think about cinephilia, and I might still write about it again; but strictly-speaking, I do not consider myself a cinephile anymore.[3] I love film, but something was still missing. My cinephilia took me down too narrow a path; my cinephilia had concealed from my vision far more than it revealed. 'That's the problem with photography', Gondry wrote, 'It records and erases at the same time. But again, I am stepping out of the subject' (2008: 19).

AUTHOR'S NOTE

I wish to thank the feedback of Michael Gillespie, Sara Hall, Chuck Tryon and of course my old buddy, Scott.

NOTES

1   In his recent book, *Show Sold Separately* (2010), Jonathan Gray discusses 'paratexts', the ancillary promotional material surrounding a new film release or television show debut, as an inseparable part of our reception of the primary text. In a sense, *Be Kind Rewind*'s YouTube site is a perfect example of this.

2   This point about pornography's impact on video's development is made as part of a larger history of the medium's legal and illegal symbiotic relationship to film commerce.

3   In his influential essay, 'Through the Looking Glass,' Willemen regards himself as a cinephiliac thinker rather than a cinephile, as someone who studies cinephilia more so than practices it.

REFERENCES

'Adam,' (2010) '10 Top 10s Part 7: Comedy,' Blog, rant, bitch, blather, gripe, and moan, http://carveyfan27.livejournal.com/133973.html.

Bazin, Andre (2000 [1948]) 'Adaptation, or the Cinema as Digest,' in James Naremore (ed.)

Film Adaptation. New Brunswick, NJ: Rutgers University Press.

Boym, Svetlana (2001) *The Future of Nostalgia*. New York: Basic Books.

Campbell, Zach (2009) 'On the Political Challenges of the Cinephile Today,' *Framework*, 50, 2, 210–13.

Ebert, Roger (2008) 'Be Kind Rewind,' *Roger Ebert.com*. http://rogerebert.suntimes.com/apps/pbcs.dll/article?AID=/20080221/REVIEWS/32638504.

Gondry, Michel (2008) *You'll Like This Film Because You're In It: The Be Kind Rewind Protocol*. Brooklyn: PictureBox.

Gray, Jonathan (2010) *Show Sold Separately: Spoilers, Promos and Other Media Texts*. New York: New York University Press.

Hilderbrand, Lucas (2009a) *Inherent Vice: Bootleg Histories of Videotape and Copyright*. Durham, NC: Duke University Press.

_____ (2009b) 'Cinematic Promiscuity: Cinephilia after Videophilia', *Framework*, 50, 2, 214–17.

Jameson, Fredric (1992) *Signatures of the Visible*. New York: Routledge.

Jenkins, Henry (2006) *Convergence Culture: Where Old and New Media Collide*. New York: New York University Press.

Kehr, Dave (2009) 'The Ballad of Blu-Ray,' *The New York Times*, http://www.nytimes.com/2010/01/03/movies/homevideo/03kehr.html.

Keathley, Christian M. (2006) *Cinephilia and History, or The Wind in the Trees*. Bloomington: Indiana University Press.

Lander, Christian (2008) *Stuff White People Like*. New York: Random House.

Martin, Adrian (2009) 'Cinephila as War Machine', *Framework*, 50, 2, 221–5.

Nakamura, Lisa (2008) *Digitizing Race: Visual Cultures of the Internet*. Minneapolis: University of Minnesota Press.

Ray, Robert B. (1995) *The Avant-garde Finds Andy Hardy*. Cambridge: Harvard University Press.

_____ (2008) *The ABCs of Classic Hollywood*. New York: Oxford University Press.

Rodowick, D.N. (2007) *The Virtual Life of Film*. Cambridge, MA: Harvard University Press.

Rombes, Nicholas (2009) *Cinema in the Digital Age*. London: Wallflower Press.

Rosenbaum, Jonathan (2009) 'Reply to Cinephilia Survey,' *Framework*, 50, 2, 181–2.

Scott, A. O. (2008) 'The Dreamer as Tapehead,' *The New York Times*, 28 Feb., E1.

Shambu, Girish (2008) 'The ABCs of Classic Hollywood,' *girishshambu.com*, http://girishshambu.com/blog/2008/05/abcs-of-classic-hollywood.html.

Shambu, Girish (2008), 'An Alphabet of Cinema,' *girishshambu.com*, http://www.girishshambu.com/blog/2008/05/alphabet-of-cinema.html.

Tryon, Chuck (2009) *Reinventing Cinema: Movies in the Age of Media Convergence*. New Brunswick, NJ: Rutgers University Press.

Willemen, Paul (1994) *Looks and Frictions: Essays in Cultural Studies and Film Theory*. Indianapolis: Indiana University Press.

Wollen, Peter (2001) 'An Alphabet of Cinema,' *New Left Review*, 12, 115–34.

INTERNATIONAL CINEPHILIAS

CHAPTER FIVE

IN THE MOOD FOR CINEMA: WONG KAR-WAI AND THE DIASPORIC PHANTASMAGORIA

Catherine Russell

The conventional view of cinephilia points toward a love of cinema that is some-how beyond reason, somewhat involuntary and deeply subjective. And yet, despite its affinities with the collector and the trivia-hound, the fetishist and the helplessly addicted, I would like to think that the recent revival of the concept might have some productive effects. I am interested in developing the idea of cinephilia into a useful concept, one that might provide the tools for the produc-tion of knowledge. Wong Kar-wai's film *In the Mood for Love* (2000) is a film through which the 'cinematic' might be explored as at once an abstraction of melodramatic language, and as a discourse on history and culture. This is a film that presents a phantasmagoria of things, drawn from a vast archive of cinematic memory and geopolitical modernity, creating a rare experience of cinematic plea-sures and historical melancholia.

In his essay on cinephilia, Thomas Elsaesser suggests that cinema might be thought of as 'one of the great fairy-tale machines or "mythologies" that the late nineteenth century bequeathed to the twentieth, and that America, originally inheriting it from Europe, has in turn passed to the rest of the world' (2005: 32–3). This peculiar formulation strikes me as somewhat similar to Miriam Hansen's (2000) notion of vernacular modernism, in which so-called classical cinema is reconceived as a discourse of modernity. Is it such a stretch to extend this under-standing of cinema to a form of cultural anthropology? The genre-system of popular cinema, overlaid with the sensuality of modern experience, is arguably crystallised in cinephilia, which in turn becomes a kind of prism of the dream-life of global modernity. Beyond the contours of national cinemas, the international circuit of film production and distribution arguably dates back to the first years of the medium, even if it has only been in recent years that the full impact of the modernity of cinema has been recognised.

The potential of cinephilia as a mode of cultural anthropology is implicit in the practice of film criticism. Film scholars over the decades have debated the vari-ous merits of interpretation, textual reading and canonical evaluation, all of which transform the passive status of cinephilia into the production of knowledge. I would like to look closely at a canonical cinephiliac text, Wong Kar-wai's *In the Mood for Love*, as an exemplary site of the cinematic phantasmagoria. This term embraces the duality of the cinematic spectacle, as on one hand a world of artifice and fantasy; and on the other, a document of social practices, rituals and audio-visual culture. By examining more closely the role of 'things' in the film, and the role of intertextuality, I hope to show how 'the cinematic' can also be thought of as a mode of cultural knowledge. Elsaesser points out that the wealth of the digital archive enables a 'dialogical engagement with the object and its meaning' (2005: 37), which might be simply a new way of thinking about a reading strategy that we once considered oppositional and resistant. Instead of resistance, cinephilia entails engagement.

In the Mood for Love is a film that tends to resist verbal description and plot synopsis. The creation of a 'mood' – through a rich textual interplay of sound, music, architectural space, colour, costume, props, performance, camera movement, lighting, and a narrative in which far more is withheld than revealed – constitutes a tour de force of cinematic expression. The story of the production is by now fairly well-known, and has only added to the mystique of the film. Shot over a fifteen-month period, it began as a sketch of three movie ideas to be shot in Beijing, Macao, and Bangkok that gradually coalesced into one film shot in Bangkok and Hong Kong, with a coda set in Cambodia. Wong's conception of the characters played by Maggie Cheung and Tony Leung was equally vague at the outset, and both actors confess to have been extraordinarily perplexed and exhausted by the production.[1] In one interview, Wong himself seemed to be completely surprised that the final print of the film delivered to Cannes only hours before the premier screening pleased the critics as much as it did (see Rayns 2000: 14).

In 2002 the Criterion Collection DVD release of *In the Mood for Love* offered cinephiles a remarkable digital version of the film along with an array of special features such as deleted scenes and a plenitude of interviews, essays, and promotional materials. Wong Kar-wai emerges from all this extra material as a quintessentially indulgent auteur, who works instinctively and impulsively for the sake his art. The story of the production is also a story of a cast and crew who were 'at home' in a cinematic world of their own creation that seems to be curiously detached from the real. At the same time, the film is remarkable for its extraordinarily detailed depiction of the everyday life of the expatriate Shanghainese community in Hong Kong in the early 1960s. Wong is said to have had special meals prepared for the cast so that they could taste and smell the character of the period that the film recreates (see Chow 2007: 73).

In an ecstatic review of the film in *Cineaste*, Paul Arthur confessed to being so enamoured by *In the Mood for Love* that he began to obsessively return to see it at the expense of other daily responsibilities. His 'swoony intimacy' with the film is described as a love affair bordering on addiction: 'Wong's movie had entered into that tiny but cherished phylum of aesthetic ravishment, governed as much by personal taste as reasoned argument, to which the lifelong movie nut will turn in good times and bad for sentimental as well as professional reassurance' (2001: 40). Four years later, reviewing Wong's less successful sequel, *2046* (2004), Arthur bemoaned his earlier inability to fulfill his impulse to write 'a lustrous epistle adorned with unaccustomed critical language' (2005: 6). He could not, in the end, do justice in writing to his cinephiliac experience.

Arthur does, however, point to some of the qualities of *In the Mood for Love* that provoke that experience in his original review. He suggests that the drama of desire played out by the erstwhile couple Su Li-zhen (a.k.a. Mrs. Chan [Maggie Cheung]) and Chow Mo-wan (a.k.a. Mr. Chow [Tony Leung]) parallels the cinephiliac desire for the image: 'the mournful procession of ecstatic moments merging into the wider river of time'; 'Our romance with the movie image', writes Arthur, 'parallels that of Chow and his lost love: impossibly vivid, suffused with desire, yet disturbingly ephemeral' (2001: 40). Betraying a certain gendering of his own cinephiliac desire, as there is no reason not to attribute lost love to Su Li-zhen as well, Arthur indicates that cinephilia is not independent of interpretation. In his cinephiliac enthusiasm, he indicates how the subjectivity of the (re)viewer and their own engagement with the film is key to the so-called 'ontology' of the medium.

The tale of two neighbours who discover that their spouses are having an affair is loaded with melodramatic conventions of social restraint and censure, and the bad timing of missed opportunity, as Li-zhen and Mo-wan fail in the end (in the final cut) to consummate their relationship, despite the powerful attraction that they clearly hold for each other. As Arthur notes, the sensuality of the film is enhanced by the 'rankly pungent atmosphere' of food, smoke, sweat and rain. 'The story', he suggests, 'emanates as if from the coils of a dream or a trance-state' (ibid.). Even for viewers who may identify more closely with Maggie Cheung's character than Tony Leung's, there is a powerful pull or entrancement enacted by the film.

Arthur's compassionate review captures the cinephiliac appeal of *In the Mood for Love*. Its spectacular ephemerality in which cinematic technique and cultural specificity are so deeply enmeshed makes it a particularly apt case study for further exploration of cinephilia as a critical concept. Paul Willeman speculates that cinephilia concerns revelation and the production of insight that he cannot quite articulate in a long and provocative discussion of the topic. He comes close to defining the term when he identifies 'films that "inhabit" ... their own cultural situation' (1994: 254). He favours directors who 'inhabit their cultures in very complex manners and that complexity is translated into a representational practice that goes beyond the narrative'; linking cinephilia to Third Cinema, Willeman suggests that 'we are talking about the articulation between representation and history in cinema. The concrete, local, historical detail shines through' (1994: 255).

Both Willemen and Elsaesser grapple with the ways that film theory in its psychoanalytic/semiotic phase of ideological critique felt obliged to deny the pleasures associated with film viewing. As Elsaesser puts it, 'the love of cinema was now called by a different name: voyeurism, fetishism, and scopophilia' (2005: 32). However, we should recall that Christian Metz himself was fully aware of the deep ambivalence of his own critical method: 'To be a theoretician of the cinema one should ideally no longer love the cinema and yet still love it' (1982: 15). He describes the acrobatic balancing act as a challenge to the 'scientific' principle of any rational social theory, but he nevertheless points out parallels in other fields. Metz particularly aligns cinematic studies with the 'subjective possibility of the ethnologist's work' (1982: 16). Cinephilia, in other words, should theoretically enable us to restore the dimensions of affect, enchantment, pleasure and emotional investment to film studies, without abandoning the theoretical goals of cultural critique that informed the discourse of apparatus theory. Instead of a deterministic, mechanical model of pleasure, perhaps we can find a more selective and subjective means of connecting with narrative cinema.

In the case of Wong Kar-wai, we are evidently in the realm of auteur cinema. We cannot say of *In the Mood for Love* that it provides 'an x-ray vision' of social disintegration as Willeman says of Douglas Sirk's films. It is true that 'people's gestures, intonations and the like' (1994: 246) are critically provocative, and indicative of some kind of social decay, but where Sirk is uncanny, Wong is canny; and where Sirk's films were commercially successful, Wong's cinema is popular only among the international community of cinephiles (an audience not to be sneezed at). On the global level, directors like this forge crucial cultural links and connections. The DVD package needs to be recognised as a luxury commodity in which the director's name becomes a kind of quality brand. In the case of this film, as it has been distributed by Criterion, the DVD package takes on added importance because of the special features that include outtakes and 'deleted scenes' that significantly alter the film. 'The secret of room 2046' includes a scene suggesting that the couple actually do make love. Other scenes include Mo-wan's wife acting hysterically, and Li-zhen's husband, both of whom are only seen from behind or heard from offscreen in the final version of the film. In interviews, Tony Leung and Wong Kar-wai both offer interpretations (or explanations) of the film that shore up the male character's agency in the affair by suggesting that he was seeking revenge for having had his wife stolen by Li-zhen's husband. The film itself carries no such rationalisation or implication, but depicts the love affair as a wholly mutual affair.

Moreover, I would argue that in order to understand the discourse of desire within the cinephiliac appeal of *In the Mood for Love* we need to situate the film within the world of things. This world includes the movies on DVD that we can buy, collect and cherish as cinephiles; and it includes the props, decors, cars and clothes that constitute the phantasmagoria, the landscape of design, that subsists in those movies. The world of things is mobilised in this film in an unusually 'cinematic' way.

THINGS

The sensuous mise-en-scène of *In the Mood for Love* is created through a rich layering of textured imagery in which architectural space, figure and camera movement and décor are intertwined. Perhaps the most striking feature of the film's display is the array of *cheongsam* worn by Maggie Cheung. These form-fitting dresses rarely escape critical comment, because they serve a far greater role in the film than costumes and fashions do ordinarily. Li-zhen's dresses change so often and so rapidly that they stand in as temporal markers, indicating that the routines of everyday life with which the film is preoccupied have skipped forward a day or perhaps an hour. The costume changes are unsettling, both visually and temporally. Her dress changes between cuts on movement, for example, from when she answers a phone call, to when she turns and enters a door. Cheung's performance is so graceful and elegant that the text is seamless despite the unusual wardrobe; and at the same time, the close-fitting high-collared style of the *cheongsam* tends to enhance that elegance by restricting the actor's movement and literally engendering an elegant performance style.[2]

Figs. 1 and 2: Two consecutive scenes from *In the Mood for Love* in which Maggie Cheung's *cheongsam* changes, suggesting an unexplained temporal discontinuity.

The fabrics and patterns that Wong and his art director Chang Suk-ping selected are vibrant, often clashing with the equally stylish background wallpapers and clutter of crowded apartments. These dresses, as gorgeous as they are, are also loaded with cultural significance, carrying a specific set of allusions to the Shanghainese community in Hong Kong in the early 1960s. They recall the movies of the period, as well as the Shanghai cinema of the 1930s. They capture the sense of a cosmopolitan bourgeois community in exile, forced into the cramped quarters of Hong Kong, not willing to let go of their illusions of wealth (see Marchetti 2002). The *cheongsam* is specifically Chinese-modern, with its revealing side-slits and form-fitting tightness and was always much more of a glamorous fashion associated with the movies than everyday wear. Gina Marchetti suggests that Li-zhen wears these incongruous dresses to show off her husband's wealth, but even the other characters in her shared apartment are surprised at how dressed-up she is to go out for noodles.

The *cheongsam* in *In the Mood for Love* are the most striking elements of an extraordinarily detailed film in which the realism of historical accuracy is infused with a sense of the fantastic. For Rey Chow, the nostalgic weight of the film's detail points beyond the film to a universal cliché of representation: 'the fundamentally unfulfilled – and unfullfillable – nature of human desire, to which history itself, even when it appears in the form of recognizable everyday phenomena, becomes subject and subordinate' (2007: 75). She suggests that the figure of Li-zhen in her incredible costumes 'stands like an uncanny doll-like fetish (in the Freudian sense)' and that 'the luxurious images become in this manner a screen for a fundamental void (ibid.)'. For Chow, to the extent that *In the Mood for Love* participates in a transcultural exchange of 'transmissible phantasmagorias', its Chineseness is infinitely dispersed. She bemoans the way the film embraces image, artifice, and commodity, and she poses the question of the value of the utopic in light of this apparent eclipse of history and cultural specificity (2007: 82).

In fact, I would argue that the utopian potential of the phantasmagoria is reconfigured in *In the Mood for Love* as a discourse of 'the cinematic' and secondly, that the film's dispersal of Chineseness is also a highly culturally specific treatment of diasporic culture. The playful and stylish fashions and décors are drawn from the repertoire of movie history. The Criterion DVD package includes a short film made from a montage of clips from the Hong Kong film archive selected by Wong Kar-wai called *Hua yang de nian hua* (*In Full Bloom*).[3] This rather fast-paced assemblage offers a series of glimpses of women wearing *cheongsam* in melodramatic poses and gestures taken from films produced in the 1930s, 1950s and 1960s. Close-ups of faces, hands and feet suggest evocative precedents for Cheung's performance in *In the Mood for Love*. This is just one of the ways that the film – in its commercial form as a DVD product – cites the history from which Chow claims it to be so eminently removed.

In the Mood for Love may be emblematically postmodern in its unanchored display of eye-candy – especially when contrasted to a much more conservative film like *The Road Home* (2000) by Zhang Yimou, which is how Chow sets up her argument. But is its discourse of desire necessarily one of fetishism? While Arthur seems to see the film through the man's eyes, Chow seems to concur by suggesting that the woman is enlisted as the object of the gaze. However, against the critical gendering of the film's spectacle by both Chow and Arthur, we can point to Tony Leung's performance as equally eroticised. His slicked-back hair and languorous poses and gestures are equally 'attractive' within the conventions of the male pin-up.

Fig. 3: Tony Leung as Mo-wan

Moreover, while the *cheongsam* clearly point to a consciousness outside the film, as Chow also notes, the film refuses the conventions of point-of-view editing that would (in a Hitchcockian universe) suture the viewer's gaze to that of a 'male gaze'. Peter Brunette notes that in this film Wong has jettisoned his usual use of voice-over narration and thus downplays individual subjectivity (2005: 88). Instead, his focus is on the social collectivity and – I would add – the intersubjective dynamics of the romance narrative in which man and woman are equally developed as subjects of desire.

The dispersed, unfocalised gaze of this film, obsessed with both the man and the woman, is perhaps more typical of the genre of melodrama than the psychology of Hitchcock. It certainly adheres to the techniques that Elsaesser identifies in Sirk and Minnelli: 'the films are built architecturally, by a combination of structural tensions and articulated pasts, and the overall design appears only retrospectively' (1991: 85). But equally important to the melodramatic discourse is the role of objects and things in *In the Mood for Love*. Elsaesser suggests that characters in melodrama are not only defined by décor, but 'pressure is generated by things crowding in on them'. Objects become 'more real than the human relations or emotions they were intended to symbolise' (1991: 84).

In the Mood for Love is a film about desire, clearly, but it seems to resist psychoanalytic interpretation. It mobilises an abstract form of the language of melodrama such that an excess of affect is produced, and the discourse of signification is countered by a discourse on 'the cinematic'. As Chow insists, the film poses certain questions about 'the everyday' despite its equal pull towards the ephemeral and the fantastic (see 2007: 80). Lesley Stern (2001) introduces an essay on the notion of 'the cinematic' with a question about the Maltese falcon: 'Does the bird desire me?' Can a film desire its spectator? For Stern this question hinges on the 'mutability of things', or the capacity of cinema to combine the materialist dimensions of everyday life with the ephemerality of cinematic time. Things in cinema are at once objects familiar from the real world and displaced from reality into the realm of thoughts and feelings.

The oscillation of the real and the fictional may be a familiar problematic from film theory with which many notable thinkers – from Eisenstein to Kracauer, Cavell and Barthes – have grappled. Chow refers to Pasolini in her discussion of *In the Mood for Love*, and his distinction between 'brute speech' or kinemes – or the profilimic – and image signs or im-signs, from which stories, memories and dreams are constructed. I do not find this model appropriate to a film such as *In the Mood for Love*, in which despite the location shooting, very little of the profilmic is not designed, constructed, dressed up and modified for the camera. The cinema has effectively penetrated the very depth of the reality before the camera, with the exception of the final, enigmatic scene in which Mo-wan travels to Angor Watt in Cambodia. Until this scene, the things in *In the Mood for Love*, including the costumes and the sets, have no prior existence to their appearance in the movie, even if they are all loaded with many levels of reference and signification.

Stern's particular twist on the question of cinematic representation is to propose a taxonomy of 'cinematic things' – objects that tend toward inflated, histrionic expression. The things she chooses to write about include raindrops and tears, foliage in the wind, kettles, and cigarettes. While these things tend toward ephemerality, her taxonomy is hardly exhaustive, as she also argues that gestures can 'move' the quotidian to the histrionic. She cites examples of detailed mundane activities such as the coffee-making scenes in Vittorio De Sica's *Umberto D* (1952) and Chantal Akerman's *Jeanne Dielman* (1975), and she also cites Robert Bresson: 'cinematography, that new writing, becomes, at the same time a method of discovery' (2001: 329). Things in cinema that evoke the senses of touch and sensuality achieve a level of affect which, in their excess, 'elude the voracious grasp of the moment (and the narrative), to reverberate beyond the frame, to generate ideas within a cultural landscape not circumscribed by the diegesis' (2001: 354).

Lest we think of this as another version of Barthes' 'third meaning', Stern's taxonomy of cinematic things insists on a materialism of 'the cinematic'. Smoking in cinema, for example, is not only visually sensuous, it is also linked to the quotidian in a circuit of gesturality: 'Gestures migrate between everyday life and the movies, but where the gestural often goes unnoticed in the everyday, in the cinema … it moves into visibility' (2001: 352). Cinematic things do not transcend history or reality; they transform the everyday into a phantasmagoria, which may well create insights into the affective dimensions of history. Siegfried Kracauer and Walter Benjamin recognised the inherent dangers of this process that is so endemic to cinema, but Benjamin also recognised how commodity culture withholds the secret of its own undoing within its always already allegorical dialectical imagery. It is precisely the idea of a cultural landscape to which Stern's notion of 'the cinematic' leads – a landscape in which the everyday (the profane) is illuminated as being a crucial nexus of forces, flows, social interaction and exchange.

Benjamin developed the notion of the phantasmagoria in his *Arcades Project*, where it was linked to the emergent display culture of the Parisian passages. The concept of cinephiliac desire should also be linked to notions of consumption, because a cinephiliac text such as *In the Mood for Love* is not independent of the marketing culture of DVD distribution and the globalised niche of film festivals that enables an art film like this to find its audience. While the fashions worn by Maggie Cheung did not (to my knowledge) have any direct consumer tie-ins, the dresses are nevertheless desirable as commodities. Their appeal to the female gaze may well refer to the potential of ownership, while the melodramatic affect is enhanced by the realisation of its impossibility. Even if one could find such a garment and afford it, the chances of it fitting well are, excuse the pun, slim.

The plot of *In the Mood for Love* actually hinges on a discourse of commodities, specifically the luxury goods that the spouses of Li-Zhen and Mo-wan purchase abroad. After a series of scenes in which Li-zhen and Mo-wan find themselves following parallel routines of lonely meals at the local noodle shop, they finally eat together in a restaurant. He asks her where she got her elegant handbag; she asks him where he got his tie. Moments later, she admits that she knows his wife already has an identical handbag; and previous conversations have established that her husband routinely brings back such items from his business trips to Japan. Based on this incontrovertible circumstantial evidence, they come to the realisation that their spouses are having an affair.

This pivotal scene establishes a new pattern of behaviour in the film, in which Li-zhen and Mo-wan assume the roles of their adulterous spouses. They wonder who made the first move, while they lightly touch each other flirtatiously, neither one actually able to make the first move. In the final cut of the film, it is never clear whether they consummate their pseudo affair, or if social propriety keeps them apart. She spends an entire day and two nights trapped in his room, afraid of being seen by the other residents of the apartment; but she remains fully clothed, alone on his bed while he sits beside her on a chair. Their romance is 'moving' precisely because of their inability to betray their melancholy identities as jilted spouses, and yet they exchange very few words, allowing the music, the swirling smoke, the food, stairways, passages, taxis, rain showers, and fashions to express their feelings for each other.

Oddly enough, while Li-zhen's *cheongsam* are accessorised with striking earrings and shoes, her handbags are played down. The purse that Mo-wan remarks on may be the pink one that appears in the scene just before their crucial conversation. Because this evidence is their only 'proof' of their spouses' affair – aside from long coincidental absences – one might expect the bag and the tie to be more visible. And yet it is equally important that they are elements in a series of gifts and goods that are exchanged over the course of the film. Li-zhen organises her boss's gifts for his wife and mistress, including handbags that she asks her husband to buy in Japan. 'The same colour?' he asks offscreen. She says, 'Yes. Who cares?'

Fig. 4: The carryout pail that Li-zhen uses to take out noodles.

Li-zhen herself often carries a black patent-leather handbag, and it is shown in close-up shortly after their first confessional meeting. Before this, she is usually only seen carrying a wallet in her hand, and the canteen for taking out noodles from the neighbourhood shop. As Marchetti notes, this object, the carryout pail 'eloquently tells a story of loneliness, abandonment, isolation and exile' (2002).

Filmed in slow-motion, swinging with Cheung's graceful stride, the stainless steel container is, in Stern's words, 'inflated'. Its everydayness is enhanced by the actor's gestures and is rendered cinematic; which is to say that its cultural significance is given a kind of affective dimension insofar as we can imagine touching it. Its historicity is likewise nudged, ever so subtly, into our presence and our present.

In the phantasmagoria of cinematic things, the handbag has a special role. Sarah Street has discussed the role of ladies handbags in Hitchcock's films in the construction of suspense and sexual tension, arguing that the purse frequently functions as a powerful object, rather a mere costume accessory (2002: 148). Hitchcock's enigmatic representation of femininity, she argues, is often concentrated in the central role played by handbags in his cinema. Focusing on these so-called 'props' opens up a space for female spectatorship within the Hitchcockian apparatus of power/vision/knowledge which is otherwise organised, as we know, around the male gaze.

In another, equally compelling article touching on the handbag in cinema, Lynne Joyrich describes the experience of seeing a vintage bag for sale on eBay dubbed 'Far from Heaven'. She explains how the circulation of films and commodities is part of a larger discourse of desire, investment and pleasure, a circuit that she argues Todd Haynes' *Far From Heaven* (2002) reflexively engages in through its radical use of the language of melodrama:

> The phrase 'far from heaven' was used here [on eBay] to signify not an actual item from the film, but a 'look' presumed to be known and appreciated by viewers of both computers and film screens. This suggests how deeply cinematic and other media texts enter our consciousness, providing us with objects in which to invest – whether materially, as in the case of the bidder who bought the purse, or more elusively, as in the case of spectators such as myself who simply invest emotionally and epistemologically in the film itself. (2004: 88)

Stylistically, *In the Mood for Love* is much closer to the Todd Haynes' 'remake' of Douglas Sirk's *All that Heaven Allows* (1955) than to Hitchcock. I have already indicated that the wandering, unfocalised gaze of the film is in the mode of melo-drama, as is the regime of detailed mise-en-scène. However, if the discourse of the handbag in Hitchcock belongs to an 'other' (female) gaze, it can also bring out the melodrama latent in Hitchcock's cinema. As Joyrich implies, fashionable commodities in the cinema open up a discourse of 'investment' for viewers. Longing and desire for objects in films are typically endowed with the sense of loss and lack – as in 'I can't possibly afford that' or in the sense that things (especially in period films) were more beautiful in the past. This, I want to argue, is part of the register of desire that constitutes cinephilia. The handbag in *In the Mood for Love* is remarkable in its absence, but that is very much in keeping with the film's atmosphere of ambiguity in which so little is self-evident. The film revolves around a handbag that is displaced by a series of other compelling, powerful objects.

INTERTEXTUALITY

When Paul Arthur suggests that *In the Mood for Love* 'emanates as if from the coils of a dream or a trance-state' (2001: 40), he links the film to other such films obsessed with memory and desire, including *Last Year at Marienbad* (1961), *Letter from an Unknown Woman* (1948), and *Vertigo* (1958). It is the last of these titles that Wong himself cites as an inspiration (see Teo 2005: 119). Like Hitchcock's *Vertigo*, *In the Mood for Love* is concerned with role-playing and a certain fascination with costume and history, even if, as already suggested, the gaze is structured very differently than it is in a film like *Vertigo*. It is the spectator rather than the male protagonist who is provoked into a desire for the characters to become a romantic couple. In the various scenes in which they 'practice' their lines, imagining themselves in the roles of their adulterous spouses, the film plays with melodramatic conventions of the 'desire to desire'. Li-zhen cries at one point 'this isn't real', and of course it isn't real at all. They are playing a scene in a movie.

Li-zhen frequently goes to films alone, returning late to the crowded apart-ment. We do not know what films she might see, but they could include the international art-house titles mentioned by Arthur. They might also include the films from which Wong excerpted clips for the short compilation drawn from the Hong Kong archives.[4] Her indulgence in film-going is nevertheless consis-tent with her attempt to imagine and recreate the romantic scenes, gestures and behaviours of her husband and his mistress. For Peter Brunette, the film's play with doubling and role-playing sheds 'new light on subjectivity'; 'Just who are we, after all, and do we ever have the possibility of saying things to each other that aren't already lines of dialogue, scripted by our culture or society?' (2005: 96). I would agree that the film poses such a question, but at the same time, the cultural milieu of the film is so carefully detailed that it seems to be directed at the very specific historical construction of subjectivity in the Hong Kong Shanghainese community.

In the Mood for Love has several intertextual sources that are more directly related to the film than *Vertigo*. Fei Mu's *Spring in a Small City* (1948) is a Hong Kong film about a romantic relationship between a woman and a friend of her sick husband. In that film the affair is strongly suggested, and the relationship is erotically charged but it is never consummated. That the 1948 film was also remade in 2002 under the title *Spring in a Small Town* by Tian Zhuangzhuang indicates the resonance of the romantic story in Hong Kong culture. According to Stephen Teo it is this later film that *In the Mood for Love* resembles most, although he also points to the resonance with Naruse Mikio's films, particularly *Meshi* (1951) and *When a Woman Ascends the Stairs* (1960) (see 2005: 119). The latter film especially, with its emblematic image of the geisha madam routinely mounting the stairs to her glamorous, yet socially restrictive, hostess bar, is strongly evoked in the shots of the well-dressed Li-zhen climbing the stairs from the noodle shop, climbing the stairs to her apartment, and climbing the stairs to Mo-wan's hotel room.

Figs. 5 and 6: Takemine Hideko in *When a Woman Ascends the Stairs* (Naruse Mikio, 1960) and Maggie Cheung in *In the Mood for Love*

Another source for the film is a short story called 'Intersections' by Liu Yi-chong, which is also included in English translation in the criterion DVD package. Wong's adaptation of this story is extremely loose. Set in 1970s Hong Kong, Liu's tale is about two characters who he traces during a few hours moving through the city. They never meet, but they do sit beside each other in the cinema. The male character is quite a bit older, having come to Hong Kong from Shanghai in the 1940s or 1950s. The woman is much younger and fantasises that she sees herself on record albums, movie posters, and finally in the movie that the two characters end up watching. The narrator alternates between the two characters' thoughts and feelings about their day and the movie they see; they go home separately and watch the same Mandarin film on TV. 'Intersections' points us again to 'the cinematic' as a point of departure for *In the Mood for Love*. The cinema provides a common space for dreaming and a public space for lonely people. In the space of the movie theatre, the characters' experiences of the city, their inchoate desires and their fantasies of beauty seem to cohere.

In the Mood for Love emerged out of the conjunction of nostalgia, desire, real estate, and mass media as they converge in the specific locale of Hong Kong. From 'Intersections', Wong distilled a nexus of memories and anticipation, of a community uncertain of its past or its future. He himself says that the novel is also an 'intersection of time: a novel published in 1972, a movie released in 2000, both intersecting to become a story of the 1960s' (quoted in Teo 2001). The diasporic population of the city seems to be only 'at home' in the cinema – which is to say, as spectators and as characters – while the melodrama of unrequited, unconsumed and unspoken desire is also the cinematic essence of such diasporic experience.

The intertextual richness of *In the Mood for Love* extends far beyond those texts that may have directly influenced Wong and his cast and crew. They extend into deeper layers of cinematic memory, confluence, and generic echoes that film critics are uniquely equipped to excavate. Gina Marchetti, for example, points to two key Hollywood melodramas of the 1950s that are evoked by the film: *Love Is a Many Splendored Thing* (Henry King, 1955) and *The World of Suzie Wong* (Richard Quine, 1960). Both star William Holden, as the love interest of a Eurasian doctor played by Jennifer Jones in the first case and a Chinese bar girl played by Nancy Kwan in the second. Both films exploit the dramatic setting of Hong Kong, and expose the racial dynamics at play in the expatriate community. Jones and Kwan dress in elegant *cheongsam*, and the romantic melodramas helped to endow the colonial cosmopolitan city with a glamorous image on the international stage.[5] *Love Is a Many Splendored Thing* further engages with the dynamics of Cold War politics, although not nearly as deeply as the original novel by Han Suyin. *In the Mood for Love* might thus be regarded as a kind of Hong Kong appropriation of the glamorous sensuality with which Hollywood embraced the city state in the late 1950s.

Love Is a Many Splendored Thing, while a fairly marginal film in the US, was hugely popular in Asia, despite the peculiar and unconvincing casting of Jennifer Jones as a Eurasian woman. Holden's character is a journalist who travels to Singapore, Macao, mainland China and Korea, where he dies covering the opening battles of the war. According to Hye Seung Chung, the film was an especially important point of reference for one of the key works of 1960s South Korean melodrama. *Stray Bullet* (*Obalt'an*, Yu Hyun-mok, 1961), she says, 'ingeniously rearticulates and recontextualizes' the earlier film (2005: 117). She draws particular attention to the climactic romantic scene in which Jones asks Holden for a cigarette. They are semi-dressed on a beach, and the lighting of the cigarette is a de-facto consummation of their burgeoning affair. By visualising the convergence of two cultures, one ostensibly bound to tradition, the other representative of modernity, this blissful contact not only seals the pact of their newfound affection but also inscribes, on a deeper level, the complex cultural hybridisation bound up in the image of the romantic couple (ibid.). In *In the Mood for Love*, the couple, of course, exists as cultural equals, and Wong manages to evade the racial and power relations that inform the William Holden vehicles. Mo-wan is sexy, but he is a far cry from the paternalistic masculinity embodied by Holden (although like the Holden character in *Love Is a Many Splendored Thing*, he also plays a journalist who is sent to various Asian destinations). And yet, *In the Mood for Love* nevertheless obliquely references the 1955 film in one of the deleted scenes that takes us behind the door of room 2046. In Mo-wan's hotel room, Li-zhen asks him for a cigarette. Through windows smeared with pouring rain, we see him lighting her cigarette, and then his. She says, 'I don't want to go home tonight', and then, with the screen still very darkly lit, with rain and glass obscuring the shadowy image, we hear the sounds of lovemaking. In contrast with the spectacular Technicolor of the Hollywood melodrama, the scene is mysterious and curiously private; following more closely the Korean treatment of the scene in *Stray Bullet*, which Chung describes as being set in 'a claustrophobic interior' (ibid.).

Deleted from the final cut of *In the Mood for Love*, this cigarette-lighting scene points to a kind of unconscious memory of *Love Is a Many Splendored Thing*. The woman in both films does not smoke until this scene. In *In the Mood for Love*, Li-zhen smokes only once more – when she leaves a lipstick-stained butt in Mo-wan's hotel room in Singapore, the only trace of her presence, like a kind of haunting. For Lesley Stern, cigarettes are charmed cinematic objects: 'There is no stopping their circulation' (2001: 345). If cigarettes are iconic of Hollywood genre cinema, their presence in *In the Mood for Love* situates the characters within that circuit of gestures which signify desire, exchange, sensuality, and of course, the quotidian. Stern notes that cigarettes are also things, and belong to the register of descriptive detail and routine. And yet, they are often deployed histrionically. Stern points out that 'the gesturality involved in smoking also contributes to a performative register that begins to delineate generic features and a certain kind of heroism' (2001: 347).

Fig. 7: Tony Leung in *In the Mood for Love*

Tony Leung, as Mo-wan, smokes constantly throughout the film, and Wong indulges in the swirling smoke, lighting it to accentuate the noirish moods and ambiguous emotions. He waits, he smokes. Smoking is also about time, and in this film it links the characters to their Hollywood ancestors, opening up passages in time.

Along with the dreamy lighting, swirling fabrics, rainy nights and labyrinthine passageways, the incessant smoking contributes to the 'mood' of sensuous visual pleasure. The dreamy atmosphere is nevertheless linked, as Stern notes, to the ritual gestures of actors like Bogart and Holden – the latter, of course, smokes throughout his two Hong Kong-set melodramas.

A TEXT WITHOUT END

Stern has also written a fascinating book on intertextuality, focused on the cinema of Martin Scorsese, which can help us to further understand the cinephiliac discourse of *In the Mood for Love*. This is a film that ends without ending, and leaves much unresolved, which Stern sees as symptomatic of intertextual film practice. David Ng writes that the film is 'an incomplete movie that, if completed, would be an inferior work' (2001). Cinema has the capacity to bring worlds into being, 'to engender bodies and transubstantiate matter', but many films falter at the cutting off point and are marked by 'a cutting edge between different regimes of reality, between different registers of the fantastic' (Stern 1995: 8).

In the Mood for Love ends with an abrupt shift to historical realism. Following a newsreel clip of de Gaulle visiting Cambodia in 1966, Mo-wan travels to Angor Watt, the ancient Cambodian temple. There, he whispers the secret of the failed romance into a hole in the monumental stone edifice and stuffs in some earth and straw to told it in. This ending poses precisely the question noted by Stern:

> What are the connections between those worlds willed into cinematic being and other worlds, histories, social milieus? This is the acute question of intertextuality, the import of asking where one text ends and another begins. (Ibid.)

Political history is alluded to in the intertextual newsreel footage which obliquely references the geopolitical struggle in Southeast Asia. De Gaulle's condemnation of the US presence in Cambodia, and his recognition of the legitimacy of the People's Republic of China (PRC) are events that led up to the 1967 riots in Hong Kong – disturbances which brought the decadent lifestyle of the Shanghai community to an end. The period covered by the film, from 1960 to 1966, was the decline of the cosmopolitan bourgeois culture preserved by the Shanghainese exiles in Hong Kong who fled the PRC in 1949. The newsreel footage follows a brief scene of Li-zhen and Mo-wan returning separately to their former apartments, missing each other, but getting a sense of the changes as all their former friends have left. Li-zhen has a small boy with her, raising questions for the viewer about her single status and the boy's possible paternity. The deleted scenes include yet another epilogue set in the 1970s in which Mo-wan's wife teases and taunts him and Li-zhen separately under the pretence of viewing the apartment now owned by Li-zhen. The former lovers meet each other briefly in the steamy setting of their old noodle shop, although they are dressed and made up very differently, and the clip ends as soon as they meet each other's eyes.

The motif of the secret whispered into the wall is taken up as a recurring visual and narrative theme in the sequel to *In the Mood for Love*, Wong's *2046*. In that film, it becomes a mode of time travel, taking the characters back and forth to the future and the past. The motif has another reference as well, though, to the final scene of *Love Is a Many Splendored Thing*: after her lover's death, Jones returns to a tree on a hillside where she and Holden had previously romanced each other. She whispers something into the tree.

Figs. 8 and 9: Mo-wan whispering into the wall at Angor Watt in *In the Mood for Love*; Jennifer Jones whispering into a tree in *Love Is a Many Splendoured Thing*

Whether or not Wong made this allusion directly or not, it nevertheless opens up another cinematic passage within the phantasmagoria of movie images. As Hye Seung Chung notes, Hollywood provided an important dream world to Asian audiences. The problems of ideological suture within the colonial text are well known, but we can also point to moments like this, of cinephilic engagement, as forms of 'cross-cultural *détournement*'. Performed from the historical vantage point of Wong Kar-wai's twenty-first century phantasmagoria, such a *détourne-ment* may be 'recuperated as a critical intervention in the cultural history and memory of the 1950s and 1960s' (2005: 125).

Yet another intertextual passage leads from *In the Mood for Love* to Scorsese's romantic melodrama, *The Age of Innocence* (1993), also a story of failed, impossible romance, set at the 'end of an era', New York at the end of the nineteenth century. Paul Arthur makes a parallel between the use of flower arrangements in this film and the *cheongsam* in *In the Mood for Love*. These things 'speak', installing in each film 'a kind of hidden syntax or paramour's code' (2001: 41). Beyond the generic discourse of melodrama, in which mise-en-scène notoriously betrays undercurrents of emotion, Wong's film is like *The Age of Innocence* in terms of its treatment of history. Stern says of Scorsese's film:

> *The Age of Innocence* does not simply connote a time before the revolution of modernity, nor does it merely register an obsession with period detail (though it

is obsessive); on the contrary, it charts the mise-en-scène and theatricalization of obsessive desire. (1995: 224)

Stern concludes her book on Scorsese by suggesting that the director has 'shown that the way to produce new knowledge is through flying off at tangents, through meticulous spatialization, through an embodied cinematic practice that flies in the face of time's covetousness (1995: 228)'. Punctuating her discussion with quotations from Maya Deren on *Ritual in Transfigured Time* (1946), Stern suggests that the significance of cinematic intertextuality concerns 'questions to do with a structuring of the social and the phantasmatic, with realms of intersection (ibid.)'. Stephen Teo (2001) also borrows Deren's film title for an essay on *In the Mood for Love*, indicating yet another layer of the palimpsest of cinematic references that circulate around and through *In the Mood for Love*. By exploring the rich layers of intertextuality, critical discourse can work through the film's phantasmagoric historiography to pursue the emotional, sensual and erotic engagement with history and/as a form of representation.

I have not nearly exhausted the list of intertextual references in the film, many of which are far more obvious and direct than the melodramas on which I have lingered. The soundtrack for example, includes a waltz theme borrowed from Seijun Suzuki's *Yumeji* (1991), as well as various tunes (authentic recordings) from Chinese opera that would have been heard on the radio in Hong Kong in the early 1960s.[6] The English title of the film comes from a Nat King Cole song that is never actually heard in the film; meanwhile, the songs he does sing in Spanish evoke the influence of Philippine musicians in Hong Kong in the 1950s and 1960s. Rebecca Pan, who plays Li-zhen's landlady and friend, was a popular recording artist from 1959 to 1975, singing in Mandarin and English. These details indicate the level of historical accuracy that lies within this otherwise ethereal, dreamy, melancholy film.

Songs, like 'things', can be tied to particular historical times and places, while pointing to more metaphorical meanings and sensuous experiences. This is, finally, the lesson of *In the Mood for Love*: that the play of reality and fiction, the real and the not-real, is not simply whimsical or fantastical. Nor is the film's reflexivity merely artistic formalism, pointing to a void of historical experience. Through the generic discourse of romantic longing, Wong is able to open up a multitude of passages through the global intersections of popular cultural history, exploring the affect of historical transformation, historical loss, and utopian desires precisely by rendering them theatrical.

Romantic melodrama is principally a woman's genre, and *In the Mood for Love* should be recognised as a woman's film. Mo-wan, like Newland Archer (Daniel Day Lewis) in *The Age of Innocence*, is a much more passive romantic hero than his Hollywood predecessors, and in my view, the film's closing voiceover is its only misstep: 'He remembers those years as though looking through a dusty window pane…' Attributing the film to Mo-wan's hazy memory retrospectively tips the gender balance away from Li-zhen as a subjective agent in the failed romance. Like the interviews cited earlier, it imposes an interpretation onto the relationship which is contrary to the subtle, mostly wordless, interactions of the two protagonists, and denies Li-zhen the privilege of memory.

The triumph of social stricture over desire is a familiar melodramatic trope, and, as we have learned from Douglas Sirk, can often be read as an allegorical indictment of bourgeois society. In the Mood for Love appropriates the aesthetics and politics of this scenario, distorting them just enough to push the generic markers into a kind of textual unconscious. Wong's nostalgic return to the Hong Kong of his youth is thus loaded with historical detail that is partially grounded in global film culture, and partially based in lived history. Despite the stylised lighting, décor and steamy weather, Wong and his crew did use locations that he felt would evoke the Hong Kong that he grew up in. The film's phantasmagoria is one of cinematic pleasure, based in the history of cinematic pleasure, and the history of a specific community at a specific point in time.

The impossibility of the love affair at the center of the film may be an allegory of the cultural loss that occurred after 1967 when the decadent Shanghainese community disbanded and dispersed; but that reading is kind of like the secret whispered into a wall or a tree. Instead, Wong invites us into a world constructed out of cinematic memories and gestures, a world in which time and space are forever shifting and unstable. Once we are inside, engaged and entranced, we cannot help but know about the loss of this world and the hopes, desires and dreams that it once contained at the intersection of so many exciting, cosmopolitan cultural flows.

In the Mood for Love is not a typical film, and yet it offers some insight into the potential of cinephilia to 'structure encounters' between people separated by language, geography and history. W. J. T. Mitchell poses the question 'What do pictures want?' as a means of exploring the role of visual culture outside or beyond the interpretive paradigms that have informed literary (and film) studies (2005: 28). He acknowledges that the question is in some sense an ironic rephrasing of the Freudian question, 'What do women want?' but a film like In the Mood for Love demonstrates that the cinema can desire its spectator, can draw one into its rapturous embrace, precisely by working through the conventions of women's cinema and the romantic melodrama.

Once we are engaged, entranced, we are able to experience history as a cinematic text folding in on itself. The history of the twentieth century is in many respects also a history of the cinematic phantasmagoria that has effectively transformed things and places into images; 'the cinematic' becomes a means of reclaiming the sensual, experiential world of audio-video culture from within its commodification. If the cinematic experience of history has congealed more strongly in some sites than others, Wong's film highlights the remarkable blossoming of the phantasmagoria in Hong Kong in the early 1960s, as a crossroads of Asian, Western, Chinese and postcolonial cultures. The film's shifting temporalities, unstable periodisation, and ambiguous ending address the spectator in his or her own historical moment. The film's emphasis on the quotidian and the everyday likewise gives it a curious grounding in an elsewhere that was only a temporary moment in time – one that was ultimately unreconciled, unconsummated and unfulfilled.

NOTES

1   The actors talk about their experience in the 'making-of' documentary for *In the Mood for Love* included in the Criterion Collection DVD.

2   Maggie Cheung says that it took her a long time to feel relaxed enough in the *cheongsam* to perform well, and that she didn't stop worrying about it until the last few weeks of the fifteen-month shoot (Toronto International Film Festival Press Conference special feature included on Criterion DVD release).

3   The short compilation film included on the Criterion Collection *In the Mood for Love* DVD carries the same title as the original title of the film, and translates as *In Full Bloom*. This is also the title of the song that plays over the montage, and is heard in the film itself playing on the radio, one of several recordings of Chinese opera that is heard over the course of the film.

4   The clips included in *Hua yang de nian hua* (*In Full Bloom*) were excerpted from Hong Kong-produced films that were found in an old Chinatown cinema in Southern California and are now stored in the Hong Kong archive.

5   The 1960 film is said to have had some influence in making the *cheongsam* briefly fashionable in the west. http://en.wikipedia.org/wiki/Cheongsam accessed July 22, 2008.

6   Yet another special feature on the Criterion Collection DVD, 'The music of *In the Mood for Love*', details the sources of the various musical fragments and themes heard in the film.

REFERENCES

Arthur, Paul (2001) 'Review of *In the Mood for Love*' *Cineaste*, 26, 3, 40–1.
_____ (2005) 'Philosophy in the Bedroom: Wong Kar-wai's *2046*', *Cineaste*, 30, 4, 6–8.

Benjamin, Walter (1999 [1927–40] *The Arcades Project*. Trans. Howard Eiland and Kevin McLaughlin. Cambridge, MA: Harvard University Press.

Brunette, Peter (2005) *Wong Kar-wai*. Urbana, IL: University of Illinois Press.

Chow, Rey (2007) *Sentimental Fabulations, Contemporary Chinese Films* New York: Columbia University Press.

Chung, Hye Seung (2005) 'Toward a Strategic Korean Cinephilia: A Transnational Détournement of Hollywood Melodrama', in Kathleen McHugh and Nancy Abelman (eds) *South Korean Golden Age Melodrama: Gender Genre, and National Cinema*. Detroit: Wayne State University Press, 117–50.

Elsaesser, Thomas. (1991) 'Tales of Sound and Fury: Observations on the Family Melodrama', in Marcia Landy (ed.) *Imitations of Life: A Reader on Film and Television Melodrama*. Detroit: Wayne State University Press, 68–91.

_____ (2005) 'Cinephilia, or The Uses of Disenchantment', in Marijke De Valck and Malte Hagener (eds) *Cinephilia: Movies, Love And Memory*. Amsterdam: Amsterdam University Press, 27–43.

Hansen, Miriam (2000) 'The Mass Production of the Senses: Classical Cinema as Vernacular Modernism', in Christine Gledhill and Linda Williams (eds) *Reinventing Film Studies* London: Arnold/ New York: New York University Press, 332–50.

Joyrich, Lynn (2004) 'Written on the Screen: Mediation and Immersion in *Far from Heaven*', *Camera Obscura*, 57, 187–219.

Marchetti, Gina (2002) 'Hong Kong in the 1960s', *In the Mood for Love* DVD essay.

Metz, Christian (1982) *The Imaginary Signifier: Psychoanalysis and the Cinema*. Trans. Celia Britton, Annwyl Williams, Ben Brewster and Alfred Guzzetti. Bloomington: Indiana University Press.

Mitchell, W. J. T. (2005) *What do Pictures Want?* Chicago: University of Chicago Press.

Ng, David (2001) 'Review of *In the Mood for Love*', *Images*, http://www.imagesjournal.com/issue10/reviews/inthemood2/ Accessed July 20, 2008.

Pasolini Pier Paolo (1988) *Heretical Empiricism* Louise K. Barnett (ed.) Ben Lawton and Louise K. Barnett (trans.) Bloomington: Indiana UP, 1988.

Rayns, Tony (2000) 'In the Mood for Edinburgh', *Sight & Sound*, 10, 8, 14–17.

Stern, Lesley (1995) *The Scorsese Connection*. London: British Film Institute.

_____ (2001) 'Paths that Wind Through the Thicket of Things', *Critical Inquiry*, 28, 1, 317–54.

Street, Sarah (2002) 'Hitchcockian Haberdashery', in Sidney Gottlieb and Christopher Brookhouse (eds) *Framing Hitchcock: Selected Essays from The Hitchcock Annual* . Detroit: Wayne State University Press, 147–58.

Teo, Stephen (2001) 'Wong Kar-wai's *In the Mood for Love*: Like a Ritual in Transfigured Time', *Senses of Cinema*, 13, http://archive.sensesofcinema.com/contents/01/13/mood.html accessed April 2011.

_____ (2005) *Wong Kar-wai* London: British Film Institute.

Willemen, Paul (1994) *Looks and Frictions: Essays in Cultural Studies and Film Theory*

London: British Film Institute.

Wong Kar-wai (2000) *In the Mood for Love* DVD published in 2002 by the Criterion Collection.

CHAPTER SIX

A HOME FOR CINEPHILIA IN BERTOLUCCI'S *THE DREAMERS*
Kristi McKim

At the beginning of his glowing review of Bernardo Bertolucci's *The Dreamers* (2003), Roger Ebert fondly remembers his personal experiences of politics, cinema, and sex of the late 1960s, finally explaining that 'I indulge in this autobiography because I have just seen Bernardo Bertolucci's *The Dreamers* and am filled with poignant and powerful nostalgia' (2004). He continues by explaining that '*The Dreamers* evokes a time when the movies – good movies, both classic and newborn – were at the center of youth culture …The film is extraordinarily beautiful … [Bertolucci] has a voluptuous way here of bathing his characters in scenes from great movies, and referring to others' (2004). In response to Ebert's swooning celebration of *The Dreamers*, Jonathan Rosenbaum recalls his own memories of Paris 1968: 'Bertolucci's movie is supposed to show us how great it was in 1968 to be young and horny and in Paris and political and smitten with movies seen at the Cinematheque. But I was all of those things, and the movie brings back none of my experience' (2004). Though Rosenbaum acknowledges that 'there's no reason *The Dreamers* has to be true to anyone's experience', he nonetheless dismisses it as 'a fairy tale designed for teenagers in Cincinnati [due to its] almost abject reliance on every American cliché about the French they can summon up' (ibid.). While Ebert loves and Rosenbaum dismisses the film, both critics indulge their readers in personal digressions about their own cinephilic days of yore.

As exemplified in this Ebert/Rosenbaum pairing, *The Dreamers*' reviewers generally respond with personal reverie instead of consideration of *how* and *why* (aside from setting, plot, citation) this film incites such reverie. This context whereby internationally-renowned film critics frame *The Dreamers* within their own true-to-life experiences is exactly the phenomena this chapter considers: how do *we* relate to the film's entrenchment in history, be it a cinephilic collection of film moments, the cinematic staging of the May 1968 Paris riots, or our current spectatorial historical moment? This chapter will look at the ways this film tries to fit into history by virtue of its cinephilia, and how cinephilia might be not only a relationship to art but also a way of writing history. I ultimately want to claim that, in creating the 1968 political, cinephilic, familial, sexual, and sensual culture as experienced *in the home*, *The Dreamers* showcases the construction and production inherent in our current home-viewing experiences. Though explicitly about cinema-going at the heart of French film history, *The Dreamers* becomes an analogy for the falsely-thought private exercise of cinephilia in the home.

CINEPHILIA AS A HISTORY OF SENSUALITY

In *The Pleasure of the Text*, Roland Barthes poses what initially seem to be ahistorical questions of sensual experience: 'Is pleasure only a minor bliss? Is bliss nothing but extreme pleasure?' (1975: 20). He proceeds to ascribe qualitative value judgments to such wordplay and finally casts an historical import to these sensual ponderings: 'Is pleasure only a weakened, conformist bliss…? Is bliss merely a brutal, immediate … pleasure? … On the answer (yes or no) depends the way in which we shall write the history of our modernity' (ibid.). Barthes argues for the temporal contingency of qualitative sensation: pleasure and bliss, in his estimation, refer to not only qualities of experience but also measures of time. In his estimation, expressing sensual *quality* involves telling *time*. At stake in time's sensual intensity is our conception of history, time writ large, as it bears upon and carries contemporary experience.

In this regard, Cinema's ability to repeat, elongate (such as through slow motion), and compress time (such as through elliptical editing) in relation to narrative or subjective momentum offers a parallel to the intimacy and intensity of Barthes' sensual history. Moreover, we might further attach this correlation of a sensual history and cinematic time with an epiphanic or revelatory relationship between spectator and film: the very *action* of film-going can itself inspire, in Paul Willemen's terms, 'the serialization of moments of revelation' – a lovely phrase by which he defines the term 'cinephilia' (1994: 233). Regarding cinematic sequences that compel one's love for cinema, Willemen claims that 'these are moments which, when encountered in a film, spark something which then produces the energy and the desire to write, to find formulations to convey something about the intensity of that spark' (1994: 235). Willemen argues that these moments share the quality of revelation – 'the realization or the illusion of a realization that what is being seen is in excess of what is being shown. Consequently, you see something that is revelatory' (1994: 236). Willemen posits an epistemological cinephilia that equates revelatory moments with learning.

Thus I want to ask: How might a 'list' of revelatory cinematic moments illustrate a sensual history? While this endeavor might seem implausible, how we measure and mark our personal experience of time (for example, the first time we met someone we came to love, the last time we saw a loved one, the sudden autumnal breeze, freshly-cut grass, perfectly-steeped tea; as many artists, scholars, and scientists have noted, these sense-experiences have the power to trigger our memory and collapse and/or expand our experience of time) arguably introduces these encounters and moments into history. More specifically, how might cinephilia evoke the historical contours of this temporal and revelatory compression?

To address this question, I recall Walter Benjamin's 'Theses on the Philosophy of History,' where he claims: 'only for a redeemed mankind has its past become citable in all its moments' (1968: 254); and 'The past can be seized only as an image which flashes up at the instant when it can be recognized and is never seen again ... for every image of the past that is not recognized by the present as one of its own concerns threatens to disappear irretrievably' (1968: 255). Benjamin's imagistic and, literally, momentous conception of history undermines otherwise linear master-narratives that inevitably privilege the powerful. Christian Keathley has noted the connection between cinephilia and Benjamin's epiphanic history, claiming that collecting cinephilic moments allows us to engage 'with history via a form that ... challenges the dominant discourses of historicism' (2006: 140). Keathley eloquently advocates a historiography of the cinephiliac 'anecdote', which 'seeks to illuminate the ways in which movies – especially moments from movies – displace themselves out of their original context and step into our own lives' (2006: 152).

Here I consider how film can illustrate a sensual history through cinephilic citation: how do these citations rupture and mystify cinematic immersion (for character and audience, alike)? To what extent does cinematic canonicity equal a sensual history? To what extent does citationality or self-consciousness equal historical awareness? A citable past, after all, doesn't necessarily always thwart a dominant history: these citations can both disrupt and reify a history.

The Dreamers both illustrates and tests this combined history and cinephilia – a history of passion that might be more accurately be defined as a history of cinematic sensuality. Set during the spring of 1968 France, *The Dreamers* begins with protests over Henri Langlois' dismissal from the Cinémathèque Française and ends with a sequence, teeming in slow-motion cinematic excess, of what we presume to be the May 1968 crowd of protestors. The plot follows the evolving erotic friendship between the young American cinephile, Matthew (Michael Pitt), and his exotic and enchanting new Parisian friends, brother and sister Theo and Isabelle (Louis Garrel and Eva Green). As the political tensions escalate in the city streets, this trio takes indoor refuge in their triangulated desire, which intensifies through their impassioned exchange of cinematic citations. Their first evening together includes a sequence laden with references to the French New Wave: the score, Jean Constantin's from *The 400 Blows* (François Truffaut, 1959); the film footage, from Jean-Luc Godard's *Breathless* (1959). As Matthew talks about his 'heart pounding' in response to some combination of a police chase and the fact that he 'was already in love with [his] new friends', the film score conflates this 2003 cinematic imagining of 1968 Paris with little Antoine's (Jean-Pierre Leaud) whimsical yet melancholic exploration of both Paris and seashore; as the music alternates between its stringed swells and piano arpeggios, Matthew claims that he 'didn't want that night ever to end', a longing we might further locate at the heart of cinema's illusory fantasy of immortality and repetition.

Having just seen the actual Leaud minutes before (in documentary footage from 1968 and also in a 2003 recreation of his 1968 vocal protest against Henri Langlois' firing), a spectator aware of his or her film history can thereby contextualise the narrative establishment of this trio's friendship within an aurally-allusive cinephilic landscape. As many reviewers have described, *The Dreamers* shows the history of its own cinematic influences as it provides the back-story for these characters: Isabel goes so far as to equate her birthday with the arrival of Patricia (Jean Seberg) to the Parisian streets of *Breathless*.

On the basis of whether or not we recognise these cinematic allusions, *The Dreamers*' heavy intertextuality has the capacity to alienate or seduce us; like Matthew, who gains entrance to the group based on his cinematic knowledge and cinephilic intensity, we become (or do not become) 'one of [them]' on the basis of our ability to not only participate successfully in their trivia games but also acknowledge Bertolucci's own stylistic allusions (e.g. *The 400 Blows*' score). The film thus rewards the cinephilic spectator by inviting them to participate in this world, if only through a jubilant passing of a cinephilic entrance exam. While *The Dreamers* seems at first to promise an historically-grounded portrait of Spring 1968 (its first clip includes documentary footage of the protests, matched with Bertolucci's staged action), this film eventually turns history into a game, upon which both Matthew's acceptance into the group and our engagement with the film are predicated.

PHOTOGRAPHIC POSES AND CINEMATIC PERFORMANCES

In relation to these concerns of style and intertexuality, two defining examples of the French New Wave further illuminate *The Dreamers*' own cinematic past particularly as related to film citation. In both *Breathless* and *Jules and Jim* (François Truffaut, 1962) mirrored and freeze-frame sequences feature characters who self-consciously yet playfully fashion themselves in stylised star portraits. In *The Dreamers*, characters more obsessively attempt to evoke, with their full bodies, moving portraits of stylised cinematic glamour. These sequences from the French New Wave emphasise their characters' *production of a still*, a moment, an event; in *The Dreamers*, the still pose expands into the seriality that is cinema.

For example, in *Breathless*, Patricia and Michel (Jean-Paul Belmondo) frequently strike glamour poses, though these now-iconic postures and expressions fit within sequences that self-consciously mock their stylisation. Regarding *Breathless*, Dudley Andrew claims that 'we who have entered the theater after ogling production stills of Belmondo and Seberg find our interest deflected from the story of the chase to the mythology of representation' (1987: 20), though one need not first have seen the stills to grasp Michel's interest in the process of becoming iconic, more than the being-glamorous, itself. Alongside the gangster/romance plot, *Breathless* tells the story of what happens *before* and *after* the glamour shot. Michel's Bogart imitations or Patricia's Renoir-esque poses suggest these characters' self-consciousness more than their self-confidence. Exemplified in Michel's and Patricia's *practicing* their poses before both reflective surfaces and each other, a film still from *Breathless* can *be* the glamour shot, while the film sequence in *Breathless* frames this glamour shot within the *story of its construction*.

Likewise, *Jules and Jim* calls attention to Jeanne Moreau's facial drama through dialogue and freeze frames. While a focused Jules (Oscar Werner) and Jim (Henri Serre) play cards, Catherine attempts to win their attention through pseudo-philosophical repartee; when these attempts prove unsuccessful, Catherine rises from her seated position, stands over them at their chess table, and animatedly describes the before and after of her involvement with her two paramours; 'I never laughed before I met you too. I always looked like this', she says, while freeze frames turn her pouty and melancholic expressions into photographic portraits that evidence her self-assessment; 'but that's over for good. Now it's like this', she jubilantly chortles, while posing charismatically in her wide-smiling and bright-eyed glee (again, doubly-frozen through both Moreau's poses and Truffaut's freeze frames). Here, Catherine poses to capture the characters' attention and, more dramatically, also that of Truffaut's camera (as in the famous ending of *The 400 Blows*, Truffaut's freeze frame of the young protagonist further emphasises the stasis). Stanley Cavell writes of these freeze frames, 'the image private to the two men appears as if materialized by their desire, which freezes her at the height of laughter, from which she then descends' (1979: 138). This latter phrase, pointing to her 'descent' from this 'height of laughter', undoes while it reifies the prior moment of her aesthetically-framed and idealised pose.

In both *Breathless* and *Jules and Jim*, these poses fit within sequences that highlight the contrived nature of these postures. In this sense, the cinematic movement (the sequentiality of these portraits) changes them from glamorous icon to *stories of humans trying to emulate* such glamorous icons. The sequence humanises these characters by showing their attempts to become the iconic faces, inevitably, these frames have launched them into being. In *Breathless*, the author Parvulesco (Jean-Pierre Melville) claims that his ambitions are to be immortal and then to die; the inverse might be said of the performances of Seberg, Belmondo, and Moreau – these characters embody a vulnerability that makes them mortal, yet the iconic status of these performances grants them the public immortality of film stars.

These performances reveal an explicit self-stylisation that historicises the 'glamour shot' still within the story of its making. If we are to think of the film *sequence* as a kind of history, insofar as images gain a temporality and momentum instead of a static film still, we might claim that, here, history humbles the characters by denaturalising their aura. Like *Breathless* and *Jules and Jim*, characters in *The Dreamers* explicitly strike poses that emulate their adored stars. Yet, unlike Michel, Patricia, and Catherine, Bertolucci's characters seem more assured of their historical and cinephilic postures. Instead of using history (or the film sequence) to humble and humanise the characters, *The Dreamers*' references to canonical films *reinvest* its characters with an historical gravity and sensual grace.

Exemplary of *The Dreamers*' performative citation, Isabelle awakens Matthew through seductive citation of Rouben Mamoulian's *Queen Christina* (1933) in yet another illustrative scene that bonds the characters and, ostensibly, seduces or alienates the audience based on the familiarity of these references. Isabelle jostles Matthew awake after their first sleepover and proceeds to caress the textured walls, to glance into the mirror, to slide her hands along the room's surfaces in gestures evocative of Greta Garbo's movement as she 'memoriz[es] this room.' *The Dreamers*' matches-on-action between Green and Garbo forge a historical cohesion available only to our omniscient point-of-view here (we can see the film that Isabelle cites through overt intercutting of *The Dreamers* with *Queen Christina*). By comparison, Matthew only sees *Isabel's* Garbo performance; he ostensibly sifts through *his* memory in order to correctly identify *her* imitation. Likewise, for Isabel to conjure Garbo's performance, she too must remember the intricate details of that film sequence (as she resourcefully transforms her surroundings into cinematic mise-en-scène).

We might read this sequence as a moment of film subjectivity for either or both of the characters; the inclusion of *actual* footage, though, allows *us* to play this game along with them; regardless of whether we can identify 'Garbo' or 'Queen Christina', we are nonetheless scanning through our catalogue of film faces and sequences, along with Matthew. Moreover, the seamless alternation between Green and Garbo doubles the performance and turns each into a repetition, thereby expanding an historical film moment to accommodate a new performance, that of Green's. The eye-line matches/point-of-view shots additionally imbricate Isabelle and Matthew into *Queen Christina*'s diegesis. The powerful yet vague seduction among Theo, Matthew, and Isabelle thus becomes further triangulated (or quadrangled, and more?) through its inclusion of film history's characters. This and other such sequences equate character interiority with spectator history, as matches-on-action establish continuity but also cinematic excess for the spectator (that the characters can only imagine and perform). *The Dreamers* portrays character subjectivity, conjures audience cinephilia, and establishes a visual/aural collection of memorable canonical clips. These sequences are removed from their own narrative story and inserted within *this* particular story as a microcosm to the film's historical manipulations. As Amelie Hastie claims, 'film histories, especially star histories, work against a chronology or linearity. As a film image is timeless, the past lives on, seemingly without change, yet this past, as history has evinced, is also ephemeral. In this way, our very history of film is produced, in effect, by cinematic time – or at least the time of the image' (2007: 13).

Here and throughout, *The Dreamers* combines the timeless yet ephemeral 'ghosts of film past' to imagine *history* as a sensualised *film* history; the characters seduce (and punish) each other in proportion to their cinephilic film knowledge. While the narrative chronicles an ahistorical and insular experience of (yearning for) cinematic immersion, the film itself rewards a spectator's familiarity with the film canon, such that she can create from its many allusions a lineage of films that hearken historicity. Film history thus emerges as *The Dreamers*' serialisation of moments of revelation, a fantasy that Bertolucci himself casts in cinematic terms: 'the challenge was to be able to absorb the clips of old movies into the body of *The Dreamers*, of the film itself … The challenge was to make organic in our story pieces of movies of the past, like if the history of cinema was only one long film made by old filmmakers … and cut together' (quoted in Thompson 2003).

In *The Dreamers*, the characters make reference to *film* history, and such citations explicitly contribute to their mystique more than to their humanisation. To return to Parvulesco's claim in *Breathless*, Bertolucci immortalises these characters by attaching them to the constellation of film stars. Yet the narrative portrays the regressive ends of such cinephilia; the characters are on the verge of starvation, for example, since they have been too busy playing film charades to bother with concerns over sustenance. The ending of the film radically challenges any such neat descriptions of history, film, and sensuality. After Theo, Isabel, and Matthew have drunkenly passed out together, Isabel realises that they (and all their naked, near-incestual, erotic and intoxicated indulgences) have been discovered by her parents. Ashamed and devastated, Isabel quietly runs the gas hose into their makeshift tent and prepares for a murder/suicide. The boys are quickly awakened, however, when a brick from the protests outside shatters their window. Upon discovering the riots, our protagonists race downstairs and argue over whether or not to take up arms with the crowd (Matthew decries Theo's and Isabel's joining the crowd, instead advocating nonviolent protest). At this point, Theo and Isabel leave Matthew – their trio, formed through their shared affection for cinematic spectacle, now ruptured by violent spectacle.

Further blurring the distinction between cinematic and historical spectacle, the film's closing minutes combine the sensualised film history with an aestheticised *history* (the May 1968 riots), therein implicitly illustrating the absurdity of conveying revolutionary politics within an extravagant film aesthetic. The fiery passions of the crowd in protest become altogether muted by Edith Piaf's anthemic 'I have no regrets'; moreover, the slow motion numbs if not cancels the fervent gestures and actions of protest. The diegetic revolt turns into a *film* revolt or revolt-as-film. Narratively, the public engagement of these otherwise house-dwelling cinephiles suggests their evolution beyond apathetic and narcissistic young performers; stylistically, this film's historical spectacle reveals the yearning to participate as historical subjects through these sensualised moments. The film as such shows the attraction and the implications of *inhabiting* a sensual history more than *sensing* history as a spectator.

As Fritz Breithaupt claims about Benjamin, 'there can only be a history of phenomena ... history is that which enables a phenomenon to last' (2002: 191). Breithaupt continues: 'phenomena have a history precisely because they are not 'entities', but rather human constructs, be they dreams, illusions, cities, institutions, or a tradition whose existence is pending on perception and make-believe' (2002: 194). This final phrase certainly bears cinematic contours. To bring together Benjamin's history of phenomena, Barthes' sensual history, and Willemen's cinephilia, we might suggest that *The Dreamers* explicitly shows the drive to create a sensual history (through and as a film canon) alongside a ghostly warning of the potentially detrimental politics involved in such a mythical history.

HOUSING CINEPHILIA

While I want to put forth this argument about *The Dreamers*' drive to *create* or *inhabit* a sensual history; such a claim – entrenched as it is in the temporal underpinnings of phenomena – should also consider the actual *spaces* in which we apprehend such phenomena, both the diegetic spaces in *The Dreamers* and our spectatorial spaces of cinematic consumption. David Denby of *The New Yorker* opens his review by naming the film's 'most interesting character' as the 'Paris flat – a worn but beautiful bohemian version of an *appartement grand bourgeois*, with olive walls, high ceilinged corridors, many pictures and books, and, here and there, a secret corner' (2004). Though this 'most interesting character' of the home introduces his review, he does not consider the implications of *home viewing* for a contemporary audience. Denby exemplifies several reviewers in his explanation that 'erotic fixation by its very nature demands an enclosed space' (2004). I want here to explore the implications of this enclosed space for home theaters. Instead of weighing whether *The Dreamers* sensually engages film history or appallingly exemplifies cultural amnesia, I want to posit *The Dreamers* as an allegory for the public production of (what we imprecisely call) 'private' home-viewing experience.

For Barbara Klinger and Laura Mulvey, cinephilia takes the form of, respectively, collecting and becoming a 'pensive spectator'. In Klinger's words, 'film's domestication has not obliterated cinephilia; rather, the conditions fueling this kind of zealotry have been relocated and rearticulated within the complex interactions among media industries, commodity culture, and the private sphere' (2006: 55). In other words, the cinephile is now a collector, whose love of film takes the form of ownership (and whose collections literally must be *produced* by the industry); as Jason Sperb and Scott Balcerzak claim, 'Klinger appears to be one of the first to suggest that studios are very conscious of, and adaptable to, cinephile behaviour' (2009: 21). Mulvey celebrates this enhanced and independent spectatorial experience enabled by emerging technologies and products; DVD indexes and the pause button, for example, facilitate 'non-linear access' to narrative and forges 'new modes of spectatorship [that] illuminate aspects of cinema that ... have been hidden from view' (2006: 27). Mulvey champions what she terms a 'cinema of delay' (which she connects with Bellour's conception of the 'pensive spectator'):

> When celluloid cinema, viewed on video or DVD, is delayed by the pensive specta-tor, the presence of the past (the look and time of the spectator) finds conscious-ness in the present (the look and time of the spectator), across the tense of fiction (the look and time of the protagonist). The place of the look in cinema gains another dimension ... leading to other kinds of pleasure, fascination, and reflection. Out of a pause or delay in normal cinematic time, the body of narrative film can find new modes of spectatorship. (2006: 191)

The Dreamers offers one unique case study of these 'new modes', which evokes both film history past and technological home-theater present.

Within a plot explicitly nostalgic for May 1968, then, *The Dreamers* actu-ally mimics contemporary experiences of cinephilia as quoting, dislocating, and upending film (history) within the confines or privacy of the home (all the while acknowledging the socio-cultural context – similar to the media industries – that *produce* this home-bound cinephilic experience). The home in *The Dreamers* becomes a private site charged with and inadvertently created by the art and politics beyond the home, less a history of 1968 Paris than a reflection of, and allegory for, our own private sphere consumption of DVDs and all their thrilling special features and remastered styles.

The obvious yet underthought verb 'play' that names the very button we push to 'play' a film (in the home) suggests the performative, *play*ful underpinnings of the home-theater experience: a 'play' that resonates both with the performa-tive and the *play*-ful (yet ultimately atrophic and regressive) cinephilia within the home of *The Dreamers*. Why not name this button 'run' or 'start' or 'project', after all? The 'play' at the heart of our home-viewing practice becomes exaggerated in *The Dreamers*, which acts out and perverts our own 'playing' films in the home: our pausing, reviewing, and clip-based experience of film whilst we live, eat meals, have sex, make friends, enjoy impassioned debates about politics and art within the place of our homes. With their bodies – Isabel, Theo, and Matthew embody and exaggerate what we now can *do* with *technology*, this isolation of a clip that we can play for each other.

To revisit Rosenbaum, he closes his review with the following: '[the film's nostalgia and narcissism] keep this story stuck in the past, frozen and intact and irrelevant. I'd much prefer a fantasy about sex, politics, cinema, or some version of all three that teaches us something new about the present' (2004). In this chapter, I have tried to show how *The Dreamers* does, in fact, 'teach us something new about the present', insofar as we self-reflexively work through the process by which we consume, model, collect, and produce moving images *in the home*, our private realm that increasingly becomes publicly produced; this nostalgic portrait of a cinema-going culture shows the extent to which we have taken our film-going indoors and decidedly produced a world therein. Not only, then, does *The Dreamers* screen the desire to inhabit a history through cinephilia, but this film also locates such a cinephilic history within a literal and figurative home.

AUTHOR'S NOTE

This essay has evolved from presentations at 'The Past in the Present' interdisciplinary conference (Glasgow School of Art, 2007), the 2008 Society for Cinema and Media Studies Conference, and the Southern Illinois University Department of Cinema and Photography (September 2009). I express warm thanks to these audiences, in addition to my students and colleagues at both Hendrix College and Hofstra University, for enriching my ideas. Special thanks to Susan Felleman for not only her invitation to Southern Illinois (where this essay grew into its more final form) but also her stimulating conversation that inspired its revision.

REFERENCES

Andrew, Dudley (1987). '*Breathless*: Old as New,' in Dudley Andrew (ed.) *Breathless*. New Brunswick: Rutgers University Press, 3–20.

Barthes, Roland (1975) *The Pleasure of the Text*. Trans. Richard Miller. New York: Hill &

Wang.

Benjamin, Walter (1968 [1940]) 'Theses on the Philosophy of History,' in *Illuminations,* ed. Hannah Arendt, trans. Harry Zohn. New York: Schocken Books, 253–64.

Breithaupt, Fritz (2002) 'History as the Delayed Disintegration of Phenomena' in Gerhard Richter (ed.) *Benjamin's Ghosts: Interventions in Contemporary Literary and Cultural Theory.* Stanford: Stanford University Press, 191–203.

Cavell, Stanley (1979) *The World Viewed.* Cambridge: Harvard University Press.

Denby, David (2004) 'They Like to Watch: Bertolucci's *The Dreamers,*' *The New Yorker,* 16 February. Online. Available at: http://www.newyorker.com/arts/reviews/film/the_dreamers_bertolucci . Accessed 15 November 2009.

Ebert, Roger (2004) *The Dreamers* (review), *Chicago Sun Times,* 13 February. Online. Available at: http://rogerebert.suntimes.com/apps/pbcs.dll/article?AID=/20040213/REVIEWS/402130302/1023 . Accessed 19 September 2009.

Hastie, Amelie (2007) *Cupboards of Curiosity: Women, Recollection, and Film History.* Durham: Duke University Press.

Keathley, Christian (2006) *Cinephilia and History, or The Wind in the Trees.* Bloomington: Indiana University Press.

Klinger, Barbara (2006) *Beyond the Multiplex: Cinema, New Technologies, and the Home.* Berkeley: University of California Press.

Mulvey, Laura (2006) *Death 24x a Second: Stillness and the Moving Image.* London: Reaktion Books.

Rosenbaum, Jonathan (2004) 'Dream On: *The Dreamers*', *Chicago Reader,* 20 February. Online. Available at: http://www.jonathanrosenbaum.com/?m=200402&paged=2. Accessed 14 November 2009.

Sperb, Jason and Scott Balcerzak (2009) 'Presence of Pleasure', in Jason Sperb and Scott Balcerzak (eds) *Cinephilia in the Age of Digital Reproduction: Film, Pleasure and Digital Culture, Vol. 1.* London: Wallflower Press, 7–29.

Thompson, David (2003) *Bertolucci Makes the Dreamers* (film included on *The Dreamers* DVD release).

Willemen, Paul (1994) *Looks and Frictions: Essays in Cultural Studies and Film Theory.* Bloomington: Indiana University Press.

CHAPTER SEVEN

A LITTLE INFEDILITY: *LA FEMME INFIDÈLE* BECOMES *UNFAITHFUL*

Susan Felleman

On 31 August 2007, a student wrote on our Film Analysis class' discussion board, apropos of nothing other than the date, 'Richard Gere is 58 today. Having grown up watching a young Richard Gere perform his art, this is very depressing.'

I know how this no-longer-young student feels. There is something poignant about seeing Gere – whom I remember as a young actor from when I was an even younger filmgoer in *Days of Heaven* (Terrence Malick, 1978), *American Gigolo* (Paul Schrader, 1980), *Breathless* (Jim McBride, 1983), and *The Cotton Club* (Francis Ford Coppola, 1984) – play the older, cuckolded husband role in *Unfaithful* (Adrian Lyne, 2002) – something poignant, yet strangely apt. The poignancy I find in that performance grows from a mood of reluctant acknowledgment of my own middle age, certainly – but it also comes from my memory of Richard Gere's life on film, including the bittersweetness that lingers between Gere and his *Unfaithful* costar Diane Lane from their earlier roles in *The Cotton Club*, in which their love and desire were clouded by illicit loyalties, risky choices, and reality. Even more apt and poignant, I find that the beautiful Diane Lane, herself on the verge of middle age in 2002, should in *Unfaithful* betray the aging Gere with a Frenchman. For her French lover awakens the dormant irresolution of another film from my youth, *A Little Romance* (George Roy Hill, 1979), and Diane Lane's debut.

Fig. 1: Richard Gere and Diane Lane in *The Cotton Club* (Francis Ford Coppola, 1984)
Fig. 2: Diane Lane and Richard Gere in *Unfaithful* (Adrian Lyne, 2002)

How do such film memories and associations that we as spectators bring to the viewing of a film affect our experience of it? And how does this experience parallel or converge with the comparable but obviously not identical film experiences that affect other viewers, and may have affected the filmmakers themselves and their choices? This is a question about cinephilia, knowledge, and memory. Movies (and television) often expect us to know. The more we know and the more we have seen, the more we appreciate the allusion, citation, pastiche, and travesty so ubiquitous in contemporary culture (for example, the Coen Brothers, Quentin Tarantino, Christopher Guest, *Shrek*, *The Simpsons*). That is the pleasure of recognition: a little payoff for our days and years of devotion to watching. But my question goes beyond the quotation marks that hover around knowing movies to the more mysterious and often obscure resonances that have to do with not just knowing, but having been intimate with movies. It has to do with intimacy, memory, the indexicality of the photographic image and the recorded sound (cinema's bases) and the plenitude of cinematic experience: pictures, sounds, stories, talent, and all the meta-cinematic clamor of pop culture. This may be a question without an answer because it is subjective to the point of obscurity and resounds infinitely, but it is intriguing nonetheless. It is about the common culture of cinema and individual affective byproducts of that culture. It is about subjectivity, resonance and pleasure. I use the film *Unfaithful* as a kind of case study.

This study occupied me on and off for a long time: a period of exploration, doubt, and experimentation, during which I presented my questions and my preliminary ideas a number of times, including twice to audiences grounded in American Studies, thus raising further questions, including 'what exactly makes a film American?'[1] It may seem a simple question, and, in the heyday of the Hollywood studio system, the answer may have appeared obvious, but these days, the ways that films are financed, staffed, and executed, they often have a mixed, more global pedigree and intended audience. In addition to the industrial and financial parameters of the production, the origins of the story, the talent, the locations, etc., all contribute to the lineage of the final product. The very title of this chapter may imply a sort of domestication or Americanisation of something originally French but, in truth, the simple compartmentalisation of film into obvious categories such as 'French film' and 'Hollywood movie' is problematic, especially as so many prejudices and simplifications are packed into them. That said, films do not, probably, get much more French than Claude Chabrol's *La femme infidèle* (1968), a devastating excavation of the vagaries and dysfunction of an *haute bourgeois* marriage set in Paris and Versailles. As for the Americanness of *Unfaithful*, there are various ways to think about this 2002 film directed by Adrian Lyne, and starring Richard Gere and Diane Lane.

I have had to think about it in terms of my own response to the film, much of which, upon analysis, I have discovered was bound up with the casting. The casual retrospective research and reflection that I, as many cineastes and cinephiles, often do upon encountering a film led me down into a rabbit hole of fascinating connections and queries. I was intrigued to discover that in Alvin Sargent's screenplay for *Unfaithful*,[2] the lover of the unfaithful wife was called Jack Pierce. And according to 'trivia' published by the Internet Movie Database, Brad Pitt and Ryan Phillippe had been offered the role but the producers ultimately decided that he should be French rather than American, and Olivier Martinez received the part.[3] Both director Adrian Lyne and actor Diane Lane in their commentaries on the DVD edition of *Unfaithful* confirm and discuss this shift of national identity during the casting process.[4] Lyne implies it was his own decision. But why should Jack Pierce become Paul Martel and Paul be French rather than American? I do not find this as trivial a question as it might at first appear. Here are some reasons.

CLICHÉ

In interviews, including his DVD commentary, Lyne admits the French lover is rather a cliché, and says he worried about it a bit, but that the positive aspects of the casting overrode his concerns. Clichés and stereotypes are, of course, themselves a basic form or symptom of intertextuality. The very presence of a French man in a role like this can conjure the ambiguous and ambivalent representations of French men – seductive, often bordering on sleazy – in American movies and popular culture, from Maurice Chevalier and Charles Boyer in their roles of the classic era to, at the more negative end of the stereotype, caricatures (often travesties of Frenchness performed by non-French actors) which are a perennial source of American comedy. Some vivid examples are: Michel Auclair (born Wladimir Vujovic in Koblenz, Germany) as the slimy 'empathicalist' philosopher, Prof. Emile Flostre, in Stanley Donen's *Funny Face* (1957); Tchéky Karyo (born Baruh Djaki Karyo in Istanbul) as Anton Depeux in *Addicted to Love* (Griffin Dunne, 1997); and Albert Brooks (born Albert Einstein in Beverly Hills) as the voice of Jacques, Marge's seductive French bowling instructor, in the 1990 episode of *The Simpsons*, 'Life on the Fast Lane', aka 'Jacques to be Wild'.

PERSONNEL

Paul's Frenchness, in addition to being a cliché, connects in numerous ways to the personnel of *Unfaithful*: its director and, especially, stars. Notably, Richard Gere appears in *Unfaithful* in his fourth, arguably fifth remake (or adaptation) of a French film: *Breathless* (1983), of course, remakes Jean-Luc Godard's seminal, *À bout de souffle* (1959); *Sommersby* (Jon Amiel, 1993) adapts *Le retour* de Martin Guerre (Daniel Vigne, 1982); Intersection (Mark Rydell, 1994) is a remake of Claude Sautet's Les Choses de la vie (1969); and, although not exactly a remake, Paul Schrader's American Gigolo (1980) – Gere's signature role – was inspired by Robert Bresson's Pickpocket (1959).[5] Although each of these movies 'Americanises' the story and Gere's character, one wonders: is there something 'French' about Richard Gere?[6]

Oddly enough, Adrian Lyne, Diane Lane, and Gere himself think that Olivier Martinez (who is, to complicate the question of Frenchness, of mixed French, Algerian, and Spanish ancestry) somewhat resembles the younger Gere,[7] with whom Lane had appeared early in her career, in Francis Ford Coppola's The Cotton Club. [I am, I confess, not overwhelmed by the resemblance between the two actors, although I do see common traits – a narcissistic cockiness, notably]. Murkier, homoerotic associations having to do with Gere's image, rumors around his private sexuality, and the narcissism of many of his screen characters mingle here with euphemisms and stereotypes associated with French sexuality and masculinity. As Elisabeth Ladenson points out, there is 'a certain pre-existing connection between queerness – in every imaginable sense of the term – and Frenchness in our culture.' The very word, 'French', itself, she points out, is loaded with slang and euphemistic meanings: 'deviant, sensuous, lewd, kinky, syphilitic, and illicit', among them (1998: 199). So the Frenchness that is behind the scenes in these remakes and adaptations merges with a certain latent aura around their leading man's sexuality and sex appeal.

Also, Diane Lane has been married to and divorced from a Frenchman: the actor Christopher (née Cristophe) Lambert.[8] How does this biographical fact bear on the Frenchness of her character's lover in Unfaithful? And what about a more textual and, for me, more poignant trace: to Lane's memorable film debut as a 13-year-old American girl who falls in love with a French boy in A Little Romance (George Roy Hill, 1979)? The connection to this perhaps slight and sentimental, but charming, love story was really the germ of this chapter. I found myself regarding Unfaithful as a kind of obscure or even unconscious sequel, a notion that implicitly complicates any sense of Unfaithful as mere reiteration or cover version of Chabrol's film, as would be implied by the term 'remake'. Is there any relevance to the fact that Adrian Lyne lives in France – in Provence – when he's not making movies?

PROVENANCE

Certainly, however – and very significantly – the lover's Frenchness points to the French origin of Unfaithful, Chabrol's La femme infidèle. Questions about sources and artistic fidelity have plagued the cinema, which has habitually adapted literary works, since its inception. As if the topic of fidelity to literary sources were not thorny enough, remakes and other film adaptations of cinematic sources have fostered a great deal of controversy and suspicion. Where does one draw the line between adaptation, exploitation, and theft? And why bother? How ought we think about the Coen Brothers' *O Brother, Where Art Thou?* (2000) in relation to Homer, when high art (James Joyce's *Ulysses*) and Hollywood comedy (Preston Sturges' *Sullivan's Travels*, 1941) stand side-by-side as intertextual intermediaries along with a hash of dozens of other movies, television shows, literary and pop cultural allusions? But the Coen Brothers, Martin Scorsese – famous for allusions and quotation (see Stern 1995) – and Brian De Palma, known for his (Harold) Bloomian engagement with the works of Hitchcock in numerous films, including *Obsession* (1976), *Dressed to Kill* (1980), and *Body Double* (1984), are regarded as auteurs, so we call their borrowings bricolage or homage, the French terms denoting artistic value. But what of adaptations, versions, and remakes with less plainly auteurist imprimaturs? And what, or who, exactly is an auteur (another French term!)?

These questions (and I am not the first to ask any of them) are thorniest, perhaps, around Hollywood remakes of 'foreign' films, especially classic 'art' films. It's easy to see both serious homage and bald exploitation in remakes like Terry Gilliam's *Twelve Monkeys* (1995), which adopts and inflates the basic plot premise of Chris Marker's French art house classic *La Jetée* (1962) or Steven Soderbergh's *Solaris* (2002), a remake of Andrei Tarkovsky's mystical and influential Soviet film from 1972. The very presence in the remakes of Hollywood stars and huge box office draws Bruce Willis and George Clooney – as with Richard Gere in *Unfaithful* – turns the film into a vehicle, a commodity. But, it must be added, big Hollywood stars are artists too and for the producers' and directors' purposes, the artistry of the original film is very likely also a form of currency which is used to lure these box-office draws to the project, as they will in turn lure ticket buyers. But just because there is exploitation involved, does that nullify the artistic interest of the product? As I have written elsewhere, the foreign film (French especially) has long connoted sex to American audiences and this,

Fig. 3: Stéphane Audran in *La femme infidèle* (Claude Chabrol, 1968)
Fig. 4: Diane Lane in *Unfaithful* (Adrian Lyne, 2002)

along with complexes about art and commerce, may contribute to the nervous-ness around the legitimacy and fidelity of the remake (see Felleman 2006: 12).

The most significant contributions to the growing body of literature about film remakes – including Constantine Verevis, as well as David Wills and Lucy Mazdon on Hollywood remaking of French films – persuasively demonstrate the silliness, snobbery, and simplicity of binary views that privilege something essential in the French art film and deride the American remake as a knock-off, a debased copy, or a poor translation, a critical tendency which remains rather reflexive and wide-spread. Fidelity and infidelity, of course, are central (indeed titular) themes of both Chabrol's and Lyne's films. I operate on the assumption that both filmmakers find these themes interesting at the literal and figural – sexual and aesthetic – levels; and that, indeed, the literal and the figural here blur. For my purposes, Lyne is treated as auteur whether or not he fits all criteria and whether or not one entirely accepts the concept. The abundant available evidence points to his having con-ceived and controlled the film from inception through post-production. It is Lyne's own cinephilia and eroticisation of influence that arouse investigation. He says of Chabrol's *La femme infidèle*, 'it has always been one of my favorite films and I thought for that reason that I shouldn't touch it, but I did'; Lyne laughs the know-ing laugh of a confessed adulterer and proceeds to excuse himself, enumerating the differences between the two films.[9] *Unfaithful* is plainly an *unfaithful* remake or adaptation. It is interesting with regard to the Franco-American relocation to think about the remake at one level as a problem of translation, in which case one might conjure the ancient polemic of 'Les belles infidèles', a term that refers to the legacy of a school of seventeenth-century French translators who adhered to the adage that, 'like women, translations must be either beautiful or faithful'. This 'conflict between beauty and fidelity', as Sherry Simon points out, 'reaches far back into the memory of Western culture (1996: 11).[10] It reveals remarkable slippage between issues pertaining to language, gender, and sexuality, a slippage that is suggestive of Lyne's dramatic and erotic re-reading of Chabrol's work.

Let us not place Lyne's film in relation to Chabrol's without locating it, in turn, in its own intertextual vortex with its literary progenitor *Madame Bovary* and in its express engagement with the films of Alfred Hitchcock. So, to return to the Frenchness of Paul, in *Unfaithful* it can invoke Chabrol, and the British-born direc-tor Lyne's avowed 'love affair' with French cinema; and also the French primal scene of *Madame Bovary* and the French 'love affair' with the British Hitchcock. Hitchcock and Lyne are both Brits whose careers began in England but achieved their maturity and greatest success in the US. Their 'Englishness', then, consti-tutes a kind of bridge, or intermediate term, which complicates in both directions any simple, bilateral contrast here between the European and the American. And, indeed, probably for each way in which Lyne's film can be characterised as 'typi-cally' Hollywood (its pronounced emphasis on the motivations and psychological delineation of individual characters, for instance), there is another way in which it must be acknowledged as equally atypical – seen in its refusal to either justify infidelity as a response to an unfulfilling marriage or to present it unsympathetically. Connie and her lover Paul may meet cute (à la Hollywood), but she and her husband Edward are left when the film ends, *in medias res* (à la française).

TRANSFERENCE

Paul's Frenchness, then, points to a way of thinking about the relationships between movies that is more fruitful and complex than these endless debates about priority, originality, and exploitation. Intertextual connections occur at all stages of production and reception. Cliché, star trajectory, homage, allusion, and debt: any and all of these reasons, and others, for Paul's Frenchness are factors, consciously and unconsciously existing in both 'producers' and 'spectators' because producers are always already themselves spectators. Many attributes of a movie are in this sense over-determined. Individual and collective memory is the crux, and love, and the way that these interact with material and historical attributes of cinema. Perhaps the cumulative intensity of countless over-determined details, motifs, scenes, or characters – the way each resonates with film history and reverberates with allusions, citations and stylistic echoes, and touches the memory of viewers – lends movies (even many seemingly routine ones) much of their peculiar fascination to those of us who are peculiarly fascinated. The relationships between movies and between spectators and movies take place not in a meta-cinematic vacuum (some schematic flow chart) or in the film buff's chat room, but in us: both individually and collectively.

Things we remember or only vaguely recall in and from other movies, other roles, books read, songs heard, a vast range of images and experiences (things as various as memory itself: a vivid shade of yellow, an eloquent camera movement, a luminous star turn, a bittersweet melody) are transferred repeatedly in our experience of movies; this must be just as true for those among the filmgoers who are sometimes behind the camera. I invoke the psychoanalytic ambience around the term transference to signal the always partly unconscious element in the genesis and reception of such intertextual relationships. For the cinephile – much more than for the casual moviegoer – that which is transferred belongs to the experience of movies.

In responding to Connie's French lover in *Unfaithful*, then, maybe some of us remember – although perhaps just faintly, or even indirectly – Charles Boyer in *History is Made at Night* (Frank Borzage, 1937) or *Love Affair* (Leo McCarey, 1939).[11] Some of us remember the curtailed juvenile, Franco-American love affair between Diane Lane and Thelonious Bernard in *A Little Romance*. And some vaguely recall Richard Gere telling Valérie Kaprisky that they will get away to

Mexico in the American remake of *Breathless* – a moment invoked at the end of *Unfaithful* – or risking his very life to try to keep his family together in *Sommersby*, the remake of *The Return of Martin Guerre*.

And a few of us recall Chabrol's *La femme infidèle*, too. Obviously, Adrian Lyne does. Others certainly know *Madame Bovary* (Flaubert's novel or one of its film adaptations, including Chabrol's own from 1991). In *La femme infidèle*, does Chabrol signal his revision of this classic story – its shift of focus away from the unfaithful wife to the cuckolded husband – by changing Emma to Hélène but retaining the name Charles? Lyne returns the favour. His film shifts the focus back toward the wife – is engrossed by the mysterious spark and inexorable momentum of her adulterous desire – and retains Chabrol's protagonists' names only to the extent of naming the Sumners' young son Charlie. *Unfaithful* ironically changes the name Hélène (which suggests beauty) to Constance (constancy, i.e. fidelity); and then Lyne changes his screenwriter's American Jack to a French Paul. In Chabrol's film, the not-the-least-bit exotic lover was called Victor, a name not without ironic effect. Curiously, Paul (the given name of Chabrol's longtime collaborator Paul Gégauff) was the name of a secondary character in *La femme infidèle* as well as one often given to the third character in a marital triangle in a number of other Chabrol films, including others in the so-called 'Hélène cycle', in which Chabrol's then wife Stéphane Audran repeatedly played women named Hélène (see Austin 1999: 49–55). Lyne 'loves' Chabrol, so maybe he knows this history.

When Lyne revisits Chabrol's scene of the two detectives calling on the unfaithful wife, is he also reprising Hitchcock, since Chabrol's scene certainly was derived from *Suspicion* (1941)? Chabrol's unfaithful wife knows neither that her lover has been murdered, nor that her husband is the murderer, whereas Hitchcock's faithful wife does not know that her husband's friend and partner has been murdered but suspects him of it. Chabrol's detective scene is an homage to and a reversal (as per the anxiety of influence) of Hitchcock's: both wives (Chabrol's Hélène and Hitchcock's Lina) are ignorant of the crime that is being investigated but while Hitchcock's is faithful and innocent, except of suspecting her husband, Chabrol's is unfaithful and guilty, except of suspecting her husband. When Lyne repeats the Chabrol scene, he too must negotiate the anxiety of influence. He reverses just the affect, substituting Diane Lane's nervous transparency for Stéphane Audran's placid opacity, consistent with his film's greater interest in the wife: her motivation, point-of-view, emotions.

It's interesting to note that this detective scene gets progressively shorter with each reprise, an interesting and probably symptomatic historical development. Despite this, one detects very close observation by Chabrol of Hitchcock's methods and of Chabrol's by Lyne. Lyne's characters here and elsewhere often stand and move about, while Hitchcock's and Chabrol's – given to more formality

– tend to sit. His greater 'efficiency' in such scenes permits Lyne, among other embellishments, a completely new first act – all about the love affair – and a third act that is longer and very different than Chabrol's film's.

As Constantine Verevis points out, 'remakes do not consist simply of bodies of films but, like genres, are located too in expectations and audience knowledge' and in 'the institutions that govern and support specific reading strategies' (2004: 89; 90). This is certainly the case with a scene like the detective visit, one that has become numbingly familiar to us in an era of *Law and Order* (1990–2010) all the time and may have been old already when Hitchcock took it up with such subtlety, humor and finesse. Verevis reminds us, too, that 'the concept of intertextuality needs … to be related to the ever-expanding availability of texts and technologies, and the unprecedented awareness of film history among new Hollywood filmmakers and contemporary audiences' (2004: 95). A side-by-side video comparison that illustrated an oral presentation of this essay instantiated Verevis's point. It enabled minute, simultaneous, shot-by-shot comparison of scenes, details of mise-en-scène, cinematography and editing, and was all but impossible prior to the introduction and wide dissemination of non-linear digital editing technology. My reliance on DVD commentaries, as well as data and user comments from the Internet Movie Database as sources of research, proves this point, too.

LOVE

'I love the French cinema', says Adrian Lyne in his commentary for the DVD edition of *Unfaithful*. 'I think that Chabrol was kind of a French Hitchcock … I love his work and I would say his movie had a kind of formality to it … it almost had a kind of stylised quality, really. I saw it in 1969 or 1970', he says of *La femme infidèle*. 'It lingered with me…' Lyne's love for French film is signaled by the French Film festival from which the private eye's incriminating photos capture Paul and Connie emerging on Bleecker Street (they tryst to Jacques Tati's *Les Vacance de Monsieur Hulot/Monsieur Hulot's Holiday* from 1953). Is this also why Connie loves Paul? On a metatextual level, of course, he can be seen as a personification of the beloved French cinema. Lyne says that he 'loved' the scene in Chabrol's film in which the husband visits the lover and indeed that this scene was one of the main reasons he wanted to remake the movie. But, as Lyne himself notes, while Chabrol's husband pretends to be cool with the affair and that theirs is an open marriage, his (Gere's) character does not. Lyne loved the scene and remade it very much the same and yet totally different. Lyne's men display a visible psychological intensity and transparency relative to Chabrol's. Lyne also says he 'loves' the mechanics of getting rid of the body, which he gets from Chabrol, and Chabrol, of course, borrowed from Hitchcock's *Psycho* (1960). But the humor (albeit black) so pronounced in Hitchcock's and Chabrol's scenes is rather anemic in Lyne. And, then, if Paul is French film personified, what does this murder and disposal of his body – the evidence – say about love and influence?

Lyne draws on influences other than Chabrol and Hitchcock, too. David Lean's *Brief Encounter* (1945) is one of his 'top five favorites of all time'. 'I looked at *Brief Encounter* very closely', he says of the presence of this poignant classic of extra-marital desire behind his (see Williams 2006). And it is clear that Lyne also loves hot emotion that shows on the body and displaying the visceral upheaval of raw eroticism. These prominent attributes of his film, like Lean's bittersweet lyricism, are utterly absent in Chabrol's chilly, almost clinical vision of constrained, civilised, bourgeois surfaces, through which the repressed ruptures. Chabrol does not illustrate Hélène's desire and is not really interested in it. Her affair is underway when his film begins – its origins totally obscure and probably irrelevant for his purposes – the most Chabrol shows of it is one discreet scene of a post-coital cup of tea and cigarette. For sensual, subjective representations of desire – the 'hardcore' (so to speak) of much of the first act of *Unfaithful* – Lyne turned his back on the remoteness and objectivity of Chabrol's critique and recalled a recent German film whose eroticism grabbed him, *Aimée & Jaguar* (Max Färberböck, 1999), borrowed its vivid image of a woman trembling with illicit sexual desire (in that case for another woman), and, while he was borrowing, hired its composer Jan Kaczmarek to create *Unfaithful*'s fulsome, emotional score, which so contrasts with the modernist *ostraneniye* of Pierre Jansen's score for Chabrol's film.

Fig. 5: Stéphane Audran and Maurice Ronet in *La femme infidèle* (Claude Chabrol, 1968)
Fig. 6: Diane Lane and Olivier Martinez in *Unfaithful* (Adrian Lyne, 2002)

The unspeakable, dangerous desire that electrifies narrative space in *Aimée & Jaguar* is evident not only in *Unfaithful*'s indebted sex scene, though. The scene between the husband and lover has a debt to Färberböck's film, too; as the two men move watchfully around the loft one senses a kind of almost erotic tension, as with a scene between the two women in the German picture. This underscores a suppressed homoerotic ambience that had already slipped into the film as an aura around Richard Gere specifically and Frenchness generally.[12] It should be noted that when *Unfaithful* was released, one of Olivier Martinez's most recent parts had been that of the gay lover of Reinaldo Arenas in *Before Night Falls* (Julian Schnabel, 2000).

Love. Lyne loves Chabrol. Freud, famously, maintained that love is transference. Transference is 'a playground of repetition', as Seán Hand recalls, suggesting it as the model for intertextuality: relationships between texts and their readers and writers (1990: 85). Lyne loves Chabrol but takes his story and shakes it so hard that the center of gravity moves from husband to wife (or at least to somewhere between the two); he takes what was cool and limpid and droll, turns up the heat and turns down the lights, recovering something of the Hitchcockian eroticism and Germanic shadows that Chabrol eschewed.

'First, let us consider a film's production history as itself one act of spectatorship', writes Tom Poe, pointing to the actual industrial conditions around and permutations of theoretical insights such as Hand's; 'In linear transmission models of communication, the producers of a text are generally figured as the binary opposite of the spectator. Before any film has a material existence, however, it is seen in the mind's eye of its creators. In most Hollywood films, the material text is the product of a number of creative and institutional points of view' (2001: 92). So the relationships between creators and spectators when it comes to Hollywood films – almost all films, actually – make for a busier playground yet. Lyne begins as a spectator of Chabrol but there is much between the fact of his loving *La femme infidèle* and us responding to *Unfaithful*.

Many more people now occupy what used to be the exclusive preserve of passionate cineastes and auteur-directors like Lyne. We are simultaneously spectators and historians of cinema. Due to 'the arrival of new technologies', according to Alain Cohen, there emerges 'a new theoretical figure who might best be thought of as the "hyper-spectator" … who can reconfigure both the films themselves and filmic fragments into new and novel forms of both cinema and spectatorship' (2001: 157). When we go to the movies, or lie down with a DVD (and its extras), our extra- and intertextual experiences in a sense mingle with those of the filmmakers. We are intimate. We cinephiles are promiscuous.

Diane Lane's film debut in *A Little Romance* paired her with Thelonius Bernard, a French boy not at all unlikely to become rather like Olivier Martinez's Paul. Lane's character, Lauren, the bright, serious, alienated daughter of wealthy Americans in Paris, meets Bernard's character, Daniel, an equally bright, cinephile son of a single, loutish, Parisian taxi-driver. The French boy combines a robust, sensual, working-class façade with Gallic charm and a sensitive, 'bookish' intellect. Olivier Martinez seems a similar mélange of traits; he is in fact the son of a mechanic, and was a boxer before becoming an actor; in *Unfaithful*, his own punching bag hangs in the Soho loft where the sensitive hunk he plays collects and deals books, and seduces Connie with his Gallic charm and poetry.

Based on a French novel, *E=mc², mon amour* by Patrick Cauvin, *A Little*

Romance crowns its juvenile love affair with a fantasy of Venice, to where the misunderstood little lovers run away in the company of their fanciful old gentleman friend, Julius, whose courtly manners and extravagant romantic tales only slightly distract from his actual disreputability. The movie ends with bittersweet goodbyes. Lauren's stepfather has been transferred to Houston, and she must leave Paris, Daniel, and Julius. Laurence Olivier, who played Julius, was very taken with 13-year-old Diane Lane, predicting that she would be the next Grace Kelly (interesting in terms of the Hitchcockian aura around her 23 years later in *Unfaithful*). Apparently, the affection was mutual. On the DVD commentary, Lane says of her distinguished co-star, who was ill with cancer during the production, 'the goodbye was my favorite scene because I really felt it. We shot it in sequence because George [Roy Hill, the director] was smart that way ... and when we were saying goodbye, I was really saying goodbye ... to Olivier.'[13]

Olivier Martinez, incidentally, comments on the DVD of *Unfaithful* that his scenes in it were shot in sequence, too. This is a relatively unusual (because usually more expensive) practice, one that directors might employ for the sake of psychological realism: to aid actors in really engaging with their characters in time. This is another link in what Constantine Verevis calls, 'the endless chain of connections – both voluntary and involuntary – which characterises film remaking' (2004: 25).

A Little Romance has its own resonant intertextual life, too; it portrays the French cinema's romance with the American, as if in a mirror. Daniel, a young cinephile, steals a lobby card photo of Robert Redford – from *Butch Cassidy and the Sundance Kid* (1969), one of Hill's own movies: one with notable debt to the nouvelle vague, Truffaut's *Jules et Jim* (1962), especially – in an obvious allusion to Truffaut's *Les Quatre cents coups/The 400 Blows* (1959). In another obvious homage (or borrowing), *A Little Romance* ends with a freeze frame of the teenage boy, who is running in traffic and leaping in air to wave at his beloved, behind the limousine taking Lauren and her family away. Hill's film was scored by Georges Delerue, whose music is the soundtrack to so much of the French New Wave and its aftermath (although very different from Jansen's).

'I've never been able to get this out of my head since its first release; it is one of the best films I've ever seen', writes one IMDb user of *A Little Romance*. 'I just looked at the DVD and was amazed at how many details I still remember from that first viewing 26 years ago ... As fine as Diane Lane has been in recent films, I don't believe she's ever been as good as she is here ... It's a real shame that Thelonious Bernard didn't have a film career, but if you can only star in one movie, this is a pretty damn good one for it. The iconic freeze-frame final shot of him leaping above traffic to wave goodbye is something one never forgets. It's like the alternate universe version of the last shot in *The 400 Blows* ... thank heavens there was no sequel'.[14]

Fig. 7: Thelonious Bernard and Diane Lane in *A Little Romance* (George Roy Hill, 1979)
Fig. 8: Olivier Martinez and Diane Lane in Unfaithful (Adrian Lyne, 2002)

Ironically, another user claims, 'this is definitely a movie that leaves you with a good feeling ... The movie is well acted with good performances by all the leads, great scenery and has a great musical score by George [sic] Delerue. Be interesting', he concludes, 'if they made a sequel to this with the kids (now adults) meeting again at 40.'[15]

Didn't 'they?', I wonder.

RESONANCE

What I mean is that I wonder whether among Lyne and his cast and crew, as with me, and perhaps other viewers of *Unfaithful* who remembered *A Little Romance*, the affair between Connie and Paul was made both more believable and more affecting by the ways it might have drawn on memory of Lane's early role. Even without the concept of transference, we all know well the way an early experience of love or loss can survive, like a spore, and inflect life experiences, hatch fantasies, unconsciously aid and abet our choices and thoughts. And if we comprehend Connie's disastrous plunge into a passionate affair in part because of the memory of the aborted little romance of the long ago girl that Lane played in 1979, is it not because this is at the same time also our own memory? Don't we unconsciously fill in characters' back stories? Memories of art, of stories told, of movies seen, are memories still.

We 'should also investigate', Janet Staiger writes, regarding spectator studies, 'not just the event of film-going but the continual making and remaking of the interpretations and emotional significances through the lives of the individuals' (2001: 29). There is a theoretical place where such an investigation might merge with a 'counter-factual' history of the sort that Christian Keathley proposes as an outcome of the cinephiliac approach to historiography in his intriguing study of cinephilia and history: 'an ongoing project of locating these alternate points of entry, nearly all of which began with some individual's experience of the movies, often in which that person watches differently, notices, something, and becomes curious about what he or she sees' (2006: 134). The boundaries between filmmakers, film viewers, buffs, cognoscenti, critics, historians, and scholars become increasingly fluid when one considers what is common in the culture, or experience of film, although this may be a threatening proposition to specialists at both theoretical and practical ends of the spectrum.

What Keathley dubs a 'cinephiliac anecdote' – a product of a loving, idiosyncratic 'counter-history' – others might call trivia. Are the connections I have drawn here meaningful, or are they trivial? Or is trivia meaningful? Does the Frenchness of the original movie to which Lyne's is unfaithful return somehow in *Unfaithful*'s French lover, as well as the Frenchness of Flaubert's canonical tale of bourgeois infidelity, the residual Frenchness of those remakes with Richard Gere, the Frenchness of Diane Lane's ex-husband and one-time co-star Christopher Lambert, and the Frenchness of the boy frozen in a bittersweet 'little romance' for over twenty years?

Might any seemingly trivial facet of a film – like this French lover – resonate, lead backward to innumerable memories, associations, and other films? Are the component parts of a movie always over-determined, like the Freudian dream image? If so, is this similar to the dream, too, in being entirely personal, subjective, private? Or is there some collective reason that movie trivia is so popular and that we want to share it? Where between the intentions of the filmmakers and the emotional resonance with a viewer does this veil of other cinematic memory and experience hang? Or is it not a veil but more like a 'film' that coats everything? Or like a delicate sinew of threads – a matrix – that connect us 'hyper-spectators' to one another and all the films ever seen? If such metaphors raise the specter of something like a 'collective unconscious', I hope it is because they speak to the more obscure aspects of the common film experience. For it is not only the canon that has 'a largely invisible cultural structure that underpins it: a tissue of quotations, linkages, assumptions and ultimately memories' (Christie 2002: 26). Feelings transfer from cinematic objects of desire and memory in ways that make even a poor cousin of a film resonant, for one, for many, but never for all. I don't want to overstate the significance of *Unfaithful*'s French lover. I'm using his Frenchness to focus on that unspeakable something – a form of cinephiliac assent, or recognition – that can occur between movie and spectator, one that seems to build on, or tie into cumulative movie experience.

I am saying that when I watch *Unfaithful*, it is not just another drop in the Hollywood bucket but is resonant with cinema, seen and unseen: not only with Chabrol's *La femme infidèle*, but also his 'Hélène cycle' and his *Madame Bovary*, with Charles Boyer's films, such as *History is Made at Night* and *Love Affair*, and other films that typify Frenchmen for American audiences (*Funny Face*, *Addicted to Love*, a *Simpsons* episode); with *Breathless* – Jean-Luc Godard's and its American remake; *The Return of Martin Guerre*, *Sommersby*, *Intersection*, *Les Choses de la vie*, *American Gigolo*, *Pickpocket*, and *The Cotton Club*, in which the two stars appeared together; and in a sense all Richard Gere's prior films, and Diane Lane's, and Adrian Lyne's; with *A Little Romance*, and through it, Truffaut's *The 400 Blows*; with Hitchcock's *Suspicion*, his *Psycho*, and in a sense his whole oeuvre, too; *Brief Encounter*, *Monsieur Hulot's Holiday*, *Aimée & Jaguar*, *Before Night Falls*; and with perhaps dozens of films I did not mention but also echo there: other films about unfaithful wives – for example, Preston Sturges' *Unfaithfully Yours* (1948), Liv Ullmann's *Trolösa/Faithless* (2000), Alan Rudolf's *The Secret Lives of Dentists* (2002), the many thrillers and domestic psychological dramas one might recollect by virtue of genre, not to mention the previous films of the secondary cast and the creative crew (writer, cinematographer, composer).

And when you watch *Unfaithful*, is it resonant, too, with traces of these or other films? These are like notes in a chord or threads that come to be woven together in the experience of the film. This composition, this tapestry, cannot sound, or look exactly alike for any two viewers but it might be vaguely similar, consonant. Maybe sometimes it is sufficiently off as to be awkward, dissonant, and embarrassing. A remake like *Unfaithful* (which is a little unfaithful to and at some remove from its not particularly iconic 'original') might induce a very different response than (seemingly) straighter remakes of more iconic movies (for an interesting discussion of Hitchcock remakes see Žižek 2003).

Probably some lovers of Chabrol loathe *Unfaithful* as I do those remakes of classics like *Sabrina* (Billy Wilder, 1954), or *Rear Window* (Alfred Hitchcock, 1954). I like *Unfaithful* more, perhaps, than such an adulterous exercise ought to be liked. I like its slippery movement from love of film to film love, and for its infidelity. It loves Chabrol's example, but not unequivocally. It observes a lack, a deficit all too familiar in films of the French New Wave, in the conception of the woman. It substitutes for the beautiful, impassive cipher – whose beauty is all the reason needed for her duplicity – an actual character: a woman whose desire, agency, and conflict become at least as central to the story as the burgeoning suspicions and unexpected violence of her husband. It seems that I am convinced by this character, and moved, in no small part because she is played by Diane Lane, because her husband is played by Richard Gere, and because her lover is French. But my *Unfaithful*, which depends on these contingencies – which satisfies my cinephilia, my feminism, and my memory – must be somewhat different than yours, or than Lyne's own. As an act of love, like Chabrol's love of Hitchcock, Lyne's love of *La femme infidèle* has its perverse and murderous side. But movie hate and movie love, like their real-life counterparts, are entwined with the vicissitudes of memory.

NOTES

1   I am deeply grateful to the audiences who submitted themselves to versions of this paper and were generous with questions and feedback, including those at the 2006 meeting of the Society for Cinema and Media Studies to the session, 'Memory and its Vicissitudes', Vancouver, March 3, 2006; the Forschungscolloquium der Abteilungen Literatur und Kultur, John F. Kennedy Institute, Freie Universität, Berlin, April 28, 2006; American Studies Brown Bag colloquium, Southern Illinois University Carbondale, February 8, 2007; and last, but not least, the brave and wondrous students in my course on Film Theory, Spring 2007, Southern Illinois University Carbondale. I am also indebted to Todd Varney, for permission to quote his offhand remark about aging and Gere; and Kevin Dettmar and Con Verevis for their generous feedback on written drafts.

2   I refer to the 11/07/00 draft of *Unfaithful* reviewed in David Goldsmith (2002) '*Unfaithful*', *Creative Screenwriting*, 9, 3, 25.

3   *Unfaithful*. Internet Movie Database. 2006. www.imdb.com/title/tt0250797/trivia

4   Twentieth Century-Fox DVD edition of *Unfaithful*, 2002.

5   As noted by Philip French, in *The Observer*, June 9, 2002: http://film.guardian.co.uk/News_Story/Critic_Review/Observer_review/0,4267,729918,00.html

6   Ethnically, Gere is evidently not French. His Anglo-Saxon ancestry goes back on both sides to the Mayflower, and connects with those of American presidents and British aristocracy. See: Gary Boyd Roberts 'Royal Descents, Notable Kin, and Printed Sources #74 'The New England Ancestry of Actor Richard [Tiffany] Gere', 2007, http://www.notablekin.org/gbr/gere.htm.

7   Charlie Rose interview, included with special features on *Unfaithful* (DVD, 2002).

8   Lane and Lambert were married from 1988 to 1994 and had a daughter together.

9   *Unfaithful* DVD (2002) special features.

10   I am indebted to Laura Bieger for directing me to this adage and to Simon's work.

11   Boyer was 'a suburban housewife's stereotype of a suave Continental lover', as IMDb user, David Melville aptly puts it (re: Fritz Lang's *Liliom*, 6 October 2004, http://www.imdb.com/title/tt0025397/usercomments).

12   I am indebted to Birgit Michaelis for this insight.

13   Lane's commentary on the Warner Bros. 2003 DVD edition of *A Little Romance*.

14   *Unfaithful*. Internet Movie Database. 2006. http://www.imdb.com/title/tt0079477/usercomments (yawn-2, 6/5/05).

15   *Unfaithful*. Internet Movie Database. 2006. http://www.imdb.com/title/tt0079477/usercomments (JohnIL, 5/16/04).

REFERENCES

Austin, Guy (1999) *Claude Chabrol*. Manchester: Manchester University Press.

Biguenet, John. (1998). 'Double Takes: The Role of Allusion in Cinema.' *Play It Again, Sam: Retakes on Remakes*. Andrew Horton and Stuart Y. McDougal, eds. Berkeley: University of California Press, 131–43.

Bloom, Harold. (1973). *The Anxiety of Influence: A Theory of Poetry*. Oxford: Oxford University Press.

Christie, Ian (2002) 'The Rules of the Game', *Sight and Sound*, 12, 9, 24–7.

Cohen, Alain J.-J. (2001) 'Virtual Hollywood and the Genealogy of its Hyper-Spectator', in Melvyn Stokes and Richard Maltby (eds) *Hollywood Spectatorship: Changing Perceptions of Cinema Audiences*. London: British Film Institute, 152–63.

Durham, Carolyn A. (1998). *Double Takes: Culture and Gender in French Films and their American Remakes*. Hanover, NH : Dartmouth College/University Press of New England.

Felleman, Susan (2006) *Art in the Cinematic Imagination*. Austin: University of Texas Press.

Hand, Seán (1990) 'Missing You: Intertextuality, Transference and the Language of Love', in Michael Worton and Judith Still (eds) *Intertextuality: Theories and Practices*. Manchester: Manchester University Press, 79–91.

Keathley, Christian (2006) *Cinephilia and History, or The Wind in the Trees*. Bloomington: Indiana University Press.

Ladenson, Elisabeth (1998) 'Gay Paree; or Thank Heaven for Little Girls', *Modern Language Studies*, 28, 3/4, 187–92.

Mazdon, Lucy. (2000). *Encore Hollywood: Remaking French Cinema*. London: British Film Institute.

Poe, Tom G. (2001) 'Historical Spectatorship Around and About Stanley Kramer's *On the Beach*', in Melvyn Stokes and Richard Maltby (eds) *Hollywood Spectatorship: Changing Perceptions of Cinema Audiences*. London: British Film Institute, 91–104.

Simon, Sherry (1996) *Gender in Translation: Cultural Identity and the Politics of Transmission*. London and New York: Routledge.

Staiger, Janet (2001) 'Writing the History of American Film Reception', in Melvyn Stokes and Richard Maltby (eds) *Hollywood Spectatorship: Changing Perceptions of Cinema Audiences*. London: British Film Institute, 19–32.

Stern, Lesley (1995) *The Scorsese Connection*. London: British Film Institute.

Verevis, Constantine (2004) 'Remaking Film', *Film Studies*, 4, XXX no.?, XXX article full page range?

_____ (2006) *Film Remakes*. Edinburgh: Edinburgh University Press.

Williams, Phillip (2006) 'The Language of Sex and Suspicion: Writer-Director Adrian Lyne returns to the big screen with *Unfaithful*', *MovieMaker* 46: http://www.moviemaker.com/issues/46/lyne.html.

Wills, David. (1998). 'The French Remark: *Breathless* and Cinematic Citationality.' *Play It Again, Sam: Retakes on Remakes*. Andrew Horton and Stuart Y. McDougal, eds. Berkeley: University of California, 147–61.

Žižek, Slavoj (2003) 'Is There a Proper Way to Remake a Hitchcock Film?' in Richard Allen and Sam Ishii-Gonzáles (eds) *Hitchcock: Past and Future*. London: Routledge, 257–74.

TRANSMEDIA CINEPHILIAS

CHAPTER EIGHT

REVISIONING CRITICAL SPACE IN THE DIGITAL AGE: CINEPHILIA, BLOGGING, AND CRITICISM
Ted Pigeon

CINEPHILIA AND CRITICISM

Theorists have ascribed various meanings to cinephilia by contextualizing it as a practice, a movement, or a way of life. In a 2008 blog entry, David Bordwell noted: 'The cinephile loves the idea of film. That means loving not only its accomplishments but its potential, its promise and prospects. It's as if individual films, delectable and overpowering as they can be, are but glimpses of something far grander. That distant horizon, impossible to describe fully, is Cinema, and it is this art form, or medium, that is the ultimate object of devotion.' Bordwell's explanation is concise and useful, but the ideological perspective toward cinema (and by extension to cinephilia) that it re-enforces limits its significance in a theoretical context. It reflects a tendency among theorists to define cinephilia as a tangible practice, lifestyle, or outlook of intangible proportions. This 'intangible tangibility' has become a central problem of situating cinephilia within film theory.

Over many years film criticism of both the journalistic and academic variety has held true to the notion that cinema can be quantified or measured on its own terms; that it is some*thing* – an artifact, product, piece of art, and so forth. A great deal of film theory is organized around the idea that a film is an object to the viewer's subject, whether that's Metzian semiology or Lacanian psychoanalysis. Even earlier European formalistic traditions assume a relationship between viewer and image largely out of necessity, since media, technology, even art were conceived as things separate from those who constructed and utilized them. Film theory was merely falling in line with an array of assumptions about lived experience by pre-supposing a scenario in which a viewer/theorist inhabits a defined space in relation to the object of inquiry, i.e. the image or the film. According to this binary model, cinematic production and consumption results from the relationships of various social, economic, and technological processes through which viewers and producers can create meaning through interpretation.

The viewer/image model has fueled both the rapid economic growth of cinema as a commercial phenomenon and the discursive explosion of theory that has brought on a number of traditions in film theory. Various theoretical spheres address cinema in a range of contexts and connotations, with cinema holding a different significance. For example, cinema has been rendered as cultural artifact, commercial product, political statement, technological assemblage, patriarchal dreamscape, art form, and so forth. These perspectives of cinema, however, are entrenched in ideological assumptions regarding cinema's external state and how it 'works'.

This conception of cinema represents an overly broad summation of Film Studies, which is far more nuanced and interesting than I have articulated here. However, my goal in emphasizing the notions of film subjects, objects, and interpretation illustrates a great flaw of film theory in regards to its often neglect of the complex negotiations of representation, visuality, and negotiation that comprise the sensory and cultural experience of cinema.

The influence of the viewer/image model is particularly evidenced by film theory's conception of cinephilia, wherein the cinephile seems to represent the ideal spectator – desiring and consuming the pleasures resulting from the experience of watching films. However, in the scope of film theory, the cinephile has long been understood as more of a passive viewer rather than a participant in the process of cinema. The extent of the cinephile's participation in cinema is limited to a love and consumption of cinematic images, whereas the theorist/critic's relationship to cinema is one defined by reflection, knowledge, and insight. While the cinephile adorns him/herself to the image, his/her access to knowledge and information regarding cinema is limited to what is produced by critics and scholars.

The dominant models for understanding and forming an inquiry into cinema leave little space for cinephilia to extend beyond an addiction to, and passive participation in, cinema. However, the notion of the cinephile has become increasingly problematic within the structures of film theory, as theorists have struggled to mold a concrete understanding of cinephilia. Instead of inquiring into the processes of cinephilia, theorists can only describe its symptoms, its qualities, and practice according to the inquiries set forth by various schools of thought regarding cinema itself.

Film theory's problem with cinephilia is consistent with and illustrative of the viewer/image model that guides many of its inquiries. Where cinema may be theorized as an object, artifact, or institution through which representations and meanings are constructed, distributed, and interpreted, cinephilia can perhaps best be conceived of as the process existing somewhere in between what is known as the 'viewer' and 'image'. The cinephile has no distance from the image, but is instead enveloped by the image. Cinephilia can thus be understood as a manifestation of the intangible accessibility of cinema, bringing forth a vision of cinema and participation in cinema that shatters the viewer/image binary.

DISCOURSE AND THE DIGITAL

In a discussion of the discourse about cinema, digital culture plays a great role in how cinephilia can be re-conceptualized with respect to film criticism. Digital culture appears to grant the cinephile a level of participation in cinema previously only available to those in the professional ranks of criticism. Access to knowledge and information are no longer based upon a line between, among other things, professionalism and non-professionalism. In the digital age, cinephilia does not simply entail an obsession over watching movies but also requires engaging cinema in discourse. It requires individuals to gain insight into a multitude of factors contributing to the enactment of cinema as not just a visual narrative device, but as a cultural practice and a process of being.

The current relevance of cinephilia is representative of a new movement in film writing and reflection. Online, writers – professional and otherwise – provide updates to web sites and blogs, offering personal anecdotes and critical ruminations on a given film or on cinema itself as an idea. There is no unity in voice, except to say that there is a multiplicity of disparate voices collectively functioning to find the gaps in film theory. The proliferation of strong writing on cinema in digital space has stuttered the language of these common critical mainstays, blurring the line between them, perhaps offering a glimpse into a Deleuzian time-image not of cinema, but of criticism. This 'digital criticism' emerges out of the multifarious lines of thought and critique through which cinephilia manifests. It enables a more reflexive inquiry beyond institutional conventions and discursive norms of professional criticism, perhaps revealing new pathways for engaging cinema in a reflexive discourse that may be enacted by professional and non-professional writers alike. This moment is positively digital – wherein the relationship between criticism and cinematic images is changing as much as the space between spectator and image. In accordance to a wide variety of cultural changes in lived experience and aesthetic potential, cinephiles are re-exploring and redefining consumption, production, and interpretation.

FOUR POSTS FROM *THE CINEMATIC ART* (http://tedpigeon.blogspot.com/)

Following are four full posts I have written for my blog *The Cinematic Art* over a one-year period. Representing my contribution to the digital front of film discourse, these essays converge various personal and critical pursuits, interests, and observations – hopefully demonstrating the versatility of digital media in a discussion of criticism and cinema. More importantly, these writings address many aspects of the argument I have introduced here. Although these pieces each concern different topics, taken together they form a narrative that addresses these issues not by situating cinephilia in relation to a particular definition or understanding of cinema, but by focusing on discourse about cinema, criticism, and cinephilia in the digital age.

Knowledge, Perspective, and the New Life of Criticism (*8 August 2007*)

I have seen only one film directed by Ingmar Bergman and have not seen any films directed by Michelangelo Antonioni. But I have learned more about them over the past week than I would have ever expected for having seen so little of their work. Why? Because of online film writing, or 'blogging' if you prefer the term. It's tragic that cinema lost two of its most prominent artists in such close proximity, but since their respective deaths there has been an explosion of online writing about them, their work, and their position in cinema history the likes of which few newspaper or magazine articles can replicate. Here in the online world of film writing, there is real discussion happening right now, and it's invigorating to be a part of in some small way. I should note that this writing is not exclusive to bloggers; after all, Jonathan Rosenbaum's editorial in the *Times* caused a ripple in film criticism. Given my ignorance regarding these two late auteurs, I can't comment on the validity of Rosenbaum's views. I can, however, observe the great amount of critical discussion that has followed, some responding to print-based writing, others not. And it is completely refreshing.

Jim Emerson has written a number of posts about Bergman and Antonioni, highlighting discussions at other blogs while contributing his own voice to the dialogue. His most recent piece, which asks the simple but difficult question, 'Who Matters?' in light of Andrew Sarris' retrospective article on Bergman and Antonioni, is the last in a string of many provocative pieces touching on subjects of auteurism and contrarian criticism in which he surveys online and print writing in what seems to be a larger inquiry into retrospective observations of cinema. Jim's posts – as well as others' such as Girish Shambu's terrific entry on Bergman (and the subsequent discussion), Zach Campbell's dissection of the Rosenbaum piece, Chris Stangl's thoughtful reflection on Antonioni, and Michael Atkinson's theory-based approach to the cultural impact of Bergman and Antonioni – have inspired me to reflect on a number of important issues that critics, movie lovers, bloggers, and scholars now face, especially as the critical discussion grows larger and more varied with blogging. One thing I have learned over the past week or so about blogging is that it has the potential to inject life into the greater discussion of film with varying perspectives. Bloggers such as those mentioned above are significant contributors to the changing face of film criticism, one that is challenging dominant theories and assumptions by asking questions of them. In doing so, it seems that online film writers are collectively yielding new critical approaches to a medium whose continual shifts and changes require these new approaches. Blogging will not displace print-based criticism, just as journalistic criticism does not displace scholarly criticism. All of these various approaches to criticism have a distinctly different viewpoint from which their members partake in criticism.

No artistic medium can really exist and grow without a strong criticism of it. Both criticism and cinema challenge, extend, and grow one another. Cinema needs its critics just as much as critics need the cinema. The current discourse on the film blogging front over the past week is a reminder of that. It also calls attention to the fact that the critical body is expanding for the better with the rise in prominence of film blogs. As for where I stand in this discussion, I am more like a sponge than an active participant; I'm trying to soak up as much information I can about these directors before I jump into their work and the films of other directors whose films with which I must familiarize myself if I am to take part in that dialogue.

The great strength of this writing form is that its interactional nature of critical discourse enables me to constantly stretch my own knowledge and participation in cinema. My exposure to this ever-growing discussion and the variety of uniquely informed individuals contributing to it allow me to challenge and question my own knowledge of the medium and the level at which I engage it in criticism. Now that I have familiarized myself with the criticism, it's time to dive into the movies themselves. Some might look at the fact that I've only seen one total film of either Bergman's or Antonioni's. Most of my life as a film lover and critic has been spent on Hollywood and Indiewood films of today and the golden age films of yesteryear. I have seen a number of international films – old and new – and now with the knowledge I have, I can swim through the cinematic treasures I have not yet been able to reach.

Scholars or bloggers, we are all of us students of cinema and the only way our own perspectives can expand is by exposing ourselves to the criticism of those whose own approaches are informed by different experiences with cinema who have engaged it in criticism.

The Hard-knock Lives of Film Critics (*9 November 2007*)

Although I do not need to point anybody in the direction of Jim Emerson's indispensable blog, I would like to take note of something that is unfolding there *right now*: critical debate.

With the release of *No Country For Old Men* (2007) today, the (mostly positive) reviews have been piling up over the last week, bringing into full focus the scattered critical glimpses of the film from when it screened at Cannes over the summer and more recently at the Toronto Film Festival. I remember Jim's enthusiasm for the Coen brothers' new film back then, so I wasn't surprised to see him visit the topic again on the day of its release. But his piece is much more interesting than your typical print review. Instead of sharing his opinion and interpretation of the film within the identifiable, safe conventions of structured journalistic film criticism, Jim instead takes issue with Jonathan Rosenbaum's more negative perspective. He does so rather defensively but with complete conviction and insight. Sure, it's impulsive and somewhat aggressive, but it's *real*, as is the debate to follow.

After reading the debate, it's clear that Emerson and Rosenbaum are each operating under different ideas and thus occupying vastly different ideological stances, not only with regards to the practice of film criticism, but in how they understand the ideas brought on by the film and how they approach seeing and responding to cinema in general. Their debate is fascinating on the grounds of pure content, with Jim's more form-based approach seemingly at odds with Rosenbaum's content-based views on examining cinema. This is of course overly simplistic; I would need to see the film about which they are debating to really probe their difference in perspective. But to me, that seems almost beside the point.

What's really important here is that how they're choosing to engage each other reflects more about the ideologies as writers and critics than what they are actually saying. These are two writers I respect immensely, and I am fortunate be to treated to a dialogue such as this, let alone be able to participate in it. And seeing them butt heads as openly as they are and in this forum is a blast. It brings to mind the harsh realities of film criticism, i.e. the very subjectivity of it all, while also highlighting the importance of this kind of writing in general; so raw and upfront and in the moment, where real ideas are discovered and eventually culti-vated through the processes of rumination and editing. But here, comments have urgency and conviction that is often filtered out of most professionally edited and handled writing. That the dialogue is between two well-seasoned professionals whose work we mostly know after those thoughts, feelings, and ideas have gone through those industrial processes is what gives it that unique flair.

Posts like this and the kind of fiery dialogue they spur reveal many of the strengths and weaknesses of film criticism, and are where real critical discourse *lives*. It is stripped down of the image of the critic sitting on a perch, walled away from real dialogue and debate, where s/he can comfortably judge and assert his/her own views. Here we see that debate in motion and can in turn under-stand the kind of life a critic leads, and the kind of discourse s/he attempts to responsibly participate in. This discourse can be both illuminating and frustrat-ing. Sometimes there is understanding, and new perspectives can be achieved. Other times, debate can be like two people speaking in different languages. This particular case seems to be a bit of both, recalling the pleasures and annoyances of trying to perceive a piece of art, interpret it according to universal meaning structures as well as personal ones, and then share with others with the hope of providing insight. This can be successful in some instances, but often it is not.

It's the life of a critic, and it's all right there in this post/discussion. It's great stuff, and yet another reason why this form of writing lends itself so well to critical commentary.

I have not seen the film yet, mind you, but after reading each comment following the post, I am motivated more to do so.

Looking Back on 2007: Analogic Reflections on the Digital (*10 January 2008*)

I have recently argued that year-end list-making and reminiscing can be worthwhile, even useful, so long that it's employed with a bit of freshness – an argument that is as vague as it is vulnerable. But I remain hopeful that good criticism can come about from these annual traditions of film reviewing. At a time when avid readers of film criticism are drowned in the numbing sameness of the unceasing 'Year in film' articles, the most productive annual retrospectives on a year in cinema are (a) defined by a more inquisitive, humble standpoint; (b) free of conventional critical jargon; and (c) wholly uninterested in naming 'the best' of anything.

The intelligent critic understands that right now is the only time of year when s/he can step out of the mode of immediacy that defines most mainstream film reviewing, and offer keen insights about the state of the art. Therefore, I would argue that useful annual cinematic reflections offer critical observations that examine a number of trends and practices in film viewing, production, distribution, and criticism. Emerging from these notes and observations is the critic's equally informed and personal insights on the films s/he has deemed important and interesting, not necessarily 'The Best'. In short, good year-end articles locate relevant ideas and themes in the cultural dialogue about cinema, critical canon, and the movies themselves.

There are a lot of good critics who are doing this, but one critic in particular has struck me as essential in light of these considerations. The always-relevant Dave Kehr recently posted his thoughts on the year that was. And while he readily admits that he hasn't seen a great number of the sea of films that were released this year, he nonetheless identifies 20 films that stood out to him, and offers sound reasoning for his choices, if not individually but collectively. Looking over his selections, they together represent (for him) the pulse of cinema, and may also offer some foresight regarding the future of cinema and cinema technologies. He writes:

> 2007 was a year in which the greatest uncovered story on the movie beat – the transition from analog to digital filmmaking – continued to be uncovered and continued to shape the kind and quality of films being produced.
>
> I think the digital revolution is most obvious in the sudden resurgence of ani-

mated films, the genre best positioned to take advantage of the new technology. For Robert Zemeckis, the digital environment of 'Beowulf' provided a way to create some of the most breathtaking and expressive camera movements since the passing of Otto Preminger; for Brad Bird, 'Ratatouille' was the occasion for some marvelously precise, classical decoupage, quite different from the frenzied cutting that has characterized so many of the new live-action digital films.

The now common use of the digital internegative to manipulate color, lighting and composition reached new creative heights in David Fincher's 'Zodiac', a film so thoroughly manipulated that it seems more at home in the animated category, a characteristic it shares with Wes Anderson's 'The Darjeeling Limited' and Tim Burton's 'Sweeney Todd'.

But the old-fashioned, Bazinian realist aesthetic also saw some triumphs this year, not just in the hardcore form of Straub and Huillet's 'These Encounters of Theirs' but also in the inconspicuously classical mise-en-scene of Quentin Tarantino's 'Death Proof' and Tony Gilroy's 'Michael Clayton'.

Not all the movies he mentioned made it into his Top 20 list, which is fine. But he made a point to highlight not just a particular movement that is now picking up steam, but also the films standing as counterexamples. He does this so simply, yet it's almost profound when you consider how many arguments are driven by some core thematic ideas, which the critic identifies in a few films around which s/he can then construct an argument. But Kehr observes that for every film ushering in 'the digital', or the postmodern, or absence of linearity, many other films (from various levels of cultural and critical relevance) embody the more analogic aspects of cinema, prizing a painterly approach to composition, longer shots.

But the analog/digital dialogue extends far beyond the physical and technological properties of a given film. Questions of how a film was shot – on film or digital video – are absolutely crucial to this discussion, as are questions of a film's narrative content and presentation of information. But equally essential is a larger sense of the cultural affective state of critics and moviegoers, and the sort of dialogue we as viewers are engaged in with the medium itself. You see these kinds of debates happening in academia, with post-structuralists and neo-formalists battling each other, as well as other social sciences and disciplines for an edge in the greater debate about cultural agency. And I think it's interesting to point out that the analog/digital discussion often times comes down to the ways in which it's discussed and the ideological and theoretical foundations of the participants in that discussion.

This is relevant now because we're currently seeing cinema change in various respects. Of course, some will say that it's not the artifact that's changing, but the viewers of that artifact. Nevertheless, cinema has evolved and progressed as its own medium for more than a hundred years, and has always reflected the underlying ideological tensions of a culture's relationship to technology and narrative. And right now, digital media play an increasingly large role in our lives, with regards to our own memories/experiences with that and those which are outside of us (e.g. digital photography, social networking, etc.), and also in terms of how we perceive and interpret information, as well as harness it to form a knowledge and construct a reality to which we must respond and on which we must always act. It's clear that with the prevalence of digital technology, any notion of the self and of a linear identity (be it individual or cultural) is becoming harder to maintain.

Yet although digital media, narratives, meaning-making practices, and information are certainly more constitutive of our social existence now than ever before, the digital does not displace the analog. In fact, the analog will continue to thrive, but always in juxtaposition with digital information, meanings, and narratives. Analog and digital have come together in challenging ways, and this convergence manifests in media, particularly in cinema, a 'medium of many media', in both its form and content. (The same relationship is probably true for form and content, in that they simply do not exist outside one another and are continually defined by each other.) Therefore, when we apply this notion to the interpretation of cinema, particularly in the amazing varieties, shapes, and sizes of cinema that now exist, we see this very convergence culminate through various media, technologies, and narrative styles.

Films like *Zodiac* (2007), one of last year's astounding achievements, explicitly wrestle with these notions. David Fincher's film does this on a number of reflexive levels, from a deconstruction of a popular cinematic sub-genre (the serial killer, police procedural), to an examination of spatial and temporal orientation; specifically exploring the notion that the way in which we communicate to a large extent determines how and what we communicate. On many levels, *Zodiac* deals with these issues – so much so, that it's impossible to unpack and arrange these concepts in a linear, or analogic fashion; which is precisely its project as a digital piece of information. It's a constant negotiation and tension, and one that cinema is directly confronting, not just with films like *Zodiac*, but also in animated movies, such as *Ratatouille* (2007), which is so proudly analogic, yet also wholly digital at the same time. It ultimately becomes something that is neither analogic nor digital, but something new entirely. One could also look at linearly structured narratives in films such as *Eastern Promises* (2007), and upon further examination uncover a deeply reflexive mediation on narrative, perception, and violence. Some documentary filmmaking also exhibits a strong sense of the digital, as is evident in *Manufactured Landscapes* (2006), a film that actively reflects on visual language, globalization, and matters of authorship in a media economy. Mainstream fare such as 2006's *Miami Vice* are also redefining a new digital space in many ways, specifically in how they invert and upend pre-existing, analogic norms of genre and cinematic vision and representation to serve a whole new kind of visual experience.

Films of all kinds are directly questioning knowledge and information, regarding cinema technologies, mediated information, the notion of a singular consciousness, and universalizing systems of knowledge and language. And it's happening right now, which is why right now is an exciting time for cinematic media, particularly criticism. Some may say that 2007 represents a great leap forward toward the digital. This may be true, but if the digital has taught us anything, it's that we are not moving *forward* to anywhere. We're not moving past or beyond the analog, but engaging it in new ways and new dialogues, creating new systems of interpretation and understanding as we move along. All of cinema is a kind of reflection on the analogic and now-emerging digital properties of aesthetic and narrative information. And as the digital becomes more prominent, so too will be possibility of cinema and aesthetics in general.

And that's why the very analogic process of looking back on a year in film is inevitable and a statement to these perpetual tensions from which great art and criticism will continue to be redefined. As a critical practice, reminiscing on a year in cinema reminds of our cultural entrenchment in analogic means of communicating. We can look back and identify a number of trends that may clue us into where we're going, but this process in itself is a linear mode of thought that cannot encompass the extent to which this new dialogue is changing how we see cinema. The sheer variety of filmmaking, both good and bad, makes the future of cinema anyone's guess. Cynics will look at this year's crop of movies and come up with reasons aplenty for why cinema is dying, while others see the diversity of perspectives and a deepening and more abstraction embrace of aesthetic meanings and styles to signify a future in which cinema in its very being will come to represent the all-inclusive art form for the decentralized collective. It all comes down to how you see the movies and how you see the world. I guess I'm a member of the latter camp, because part of why I love cinema is precisely because it eludes essentialism and universalized meaning structures. I strongly believe that great cinema is not a measurement or pre-determined meaning, but an intangible state of mind and aesthetic potential. In other words, every great movie, in some way, reminds the viewer (or critic) that cinema's potential as an art form, a technological medium, and a cultural artifact is without limit.

A Scholar Amongst Bloggers: SCMS Part II. (*7 April 2008*)

As I said in the first account of my experiences at the Society for Cinema and Media Studies annual conference, my day at the meeting was so overwhelming that it was almost too much to process all at once. I wish I had been there for a couple of days, if only to digest all the lectures, workshops and encounters. At the end of that day (4:00 PM), I was to present first in a workshop called *The Presence of Pleasure: The Work of Cinephilia in the Age of Digital Reproduction*. I was asked on to the panel by co-chairs Scott Balcerzak and Jason Sperb, who were seeking the input of a 'prominent, academic blogger', even though I may boldly disagree that I am academic or prominent. Nevertheless, I was more than honored to receive the invitation, if a bit nervous. Panel members included myself, Jason and Scott, as well as Catherine Russell and Robert Burgoyne, both respected figures in film scholarship.

As both a student and as a blogger, I felt out of my league. But my presence alone at this workshop may be a reflection of some of the issues I've decided to talk about. Unlike most other presentations on the workshop, each of whom took on the notion of cinephilia in a uniquely focused manner, I elected to speak more broadly about the institutional frameworks that influence the variety of outlets for film criticism. Connecting this discussion with a distinct proposal for a kind of dig-ital criticism, i.e. blogging, I tried to examine film criticism both as a practice and as a concept, specifically addressing the question of what defines film criticism at all. What interested me most in this discussion was the odd prominence of binary structures in influencing forms of content and expression of film criticism. I examined the rhetorical and critical styles of both academic and journalistic criti-cism, as well as their respective interfaces and formats.

Given that this was a workshop, presentations were expected to be shorter and so I spoke for about 15 minutes roughly on these topics. While I tried to cover as much as possible in outlining the odd place within which blogging is situated as a medium for communication and a possible model for film criticism, ultimately, I could only introduce a lot of these concepts. My development of them will probably take place over time, perhaps in my thesis preparation and proposal next semester. But for the moment, at least, I had to keep it broad and simple, which was extremely difficult to do because I was appealing to a particu-lar audience with my presentation. I didn't adopt a distinctly academic or journal-istic rhetorical style, and many of my observations I was able to make because of my unique involvement in many facets of film journalism and criticism, as both a reader and performer. I was more interested in the inter-relations among the variety of film criticism modalities, which is not a discussion in which many film enthusiasts seem interested. Depending on our training and expertise, many of us can address conflicts and issues within a particular body of criticism, which is useful and important, but to understand the larger social policies of film criticism, one must extend that discussion to external factors.

As it turns out, varying levels of professional criticism are not just at war with themselves – i.e. journalistic criticism becoming ever-cutthroat, and academic criticism sectioned off into so many theoretical viewpoints – but also with each other. Academic critics rip into journalistic critics routinely, critiquing their critical values and structures. The same is true vice versa. So what we have are a number of 'pockets' of film criticism, each with its own language and rhetoric, engaging views that are designed to fit that scheme (positively or negatively). These are concepts I mentioned in a blog post last October, in which I made many sweeping, mostly unfounded claims, but may have found the beginnings of a larger, more significant argument:

> [T]he end result is a spectrum of sectioned off critics, scholars, and writers, all subscribing to different norms and practices within that larger spectrum, engaged in masturbatory dialogue wherein those who subscribe to the same theories, views, and opinions love the sound of their own voice, and those who disagree simply do not associate. And never once is the makeup of that larger spectrum that keeps them so divided ever challenged.

These systems have been in interaction for quite some time, as each has evolved over many decades and developed their own styles and sub-styles of critical commentary and theorizing. So how does blogging situate in this discussion? Rather intriguingly, it seems. The following paragraphs strike more to the core of my argument, or at least my articulation of the problem:

> These pockets of film writing culture rarely breach other, but they have nearly unanimously made certain to frame the debate over web discourse and critical validity as if it must 'earn' some respect via the same means that enables published writers to lay come claim to validity or qualification. The blogging debate is continually engaged on the level of asking the question as to digital democracy, which is indicative of publishing trends that too many writers and readers have bought into. Proponents of digital media and blogging are forced to enter the dialogue by defending this supposed wasteland that is the internet. In doing so, they are immediately handicapping themselves to the dominant underlying assumptions as set forth by published writing. The only way of seemingly entering this dialogue is to accept the pre-established position of skepticism regarding digital media and web interaction. That's not to say that blogging is a 'whole new realm', since this too is a rhetorical device emerging as the fierce alternative to the 'internet is inherently bad' mindset that permeates the debate. Those who blindly sing the praises of the internet, hailing it as a bold new medium of communication, are essentially playing right into a dominant ideology to which they are positioning themselves in direct contrast, thus sustaining a binary level of discourse that is required to preserve that ideology.

I expanded on this notion, in particular, observing that blogging can be a form of criticism subject to many of the same problems and conflicts of the existing models of criticism, plus a whole other series of questions with regards to its status as a discursive medium. Speaking more to the connection of blogging and professional criticism, I noted that the model of journalistic/academic has undeniably set the course of criticism, and that won't change. Digital criticism doesn't displace other forms of criticism. It should, however, change how they function and facilitate growth via reflexivity and re-calibrate our modes of vision and analysis for the ever-changing medium of cinema.

For instance, it is possible that the blog embodies a more immediate, flawed, and urgent criticism, one that is arguably more in-demand given the sheer amount of cinema that is now available to critics and consumers. Of course, we need to take care not to resort to the romanticized approach that online writing is the brand new frontier where true critical democracy lives. This is dangerous rhetoric, because, after all, the majority of blogs offer little insight beyond that of mainstream journalistic criticism. Furthermore, as Matt Zoller Seitz recently pointed out in a discussion over at the House Next Door about the fragile state of journalistic criticism, most blogs with high readership and prominence are commercialized and homogenized in their content and format. On my best day here on this blog, I may get 300 hits, most of which come from image searches.

But let's return to this notion of the immediate, flawed, and urgent criticism, because there seems to be something developing on the non-commercial blogging front that's particularly interesting. For bloggers with or without professional experience, the blog in many ways represents the sort of bare-bones criticism that is sorely needed. It's criticism without the gloss and glean of the finished product. It's more about the process of engaging ideas and challenging concepts, wherein all of the flaws of arguments in process are on display. One could argue that if we don't engage perspectives at this stage, we would become too attached with the conventional theories and styles of criticism that have become so internalized amongst professional critics of all types; which may partly account for the degree of fierce division I mentioned earlier. With the blog, we are seeing an erasure of the line of professionalism between so-called 'critics' and 'cinephiles'. With digital criticism, the meaning of those terms is not all that far off, and depending on your position as a critic and/or cinephile, your comfort with this notion may vary.

These were a few of my talking points during my presentation. In retrospect, I wish I had provided a more focused argument about the state of film criticism, because it felt like I was rushing through a lot of it. But when you're dealing with a subject matter such as this, there's no easy way to streamline it. Regarding the discussion afterwards, I should first note that it was a pleasure meeting some fellow film writers: Jason and Scott, obviously, but I also met Zach Campbell and Chuck Tyron, with whom I talked further about blogging and criticism. I was also struck with the amount of attendees who were almost completely oblivious to the goings on of the film blogging community, let alone journalistic criticism. The disparity of reactions – from those who have not read a blog to those who do so adamantly – is fascinating, as some of perspectives from those who have 'dabbled' on blogs seemed to embody that academic elitism of which I am so critical. The responses from those who do not associate with journalistic criticism, or the internet for that matter, were equally interesting as firsthand evidence of a popular critique of blogs as a self-enclosed community lacking relevance to the overall discussion of film criticism. Although I did discuss the question of relevance earlier in my talk, I wish I was able to articulate my concerns about it; because it's a question not only facing bloggers, but film writers of all kinds.

Despite my own shortcomings and feeling like we only scratched the surface, I was pleased with the presentation and discussions. As I said, the goal was to illuminate central questions and concerns facing critics and cinephiles of all professional backgrounds as we move into the digital age of cinema and criticism. I've tried to explain why it's become essential that we evaluate different modes of criticism and cinema, as well as the implications for the ever-changing relationship of cinema and criticism. Catherine Russell's comment regarding demographics with respect to online writers is one we will always have to deal with; however, based on my surveying the more serious circles of film critic blogs are not as male-, white-dominated as one would think. These concerns are absolutely essential to any discussion of the blog's validity as criticism, but they should also be directed toward the established modes of criticism.

I find it hard to try to tie together the many threads I've introduced here in trying to explore the interconnections of digital culture, cinema, and criticism. Perhaps the best way I can do this is to reference philosopher Gilles Deleuze, whose cinema and non-cinema writing is swiftly gaining relevance in film and media studies. One of the central concepts of Deleuze's writing that informed his logic of cinema is the notion that we should become foreigners to our own language, and to become multilingual with a single language. Deleuze routinely spoke of making language 'stutter', of forming new relations within systems of signification. This idea applies to cinema, but also to discourse and criticism. We shouldn't be looking outside the binary of academic/journalistic model of criticism, but *within it*. We need to find the 'lines in between', as Deleuze might say. For that is the essence of digital cinema, criticism, and culture.

Moving ahead and advancing these Deleuzian notions of digital criticism will not be easy, since that would require a fair amount of reflexivity about what we do as film spectators and theorists. But if we expect to enact a digital criticism that transcends discursive formats and technological capacities of media, reflexivity is necessary.

I have always thought of criticism as a discovery of ideas, not a vehicle for conveying them. Good criticism, like good art, is always in the process of constructing itself. Like the cinematic image, criticism should be in the perpetual state of becoming. Sometimes all that separates critics and cinephiles is the rhetoric associated with them. And as digital culture and media become more constitutive of our critical, analytical, and professional capacities, we must constantly challenge ourselves to widen our perspective and understanding of the media with which we actively construct these models of criticism.

CHAPTER NINE

ACADEMIC BLOGGING AND DISCIPLINARY PRACTICE: IMPLICATIONS FOR FILM AND MEDIA STUDIES
Chris Cagle

In the summer of 2006, I began a weblog called Category D, devoted to discussing the fields of film studies and humanities-based media studies. When I started it, there were few academic blogs on the subject (fewer in film than in media studies). As I write, there are still not many; at a most generous count, the English-language film or media studies blogs – by scholars and with scholarly focus – number less than 75, and the majority are written by graduate students or junior scholars. One can imagine a range of reasons for the lack of interest in blogging. An immediate and unedited activity, the practice runs counter to the time-honored process of peer-review and the academic premium on careful reflection. The very idea of blogging seems trendy or frivolous, associated with confessional tone and professional inappropriateness. Most of all, blogging means yet again more writing and demands time from those already facing competing demands in teaching, writing, and research. I do believe, however, that academic blogging promises great benefits to individual scholars and to the field as a community, and that through a network effect these benefits will grow as more scholars blog. This chapter is, thus, in part an attempt to sell the virtues of blogging and to map-out some useful future directions.

At the same time, academic blogging is new, and the very notion deserves examination. A weblog, after all, is simply defined by two facts alone: the reverse-chronological entry format (the 'log' part) and the user-friendly software that allows for easy web publication updates in a static web page template. Nothing about these qualities necessitates a greater formal structure to a blog, but in practice bloggers have developed conventions of writing and dialog that adapt the software and entry format to suit different arenas. After an initial period of specialist and trade use by computer technicians, blogging first took a prominent form in the current events blogging to emerge after the September 11 attacks. From there, the activity was adopted and adapted to new ends: personal online diaries, gossip sites, restaurant reviews, and real estate offices. From this, it is not obvious what academic blogging would mean, or how it adopts the conventions of online conversation and adapts popular blogging to a discourse with different demands. Fortunately, we have models in our field and in other disciplines like economics or philosophy, where academic blogging is more popular and central to disciplinary conversations. By highlighting instances of academic blogging as it currently exists, we can better define the practice and imagine its utility for the disciplines of film and media studies.

THE DIARISTIC SKETCHPAD

The most obvious use of timely web publication is to share work in progress. One disadvantage of peer-reviewed and paper publications is the lag time between research and its printed form. For this reason, online preliminary publication is common in the sciences. Timeliness may matter less for humanities scholars, who measure disciplinary progress on a different time scale (see Booth et al. 2008: 78). It is no accident that television and new media scholars have been quicker to adopt the blog than their counterpart film historians or theorists. Even if the field does not require the same timeliness of data, models, or findings in other fields, some scholars do circulate work before publication: Michael Newman has posted chapters from his dissertation on independent cinema, Chuck Tryon puts up article drafts, and Jason Mittell frequently shares work in progress. Sharing of course can have drawbacks, particularly those concerned about guarding original research, but it does allow for wider feedback. For some publications, such as textbooks, the ability to foresee objections may be important.

Ultimately, humanities scholars are less likely to blog and share findings than to air ideas in their infancy and development. I frequently liken the blog's function to a diaristic sketchpad. Like a diary, it serves as a record, for the writer as much as the reader (and, important to remember, for the Google searcher). For instance, as part of my research, I have blogged my viewing project of 1947 Hollywood features. Not only does this project give me a chance to present my research interests to others in the field and to share my process of discovery, it also reminds me of what I noticed after watching particular titles.[1] Traditional notetaking can serve this role, too, but often notes take the form of raw data, while the blog demands an initial summary of the material. For that reason, Jason Sperb (2007) posts reactions to key theoretical articles he reads for his project. Elana Levine (2008) articulates key research challenges and methodological concerns in her ongoing research on American soap opera television. Bob Rehak (2009) assesses visual effects trends and franchise storytelling in current film and television works. Much of blogging's value lies in the initial synthesis of ideas.

Sociologist and blogger Kieran Healy puts forth a case for the intellectual diary approach to blogging. Against those who would say blogs waste time, he notes their utility by quoting C. Wright Mills' famous call for 'intellectual craftsmanship' (1959: 195) and substituting the word 'blog' for Mills' use of 'diary':

Many creative writers keep blogs; the sociologist's need for systematic reflection demands it. In such a blog as I am going to describe, there is joined personal experience and professional activities, studies under way and studies planned...

By keeping an adequate blog and thus developing self-reflective habits, you learn how to keep your inner world awake. Whenever you feel strongly about events or ideas you must try not to let them pass from your mind, but instead to formulate them for your blogs and in so doing draw out their implications, show yourself either how foolish these feelings or ideas are, or how they might be articulated into productive shape. The blog also helps you build up the habit of writing. You cannot 'keep your hand in' if you do not write something at least every week. In developing the blog, you can experiment as a writer and thus, as they say, develop your powers of expression...

But how is this blog – which so far must seem to you more like a curious sort of 'literary' journal – used in intellectual production? The maintenance of such a blog is intellectual production. It is a continually growing store of facts and ideas, from the most vague to the most finished. ... I do not know the full social conditions of the best intellectual workmanship, but certainly surrounding oneself by a circle of people who will listen and talk – and at times they have to be imaginary characters – is one of them. (2008)

Mutatis mutandis, the same idea applies to humanities scholarship. One can argue that an offline diary or notepad would serve the same purpose, and indeed Mills is writing for a pre-digital age. Opening up one's intellectual diary can be a tough decision (showing our foolish ideas rubs against our better guarded instincts), but it allows for valuable input from fellow scholars. Others can elevate useful insights, challenge us in productive ways, and provide encouragement and pointers. With blogging, the people who will listen and talk need not be imaginary characters.

THE VIRTUAL SEMINAR

One might liken this larger community of scholar-readers to a virtual seminar or colloquium. I suspect most scholars would recognize that while the value of scholarship is measured in formal, peer-reviewed outlets, so much of our education, inspiration and insight come from interaction with other scholars. I think back to my graduate school days and the role my colleagues had in challenging and encouraging me, in introducing me to ideas I had not encountered. I think, too, of the academic conferences I have attended showcasing the variety and sharpness of work being done by other film and media scholars. What academic blogging can do is extend these kinds of informal conversation beyond the confines of the geographical and institutional limits we all face.

If the blogging format *per se* entails few necessary conventions, the model of current events and personal diary blogging converge around three practices of blogging: (1) the informal, personal voice; (2) the role of comments and links to create a dialogue out of self-standing blogs and blog posts; and (3) the citational structure in which the writer reacts to responds to quoted statements or arguments. The first dovetails neatly with blogging's role as diaristic sketchpad, while the latter two foster a virtual seminar. Just like the actual seminar (if my graduate experience was representative), the virtual seminar is both a dialogue and a conceptual engagement with claims. For the dog-eared page and the highlighted book passage, the blog substitutes the link and the blockquote. Citation, comment, and link cooperate to facilitate a 'discussion' that may be sustained or brief. It is as if the seminar topic changes by the week, by the hour, or by the blog.

The type of discussion varies across the blogosphere. Not every current event blog welcomes comments or engages with other blogs; similarly, certain film and media blogs, like David Bordwell and Kristin Thompson's, serve primarily to publish detailed essays online. Even still, as online writing, freely available with permanent links, these blogs can foster discussion in other online venues. Most academic blogs, moreover, do maintain comments and regularly link to other sites. The resulting discussion might not build into an interaction of much significance; blogging is not a structured conversation like an actual colloquium or seminar. Then again, it may flourish and develop in unpredictable ways, lifting the constraints of time and place off the exchange of ideas. Blogging is a less linear academic conversation than a true seminar, but it is also a less bounded one.

Film and media studies blogging is still in its infancy, but other fields suggest what this analog to a seminar might look like. Their academic blogs embody an academic practice that serves several functions familiar to most scholars.

Blogs flag new ideas and new research. Eszter Hargittai (2004) and Henry Farrell (2008) highlight research on the politics and sociology of blogging. Tyler Cowen's and Alex Tabarrok's Marginal Revolution frequently elevates specialist research in economics and economics-informed social science; they have a particular eye for research with surprising results. The Modern Kicks blog points out current work in art history journals, particularly issues dealing with interesting questions of theory or historiography.

Blogs provide methodological debate. Historian Mark Grimsley, for instance, uses his blog to put forth a polemic for the integration of social history and military history; the multiple-contributor history blog Cliopatra has featured Grimsley's call and responded with a conversation about military historiography.[2] Anthropology and other social science blogs used Jared Diamond's *Guns, Germs, and Steel* as an occasion for a methodological debate about causation (see Farrell 2005; Friedman 2005; Lowrey 2005).

Blogs debate the merits of specific scholarly works. Crooked Timber's book events are a good example, with roundtable discussions of interdisciplinary books like Yochai Benkler's *The Wealth of Networks* (2007) and Steven D. Levitts *Freakonomics* (2005); similarly, literary studies blog The Valve hosted an event around Daphne Patai and Wilfrido Howard Corral's *Theory's Empire* (2005), a book challenging the dominance of high literary theory.[3] These discussions weigh the merits of popularization and the nature of interdisciplinary work. Blogs can also host reading groups, like Unfogged's blogging devoted to Martin Heidegger's *Being and Time*.[4]

Blogs interrogate the contours of the discipline. A number of economics blogs participated in an inter-blog discussion on heterodox economics (see Hayes 2007; Davies 2007; Cowen 2007a and 2007b). Steve Vaisey (2008) recently asked sociologists to reexamine the concept of individual motivation by comparing the field's notion of motivation to that of economists and psychologists.

The examples I have given are admittedly limited. Essentially, they are the academic blogs I have bookmarked for my own use and interest. This limitation, however, is partly the point: as academic blogging expands, more of these conversations are likely to happen. As is, they undoubtedly are currently going on in fields and subfields beyond any one individual's view.

Even with fewer bloggers, the fields of film and media studies have begun similar conversations. Michael Newman (2008d) has reviewed Carl Wilson's *Celine Dion: Let's Talk About Love: A Journey to the End of Taste* (2007) and suggested why it is a useful contribution to our understanding of media taste formations. Chuck Tryon, Alexandra Juhasz, and I (2008) have discussed and debated montage in the YouTube age. David Bordwell (2008) has reflected on how copyright has influenced the starring role for *His Girl Friday* (Howard Hawks, 1940) in the field of film studies. The writers at a group blog, Dr. Mabuse's Kaleidoscope (2008), have assessed the political imperative of media scholarship, suggested that notions of cinephilia need to include contemporary cinema, and have reflected on narration and film sound.[5]

Ultimately, the blog can help manage a tension scholars inevitably feel between specialization and disciplinary community. As the field of film studies becomes a more genuinely specialist field and as humanities-oriented television and media studies gain institutional autonomy from a previous and often uneasy appended status to cinema studies, the common grounds for disciplinary conversation can become more difficult to have. Of course, the various corners of the discipline do not suddenly cordon off into subfields because of scholars' lack of interest in the developments elsewhere; they atomize for largely structural reasons, since specialization and institutional structures impose their own logics on scholarly inquiry. Blogging is not a full solution to atomization, nor the only solution, but it has an ideal level of scholarly communication. Where the academic paper or book in a specialist subfield takes sufficient time to find and digest, the blog post is likely to be synoptic – a quick observation or concise summary. (Dan Ryan's 2008 summary of his sociology of information project represents this concision at its finest.) Thus, the blog reader can efficiently read material from a variety of scholars, whether through automated feeds or through trusted blogs. The benefits also accrue to interdisciplinary dialogue, which has always been easy to desire yet hard to achieve. Again, the blog is no magic bullet for cooperation between fields, but it does provide one link for sharing ideas where departmental and professional structures do not.

THE BIBLIOGRAPHIC RESOURCE

The 'bleg' is one neologism of the blog age. A portmanteau of 'blog' and 'beg', bleg means a request for suggestions or information from blog readers. Surprisingly, academic bloggers have been less quick to resort to the bleg than their counterparts blogging on current events, yet the collective bibliographic resource of academic bloggers could be an asset. As specialists, academic bloggers embody the training of our fields and extensive, deep reading. In our daily lives, we share suggestions with colleagues and with those at conferences; blogging allows for new lateral connections and more ease in sharing. Alisa Perren (2010), for instance, has opened a class book-review assignment for recent work on media industries, and her post serves both as a bibliographic resource to readers and a bleg for further additions. My blogging on the films of 1947 elicited a useful suggestion for similar projects in literary studies (Anon. 2007). In this process, academics should not have to shoulder the sole work as bibliographic resource. In fact, one of the promises of increased blogging is the possibility for fuller interaction between the discipline's scholars, archive professionals, and librarians and information specialists.

The connection between disciplinary practice and informational architecture is a pressing concern. As digitally-coded and network-distributed information sources grow in number and penetration, our practice as scholars is changing. We are asked to build information literacy into our classes, and we face a generation of students for whom search engines and online reference take priority over more traditional means of finding knowledge. Blogs can conduct useful online materials to scholars and students alike; moreover, the blog can in its best instances contextualize these resources. Catherine Grant at Film Studies for Free regularly collects available online academic writing and film criticism, grouping links by topic; recent areas include depth of field, horror films, and Chris Marker.

At the extreme, bibliographic discussion can serve as a kind of supplemental peer review. Peer review does not catch every potential problem, of course, and the wisdom of crowds may enable a better record of statement within the field.

On her blog, for instance, Historian Rachel Leow (2008) noticed a misleading quotation in one article in the *Journal of History of Ideas*. Meanwhile, blogging can preemptively solicit scrutiny. Jason Mittell shared his then-television studies textbook-in-progress; among the reactions was an objection from a scholar that Mittell's account of media ecology was reductive (2007b). Mittell could take this argument as he wished, but whether he agreed with the assessment or not, it potentially aided in revising the textbook to take into account the temperature of the field.

THE PEDAGOGICAL FORUM

Film and media scholars are usually teachers in addition to researchers. However, save for the occasional 'In Focus' section of *Cinema Journal*, traditional academic publishing in our field does not provide much detailed, practical discussion of film and media pedagogy. Film and media studies may in fact be less invested in publishing pedagogical discussion than other disciplines. Blogs provide a natural forum in which to discuss pedagogical matters, since they are timely and personal. They network writers to other scholars facing similar issues. From sharing syllabi to detailing experience with in-class use of the blog, as Michael Newman (2008b; 2008c) has done, the discourse on teaching need not fulfill a preset genre of pedagogical writing. Instead, scholars can be free, within the constraints of tact and professionalism, to discuss issues how they see fit. For instance, seeing no central place where introduction-to-film-analysis textbooks were reviewed, I reviewed the major textbooks on my blog (2006). Such reviews can aid potential adopters but can also help writers themselves anticipate the books' uses; Jeremy Butler, for one, has called for a similar review of television studies textbooks (2007). The title of Chuck Tryon's post 'teaching in the information age' reveals one of the central interests of his blog – how to incorporate the way the Internet is consumed by students into a media studies pedagogy (2007).

PROFESSIONAL ASSOCIATION AND COMMUNITY

Blogging is by convention both an individual and communitarian activity. By blogging, academics can extend the collegial conversations subtending academic knowledge. However, beyond fostering intellectual community, the academic blog can develop three broader communities: the discipline, a film or media culture, and a university citizenship.

The discipline, to begin with, is as much a networked body of scholars as it is an abstract terrain of ideas. Across institutions, blogging can carry on conversations difficult to hold in any other way. As professional associations like the Society for Cinema and Media Studies grow, a true deliberative discussion

– whether over particular issues or strategic goals for the association – becomes difficult; here, blogs can facilitate deliberation and help make the field's scale more manageable. The greatest service, though, can come with its networking capabilities. Calls for papers, conference news, and personal contacts happen in new and different ways online than they do in the face-to-face world.

Film studies bloggers also engage with a wider film culture. Here, the influence runs two ways. Cineliterate and philomath film weblogs like Girish Shambu's blog mix academic and cinephile insights, while others like Pullquote are penned by authors with one foot in the academy, one foot in a larger film culture. Internet-based film criticism is reenergizing the moribund practice of an autonomous film criticism – criticism that is theoretically and historically informed yet not academic in aim. With the arrival of online criticism, film scholars may continue their long-standing communion with a wider film culture, or they may reflect on the gap with this culture under the pressures of specialization. Either way, the proximity of nonacademic cinephile writing to scholarly writing can spur the discipline in productive ways. Here, the realm of art blogs can suggest new, productive kinds of dialogue between scholarship and arts culture. In the visual arts, the online presence of artists, curators, periodicals, academics, and other observers frequently cross paths.

The stakes are even greater for television scholars or digital media scholars interested in a sympathetic media culture. Admittedly, a community reclaiming popular television as art is much more fledgling (though it exists); its newness gives academic media studies blogs an even greater role in engaging in a wider subculture. Henry Jenkins' Aca-Fan blog genuinely straddles disciplines and constituencies, an asset he plays up with regular interviews of scholars, media makers, and other figures in online and participatory culture. Michael Newman started an online debate about television spoilers (2008a). Jason Mittell has called for the start of a discussion of televisual aesthetic value (2007a).

Finally, media scholars also are members of a wider university. Like other scholars, we can be invested in the governance of our institutions and the directions higher education is taking (or should take). We may have a particular take on these questions based on our field and its needs. Tim Burke's Easily Distracted exemplifies the continuity between scholarly pursuits – Burke is a historian specializing in sub-Saharan Africa – and what might be called university citizenship – he continually interrogates what liberal arts education should do, and which of the critiques leveled against the university have merit, which ones are cant. He includes among his reasons for blogging:

1) Because I want to introduce some unexpected influences and ideas into my intellectual and academic work...
2) Because I want a place to publish small writings, odd writings, leftover writ-

ings ... things I think have some value but not enough to constitute legitimate scholarship...

3) Because I want to find out how much of my scholarly work is usefully translate-able into a wider public conversation...

4) Because I want to model for myself and others how we should all behave within in an idealized democratic public sphere... (2005)

From his blog, it is clear that Burke sees the college or university as a public sphere in its own right. In addition to such deliberative questions, his writing suggests the potential of blogs to popularize a scholar's work and, with it, the work of a discipline. The role of blog as popularizer is clear in other fields, as well. The most immediate application comes from disciplines with clear public policy dimensions, such as the climate scientists at Real Climate, but purer disciplines can adopt a popularizing function, too. Marginal Revolution is a good example, as a blog devoted to economic analysis and theory, yet one with a wide reader-ship (in and out of the academy) and often nonspecialist in its address. I myself learned of Tyler Cowen's work on cultural economics through the site. Perhaps not incidentally, it has done much to raise the public profile of George Mason University's economics department.

CONCLUSION: THE DEMAND SIDE OF SCHOLARSHIP

In each of its capacities – as diaristic sketchpad, as virtual seminar, as biblio-graphic resource, as pedagogical discussion, and as means to connect scholar to his or her larger community – the academic blog has shown promise already in film and media studies. It has shown even more in other disciplines. Currently, academic blogs adapt a publishing format better known for the trade forum or topical debate in order to sustain a rich and substantive contribution to their aca-demic disciplines. In this regard, their full potential is yet untapped. Since the positive effects rely extensively on the connective force of the link, the blogroll, and the comment, the increase of academic bloggers will likely increase dispro-portionally the utility of academic blogs.

For all the concern that academic bloggers are pretenders to a peer-reviewed throne (see, for instance, Hargittai 2004; Mortensen 2004), blogging's impact may be less in its production of scholarship than as a new way of consuming scholarship. There is increasing talk of a crisis in academic publishing, with *Cinema Journal* weighing in with a forum and the Modern Language Association drafting guidelines calling for changes in tenure review and requirements (see-Juhasz 2005; Modern Language Association 2002). Not to take away from the structural factors at play in academic employment, I would say the crisis is not merely one of production but of consumption. Too many scholars are chasing too few readers. We may not have any profound way to address the overly harsh gate-keeping that results from the overproduction of PhDs, but as a community of scholars we can do a better job of serving as a receptive audience for each others' work. By hosting our debates, our conference reactions, or our capsule book reviews, academic blogs can expand our collective sense of investment in scholarship as something meant to be used. Just as surely as poetry blogs or websites on experimental film carve out surprisingly vibrant niche audiences and communities, the academic blog can foster readership for even the most monographic of scholarship. As the field of film and media studies becomes more specialized, and as our conferences grow to Modern Language Association proportions, there is the danger of a giant sea of young scholars giving papers to the ether while atomization paralyzes intellectual dialogue. While imperfect, the academic blog may help the discipline avoid that fate.

WEBLOGS MENTIONED IN THIS CHAPTER

Film and Media Studies
Category D (Chris Cagle): http://categoryd.blogspot.com/
The Chutry Experiment (Chuck Tryon): http://chutry.wordherders.net/
Confessions of an Aca-Fan (Henry Jenkins): http://henryjenkins.org/
Dr. Mabuse's Kaleidoscope (group): http://www.dr-mabuses-kaleido-scope.blogspot.com/
Dr. Television (Elana Levine): http://drtelevision.blogspot.com/
Film Studies for Free (Catherine Grant): http://filmstudiesforfree.blogspot.com/
Graphic Engine (Bob Rehak): http://graphic-engine.swarthmore.edu/
Just TV (Jason Mittell): http://justtv.wordpress.com/
Media Industries (Alisa Perren): http://www.themediaindustries.net/
Media Praxis (Alex Juhasz): http://aljean.wordpress.com/
Observations on Film Art (David Bordwell and Kristin Thompson): http://www.davidbordwell.net/blog/
Zigzigger (Michael Newman): http://zigzigger.blogspot.com/

Film Culture
Girish Shambu: http://www.girishshambu.com/blog/
Pullquote (Amy Monaghan): http://pullquote.typepad.com/

Other Disciplines
Blog Them Out of the Stone Age (Mark Grimsley): http://warhistorian.org/wordpress/
Brad DeLong's Semi-Daily Journal: http://delong.typepad.com/sdj/

CLIOPATRA (group): http://hnn.us/blogs/2.html

Crooked Timber (group): http://www.crookedtimber.org/

Easily Distracted (Tim Burke): http://weblogs.swarthmore.edu/burke/

A Historian's Craft (Rachel Leow): http://idlethink.wordpress.com/

Kieran Healy: http://www.kieranhealy.org/

Marginal Revolution (Tyler Cowen and Alex Tabarrok): http://www.marginalrevolution.com/

Modern Kicks (pseudonymous): http://modernkicks.typepad.com/modern_kicks/

Org Theory (group): http://orgtheory.wordpress.com/

Real Climate (group): http://www.realclimate.org/

Savage Minds (group): http://savageminds.org/

The Sociology of Information (Dan Ryan): http://soc-of-info.blogspot.com/

The Valve (group): http://thevalve.org/

Unfogged (group): http://www.unfogged.com/

NOTES

1 Chris Cagle, Category D blog, http://categoryd.blogspot.com/search/label/1947 project/.

2 Mark Grimsley, Blog Them Out of the Stone Age blog, http://warhistorian.org/wordpress/; Schwyzer (2006).

3 Crooked Timber blog, Levitt and Benkler seminars, http://www.crookedtimber.org/category/levitt-seminar; http://crookedtimber.org/category/benkler-seminar/.

4 Ogged [pseud.], *Being and Time* reading group, Unfogged blog, http://www.unfogged.com/beingandtime/

5 Dr. Mabuse's Kaleido-scope blog, http://dr-mabuses-kaleido-scope.blogspot.com/, see especially posts and comments of August 10, 2006, November 15, 2006, and August 22, 2008.

REFERENCES

Anonymous (2007), comment on '1947 Project', Category D blog, 30 March. Online. Available at: http://categoryd.blogspot.com/2007/03/1947-project.html (Accessed 10 March 2010).

Booth, Wayne C., Gregory G. Colomb, and Joseph M. Williams (2008) *The Craft of Research*, third edition. Chicago: University of Chicago Press.

Bordwell, David (2008) 'Creating a Classic, with a little help from your pirate friends', Observations on Film Art blog, 21 February. Online. Available at: http://www.davidbordwell.net/blog/?p=1809 (Accessed 10 March 2010).

Burke, Tim (2005) 'Burke's Home for Imaginary Friends', Tim Burke's blog, 26 January. Online. Available at: http://www.swarthmore.edu/SocSci/tburke1/perma12605.html (Accessed 10 March 2010).

Butler, Jeremy (2007) 'Comparison of Intro-to-Film Textbooks', forum, ScreenSite, 12 June. Online. Available at: http://www.screensite.org/index.php?option=com_fireboard&Ite mid=52&func=view&id=292&catid=7 (Accessed 10 March 2010).

Cagle, Chris (2006) 'Intro Textbook Comparison', Category D blog, 15 November. Online. Available at: http://categoryd.blogspot.com/2006/11/intro-textbook-comparison.html (Accessed 10 March 2010).

Cagle, Chris (2008) 'Compilation and Mashup Montage', Category D blog, posted May 20, 2008. Online. Available at: http://categoryd.blogspot.com/2008/05/compilation-and-mashup-montage.html (Accessed 10 March 2010).

Cowen, Tyler (2007a) 'Feminist Economics', Marginal Revolution blog, 6 June. Online. Available at: http://www.marginalrevolution.com/marginalrevolution/2007/06/feminist_econom.html (Accessed 10 March 2010).

Cowen, Tyler (2007b) 'The Value of Heterodox Economics', Marginal Revolution blog, 3 June. Online. Available at: http://www.marginalrevolution.com/marginalrevolution/2007/06/the_value_of_he.html (Accessed 10 March 2010).

Davies, Daniel (2007) 'Profits and Loss', Crooked Timber blog, 7 June. Online. Available at: http://crookedtimber.org/2007/06/01/profits-and-loss/ (Accessed 10 March 2010).

Farrell, Henry (2005) 'Nobbled Savages', Crooked Timber blog, 26 July. Online. Available at: http://crookedtimber.org/2005/07/26/savaged-minds/ (Accessed 10 March 2010).

____ (2008) 'Blogs, Participation and Polarization', Crooked Timber blog, 1 July. Online. Available at: http://crookedtimber.org/2008/07/01/blogs-participation-and-polarization/ (Accessed 10 March 2010).

Friedman, Kerim (2005) 'Guns, Germs, and Steel Links', Savage Minds blog, 26 July. Online. Available at: http://savageminds.org/2005/07/26/guns-germs-and-steel-links/ (Accessed 10 March 2010).

Hargittai, Eszter (2004) 'The Academic Contributions of Blogging?' Crooked Timber blog, 18 November. Online. Available at: http://crookedtimber.org/2004/11/18/the-academic-contributions-of-blogging/ (Accessed 10 March 2010).

Hargittai, Eszter (2008) 'Gender differences in sharing creative content online', Crooked Timber blog, 25 June. Online. Available at: http://crookedtimber.org/2008/06/25/gender-differences-in-sharing-creative-content-online/ (Accessed 10 March 2010).

Hayes, Christopher (2007) 'Hip Heterodoxy', The Nation, 24 May. Online. Available at: http://www.thenation.com/doc/20070611/hayes (Accessed 10 March 2010).

Healy, Kieran (2008) 'On Wasting One's Time'. Kieran Healy blog, 7 February. Online. Available at: http://www.kieranhealy.org/blog/archives/2008/02/07/on-wasting-ones-time/ (Accessed 10 March 2010).

Juhasz, Alexandra (2008) 'YouTube Specificity/History', MEDIA PRAXIS blog, 21 May. Online. Available at: http://aljean.wordpress.com/2008/05/21/youtube-specificityhistory/

(Accessed 10 March 2010).

Juhasz, Alexandra (ed.) (2005) 'In Focus: The Crisis in Publishing', Cinema Journal 44, 3, 81-98.

Leow, Rachel (2008) 'On Bad Citation', A Historian's Craft blog, 23 August. Online. Available at: http://idlethink.wordpress.com/2008/08/23/on-bad-citation/ (Accessed 10 March 2010).

Levine, Elana (2008) 'Soapy Research Questions', Dr. Television blog, 27 May. Online. Available at: http://drtelevision.blogspot.com/2008/05/blog-post.html (Accessed 10 March 2010).

Lowrey, Kathleen 'Ozma' (2005) 'Anthropology's Guns, Germs, and Steel Problem', Savage Minds blog, 24 July. Online. Available at: http://savageminds.org/2005/07/24/anthropology's-guns-germs-and-steel-problem/ (Accessed 10 March 2010).

Mills, C. Wright (1959) The Sociological Imagination. New York: Oxford University Press.

Mittell, Jason (2007a) 'Lost in a Great Story', Just TV blog, 23 October. Online. Available at: http://justtv.wordpress.com/2007/10/23/lost-in-a-great-story/ (Accessed 10 March 2010).

Mittell, Jason (2007b) 'Medium Theory', Just TV blog, 13 August. Online. Available at: http://justtv.wordpress.com/2007/08/13/medium-theory/ (Accessed 10 March 2010).

Modern Language Association (2002) 'The Future of Scholarly Publishing', report of the Ad Hoc Committee on the Future of Scholarly Publishing, Profession, 172–86. Available at: http://www.mla.org/issues_scholarly_pub (Accessed 10 March 2010).

Mortensen, Torill (2004) 'Blogs as Academic Publishing?' Thinking with My Fingers blog, 19 November. Online. Available at: http://torillsin.blogspot.com/2004/11/blogs-as-academic-publishing.html (Accessed 10 March 2010).

Newman, Michael (2008a) 'Spoilers', Zigzigger blog, 13 March. Online. Available at: http://zigzigger.blogspot.com/2008/03/spoilers-cui-bono.html (Accessed 10 March 2010).

Newman, Michael (2008b) 'Intro', Zigzigger blog, 2 January 2. Online. Available at: http://zigzigger.blogspot.com/2008/01/intro.html (Accessed 10 March 2010).

Newman, Michael (2008c) 'Lessons from the Class Blog', Zigzigger blog, 21 May. Online. Available at: http://zigzigger.blogspot.com/2008/05/lessons-from-class-blog.html. (Accessed 10 March 2010).

Newman, Michael (2008d) 'Let's Talk About a Book About 'Let's Talk About Love'', Zigzigger blog, 10 January. Online. Available at: http://zigzigger.blogspot.com/2008/01/lets-talk-about-book-about-lets-talk.html (Accessed 10 March 2010).

Perren, Alsia (2010) 'Books on the Media Industries', Media Industries blog, 5 March. Online. Available at: http://www.themediaindustries.net/2010/03/books-on-media-industries.html (Accessed 1 June 2011).

Rehak, Bob (2009) 'Watching Avatar', Graphic Engine blog, posted 30 December. Online. Available at: http://graphic-engine.swarthmore.edu/?p=372 (Accessed 10 March 2010).

Ryan, Dan (2008) 'The Theory of Notification', The Sociology of Information blog, 12

September. Online. Available at: http://soc-of-info.blogspot.com/2008/09/theory-of-notification.html (Accessed 10 March 2010).

Schwyzer, Hugo (2006) 'More on Military History', CLIOPATRIA: A Group Blog, History News Network, 16 October. Online. Available at: http://hnn.us/blogs/entries/30875.html (Accessed 10 March 2010).

Sperb, Jason (2007) 'Cinephilia and Disappointment', Dr. Mabuse's Kaleido-scope blog, 22 May. Online. Available at: http://dr-mabuses-kaleido-scope.blogspot.com/2006/08/politics-of-cinephilia.html (Accessed 13 September 2008).

Tryon, Chuck (2007) 'Teaching in the Information Age', The Chutry Experiment blog, 28 October. Online. Available at: http://www.chutry.wordherders.net/wp/?p=1742 (Accessed 10 March 2010).

Tryon, Chuck (2008) 'A YouTube Theory of Montage', The Chutry Experiment blog, 16 May. Online. Available at: http://www.chutry.wordherders.net/wp/?p=1917 (Accessed 10 March 2010).

Vaisey, Steve (2008) 'Motivation, Markets, and Manipulation', OrgTheory blog, 28 August. Online. Available at: http://orgtheory.wordpress.com/2008/08/28/motivation-markets-and-manipulation/ (Accessed 10 March 2010).

CHAPTER TEN

THE KITSCH AFFECT; OR, SIMULATION, NOSTALGIA AND THE AUTHENTICITY OF THE CONTEMPORARY CGI FILM

Greg Singh

Audiences do make demands on special effects that they don't make on other types of computer-generated images, and this has put the producers of this imagery in the position of having to find new ways of soliciting audiences' attention once the aesthetic novelty of a particular technique has worn off.

– Michele Pierson (2002: 63)

The most progressive works [of] individual style, cunningly tricked out of the requirements of construction, take on the quality of a blemish, a deficiency, or at the least a compromise. This is one of the most important reasons why advanced artistic production aims less at originality in a particular work than at the production of a new type. Originality is in the process of being transformed into the act of inventing types.

– Theodor W. Adorno (1997: 172–3)

Growing up, there are two particular moments that I can clearly recall as being definite 'cinephiliac' moments for me. One of these happened when I was eleven years old. It involved watching *The Stuff* (Larry Cohen, 1985), a comedy-horror in which one of the characters – Chocolate-Chip Charlie (Garrett Morris) – inadvertently eats a malignant alien substance loosely resembling yoghurt, and ends-up being himself eaten from the inside out. Another moment occurred for me much earlier, when I was about six: at school we had been primed for *The Wizard of Oz* (Victor Fleming, 1939), because a live production was being put on at one of the local theatres. The moment came when, at a friend's house party, we kids were sat down and made to watch the film version, because such a fuss had been made about *Oz* at school. The 'cinephiliac' moment occurred when Dorothy (Judy Garland) first steps into the Technicolor world of Oz and is greeted by Glinda the Good Witch (Billie Burke). Dorothy asks: 'Are you a good witch, or a bad witch?' presumably because she did not know whether or not to trust the witch. This was perfectly understandable, given the trauma that she had just endured and the fact that this simple farm girl from rural Kansas was being confronted by a fairy-type creature with wings, who just happened to mysteriously appear in a bursting bubble of psychedelic lights and glitter. I vividly remember sharing Dorothy's fears, or at least, I was fearful for her.

Although perhaps not on the face of it, these two moments share a number of things in common for me as a critic and a consumer. Firstly, they are moments that had a lasting impact on my fascination with film. They are, if you like, defining moments in my viewing past. Secondly, both clips produced similar affective responses from me, as a viewer: those of fear in particular. Thirdly, both moments are shaped by, indeed owe their existence to, their use of special effects. Charlie's mouth becomes unhinged and gallons of the 'stuff' ooze out of his head, while Dorothy emerges from her farmstead in full colour after a few minutes of monochrome, and the Good Witch appears through a series of magical superimpositions, dissolves and other ingenious visual devices. The sense of wonder at these special effects did add to the affective nature of what I was experiencing, although, to what extent I am now uncertain. Memory tends to play tricks in hindsight, and the 'interference' of nostalgia in recalling how I felt at these moments plays its own part in shaping how I feel about them now. This aspect of experience through memory and pleasure raises some interesting questions concerning the role of nostalgia in the mediation of affective responses to such moments, and serves as the starting point for this discussion.

I felt it necessary to recount these moments of my own cinephilia, as they inevitably played an important part in the way I now think about film. I do not wish to dwell on the nature of cinephilia as a concept too much here, as it is the focus of debate elsewhere in this collection. However, the term has been discussed recently by Jason Sperb and it is useful to quote him here in relation to the phenomenon of the 'cinephiliac anecdote', a term originally coined by Christian Keathley. Sperb suggests that this is 'something whereby a particular fragment builds, almost stream-of-conscious-like, into a more substantive discussion of the film in question and even film history more generally' (2008). Reid Davis, who relates his own *Oz* viewing experience to sexuality, camp, and pleasure through repeated viewing, articulates cinephilia slightly differently:

> To go to a movie repeatedly is to reenter a previously inhabited world – a darkened space constructed of conscious fondness, unconscious memory, the materiality of visual representations, the subjectivity of identifications with one's spectator-companions. (2001/2: 3)

At the beginning of his essay, Davis is taking on a specific phenomenon – repeated viewing – and using it to examine issues of pleasure, memory and the experience of watching a particular film. I have watched *Oz* countless times since that first encounter, and although every experience is unique, they each in some way refer to the first feelings I felt about Dorothy and her exchange with the Good Witch. This is why it is crucial to remember that, as Davis continues: 'Reviewing film is a negotiated practice, upsetting and figuring stable definitions of time (as linear), history (as fixed), spatial relationships (as synchronic), identity (as transcendent)' (ibid.). Here, I do not wish to dwell on identity, as much as the first three elements of reviewing practice, as these are of more immediate interest to me. Although my recollection is key to my identity as a critic and consumer, the first three elements mentioned here feed into Keathley's concern with cinephilia as having the potential to reveal something about film history itself. In relation to my *Oz* recollection, a more recent experience in film viewing compelled me to rethink my earlier encounter with this scene, and in particular, to rethink the viewing relationship with visual effects in cinema holistically.

There is a sequence near the beginning of Kerry Konran's *Sky Captain and the World of Tomorrow* (2004) that stays in the memory thanks in some part to its overt and multi-layered references to film history and technology. This sequence informs the narrative trajectory of the film for the rest of its duration, and in a number of interesting ways. Firstly, we see *The Wizard of Oz* playing on screen in the background as Polly Perkins (Gwyneth Paltrow) walks into a movie theatre in Radio City Music Hall. It has already been established that Perkins is a journalist and that the film is set in New York *circa* 1940. Paltrow's costume, hair and make-up give off an air of authenticity, of a mix between a *femme fatale* and a plucky derring-do. She here has more than a passing resemblance to a number of blonde bombshell stars of the period, such as Lauren Bacall, Veronica Lake and Lana Turner. As we follow Perkins into the theatre, we are able to notice how *The Wizard of Oz* is slightly out-of-focus, simulating an 'authentic' depth perception that occurs through cinematic projection. What is significant about the scene being shown is that it is the moment when Dorothy wakes up in Oz. This is also the moment when the colour scheme of that film switches from monochrome to Technicolor. Doubly significant is the fact that the film-within-a-film technique being employed here is not generated through traditional back-projection techniques, but through CGI technology in post-production. In other words, the scene from *Sky Captain* (taken in total) was never a pro-filmic event. It is an example of image manipulation and computer generation working within the frame to give the impression of a filmed event (the expository scene in the theatre), yet challenging traditional positions in film theory on photorealism. Following Stephen Prince, here we have a paradox in the creation of 'credible photographic images of things which cannot be photographed' (2004: 271). We are seeing, in effect, a 'realistic' screening of *The Wizard of Oz* in 1940s Radio City.

It is evident that we as an audience are dealing with a complex filmic, textual, and spatial relationship here. It is evocative of Reid's four-layered time, history, space, and identity structure. We are watching a film, a film-within-a-film and the perceptibly self-conscious interplay between the two, in which old and new come together through a complex relationship involving narrative, dialogue, music, and textual layering. We are also engaging in a multi-layered interplay of 'audience', diegesis, and knowledge of the narrative. We, as an audience, are watching all this unfold in *Sky Captain*; however, there is also a second audience, in Radio City, watching *The Wizard of Oz*, unaware that we are watching them, but, we may assume, aware (as real-world audiences were at the time) of the technological significance of this then-new film (*Oz*).

Although relying a little on speculation here, the coincidence of subject matter in *Sky Captain* with the historical period of the film's diegetic world and the use of *Oz* specifically as a cultural and visual referent is difficult to ignore. *Sky Captain and the World of Tomorrow*, with its science fantasy motifs reminiscent of movie serials such as *Flash Gordon* and *Buck Rogers* (the modern metropolis, flying machines, death rays, and so forth) plays with filmic nostalgia on several levels. J. P. Telotte, in an essay discussing science fiction film and the inter-war period (the precise historical period of *Sky Captain*'s setting), notes that this 'machine age' is not a purely historical moment, but also a cultural turn of sorts; he states that this period is 'the moment at which the modern world first discovers its specifically modern character' (1999: 1). One of the defining characteristics of this cultural turn, in North America at least, would have been the phenomenon of successive World's Fairs, according to Telotte. It so happens that *Oz* premiered in August of 1939 in New York (after Wisconsin and LA), the same year that the city of New York held its own World's Fair, the location and timing of the opening sequence of *Sky Captain*. Also important, for Telotte, 'We might also note that the first World Science Fiction Convention was held in New York in 1939' (1999: 190, n. 9). This is significant for a number of reasons, not least of which is the World's Fair's affinity with science fiction film and its generic conventions, as attested to in a documentary on the Fair, entitled *The World of Tomorrow* (Lance Bird and Tom Johnson, 1984) – importantly, named after the Fair itself.

Robots, vehicles, cityscapes and ultra-modern architecture such as the 'Perisphere', and the testimony of scientists such as Albert Einstein (in this case), are all features of the documentary, because they were all features of the Fair. They also happen to correspond with conventions and iconography present in several science fiction films of the period, such as *Just Imagine* (David Butler, 1930) and *Things to Come* (William Cameron Menzies, 1936). These correspondences converge at a stylistic level, nodding to the audience and engaging knowledge of genre, sensibility, and film history. In this sense, *Sky Captain*, and its evocation of nostalgia, of science fiction film-past and the end of the 'machine age', is as much a film of 'facts' as is *The World of Tomorrow*. As Telotte writes, '*The World of Tomorrow* aims not so much at an ironic evocation of the past or of cultural history'; rather, it 'seems intent on reclaiming something of the past, on tracing out a manner of thinking and presentation that still echoes in our present modes of thought about the technological' (1999: 166–7).

Less likely to reclaim the past, but more precisely to reinvent it through both fantasy and verisimilitude, *Sky Captain* chooses to cannibalise elements of film history and real-world history in order to show us the past. Nevertheless, one might argue, through the pursuit of nostalgia, both films are attempting to emphasise the importance of visual technology and its place in the popular imagination. The soundtrack for *The World of Tomorrow* utilises 'Somewhere Over the Rainbow', the title theme in *Oz* repeatedly, as if to seal its connection with the history of film and with the nostalgic cinephiliac practices of the real world. *Sky Captain* performs a similar trick, by using a new recording of the song over its end credits, thus demonstrating a connection and a discontinuity with *Oz* at the same time. The 'world of the film' of *Sky Captain* – working both diegetically and extra-diegetically – may therefore be said to engage the fictional imagination of *Oz* as well as the historical imagination of film technology, shaping in some small way, nostalgia as a sensible presence in the text.

Michel de Certeau describes this attendant nostalgia such as found in contemporary or near-contemporary documentation of the past:

> Any autonomous order is founded upon what it eliminates; it produces a 'residue' condemned to be forgotten. But what was excluded re-infiltrates the place of its origin … It resurfaces, it troubles, it turns the present's feeling of being 'at home' into an illusion … and it inscribes there a law of the other. (1986: 4)

It is little wonder that fellow postmodern theorists such as Jean Baudrillard and Fredric Jameson stick to a definition of the postmodern as principally characterised by an absence of history, an endless, almost psychotic present. In representational terms, this residual (but ever-present) homely-otherness dialectic has found its way into many feature films, including *Sky Captain* itself. Even as Perkins enters Radio City, a poster, advertising the *Sky Captain and the World of Tomorrow* movie can be faintly seen outside the theatre. Therefore, the film represents a rupture – less with science fiction film-past – and more with a sense of real continuity with what has gone before. As Jameson has described in *Postmodernism: Or, the Cultural Logic of Late Capitalism* (1991), the gap left by the absence of history and historical memory is filled with a past simulated through film iconography and generic markings.

As the dialogue in the movie theatre between Polly Perkins and Jennings unfolds, it also soon becomes apparent that the scene is mirroring the narrative and spectacle elements of the 'screened' film in the background and is thus a much more complex version of absence and simulation than Jameson appears to allow. The scene happens to be *Sky Captain*'s 'info-dump': a scene of expository dialogue very common in science fiction film, particularly of the historical period represented (i.e. the 'machine age') but still common today. In this expository function, the choice of scene from *Oz* seems particularly powerful since we are invited to re-imagine *Oz*'s narrative in terms of something almost sinister – lurking around the corner in the world of *Sky Captain*. *Oz*, with its underlying allegories of pubescence, anxiety, and sexual awakening is interesting itself; but when integrated into the story of *Sky Captain*, it becomes a signifier for impending, and significant change. In Roland Barthes' terms, this scene (in the inclusion of the scene as played in the background) is crucial to the narrativity of *Sky Captain*. Both films are presenting *cardinal* functions of their particular narrative, thematically significant, and temporally placed in the plot to open up alternatives of consequence in the development of their stories. The manner in which these events are presented (i.e. the *interplay* of two cardinal functions) is itself a *catalyser*, suggesting that narrative and narration, or story and discourse, are here conflated to an extent. There is thus a kind of presence through the simulation of *Oz* playing at Radio City (rather than a straightforward absence), in which audience knowledge of the film and the pleasure in recalling the experience of watching that film (and knowing its plot concerns) are foregrounded. That presence is nostalgic in tone and, therefore, a species of turning the 'present's feeling of being "at home" into an illusion' (Certeau 1984: 4). Not all is that homely in the scene as to be unproblematically pleasurable. Even if we have no prior knowledge of *The Wizard of Oz*, its presence in the scene is still troubling, because its aesthetic is so firmly embedded in its own historical technicity. It is definitively of its time, and yet, without a reference to this knowledge; it is cast adrift and becomes an empty gesture, the return of a Jamesonian absence, perhaps.

As an audience, we are invited to relive a moment of awakening through new eyes. As Jennings describes a sinister Nazi plot, hinting at inhumane experimentation for malign purposes, Polly's knowledge of the magnitude of these events grows. At the same time we, as the audience, get a sense of backstory, and the conventions of science fiction are such that we may expect a significant plot development immediately following this exposition. So too, are Dorothy's eyes opened to a world of magic and wonder in the scene playing in the background. That scene is also mapped out through the use of expository dialogue (Dorothy's quest) significant to the plot, and likewise the diegetic audience in Radio City is given information as to the next few plot developments in *Oz*.

The double spectacle of Technicolor and intertextual reference (and interplay) through CGI rendition explicitly engages a reciprocity and tension between narrative and narration (in this case taking the form of technological spectacles, and nostalgia). Like most of the backgrounds in *Sky Captain*, the theatre, and the 'projected' film itself are part of one big CGI backdrop, made up of stylised, 'authentic' 1940s environments and objects. When Garland then delivers her magical line: 'Toto, I've a feeling we're not in Kansas anymore', the provocation of the uncanny as her feeling is simulated through the deconstruction of the either/or aspect of the old and the new converging. When point-of-view is switched from the conventional shot/reverse-shot to that of the on-screen audience behind Polly and Jennings, coinciding with Dorothy's words 'We must be over the rainbow', the remaining dialogue takes place to the orchestral motif of *Oz*'s signature tune 'Somewhere Over the Rainbow'. Thus evocation of the past through the nostalgic use of this classic signature tune, along with the simulation of the past (set design, aesthetics, and sci-fi plot conventions) through contemporary technologies, sets the nostalgic tone for the rest of the film. In reference to another Millennial CGI franchise, *The Matrix* (Andy and Lana Wachowski, 1999), there is a clear sense that somehow, we are seeing the homely certainties of farmstead-era Kansas go 'bye-bye'; replaced by a residual otherness that nevertheless persists and permeates the simulated CGI rendition of the past. It is this affective dimension of uncertainty that evokes a sense of nostalgia in this scene, at least as much as the straightforward visual reference to *Oz*.

The sequence walks a fine line between diegetic coherence and rupture whereby, although the diegetic spaces are quite distinct, the movie-within-a-movie trick enables a textual engagement with the remediative possibilities of using such historically-specific material as *The Wizard of Oz* within a contemporary film text. This dialogue sequence – of vital importance to *Sky Captain*'s plot – happens to coincide with the moment when Dorothy wakes up in the Technicolor world of Oz. The division of spectacle and narrative once so keenly accepted within film scholarship as fundamental to understanding the difference between the presentational and representational, is shown here (through the interplay of dialogue, sound and textual layering) to be a misapprehension of the way narrative film in general often plays somewhere between the two. From this scene onwards, the interplay between the dramatic tension in *Sky Captain*'s romantic action-adventure plot and the child-like fantasy of *The Wizard of Oz* becomes almost comical. It is a pastiche of awakening innocence. The sense of wonder, often articulated in popular discourse as the 'magic of the movies', is aligned against the knowing manipulation of cinema history and the epistemic spaces of production and consumption. Spectacle is here only fully realised as an epistemic relation between the assumed knowledge of the older film on the part of the audience, and the expectation of what is to follow in the conventions of contemporary science fiction film. Whether the intention is to place Polly in a surrogate Dorothy role or not, the register of nostalgia is evoked through knowledge of *Oz*, and the kind of experience *Oz* seems to exemplify is the notion of 'movie magic' so beloved of Hollywood. Indeed, Polly is plunged, Alice-like (or Dorothy-like), into a world of science fantasy involving giant flying robots, ray guns and airborne aircraft carriers in scenes immediately following this one, thereby intensifying the scene and its resonance, through repeated viewing.[1]

Several writers have commented upon the tension of narrative and spectacle (notably, Pierson 2002) without really engaging with what is happening affectively when the epistemic space between audience and text is so carefully and self-consciously marked out. This self-consciousness is not just textual, but also bears out the lengths to which the reception process is anticipated in post-production assembly. It is not necessarily a case of meaning-intention, nor is it a question of a specific emotional effect intended to be elicited on the part of the producers. It does, however, explicitly negotiate an affective response that feeds off knowledge of the older film and its place within this new context, or at the very least, a feeling that old and new are being intentionally juxtaposed for a narrative-related purpose. It is non-specific intention in terms of emotion, as the nostalgic register engages any number of emotions from the incredulous to the sincerely moving. Therefore, what is needed in order to fully account for some of the problems raised here, in relation to the critical engagement with this sequence, is a theory of affective response that incorporates debates on spectacle – narrative and film culture from an audience perspective. What I mean by affective response is a negotiated relationship between excessive textual elements, that is, kitsch elements, and audiences, that engages the consumer epistemologically.

To give an example of this from the discussed sequence, Polly and Jennings are at one point seen in profile. This type of two-shot, when used, performs a function of establishing spatial relationships between the characters, and their relationship to the space around them. This two-shot is then intercut with a shot/reverse-shot, each actor framed close-up, to heighten the drama of the exchange in a familiar technique of emotional action/reaction between characters. In the two-shot, the spatial orientation has a point-of-focus: the object of fascination and the visual interest of this shot are located in the background. We, as the audience, are positioned as a member of the diegetic audience in Radio City, perhaps in the seat immediately behind the two characters and privy to their exchange. The interplay continues within the camera's field-of-vision, and various audio cues (snippets of dialogue and soundtrack) work as hints towards emotional response between characters. Facial expressions, whilst obviously present, are secondary to these cues, and the spectacle of textual interplay. Jennings describes the research facility in Berlin within which scientists were compelled to work for the Nazi regime: 'The things we were made to do there…', he says, in a barely plausible German accent.[2] He pauses. The Good Witch of the North first appears at this moment in the background, accompanied by the end of Jennings' sentence: '…terrible things'. He looks towards the screen (away from us) at that moment. There is the briefest of hints in that look, that the actor is cuing the interplay between the two story worlds. However, this may be put down to guilt in the acknowledgement of his past crimes (as a character, Jennings cannot bear to face Polly as he admits them) or more simply a reflection of real-world viewing patterns (those annoying little conversations that other people seem to have in the theatre that distracts viewing).

As he continues talking, the background film cuts to a close up of Dorothy, with Jennings' words, 'I shouldn't have come'. Then Dorothy says, 'Now I *know* we're not in Kansas', enticing us to speculate that an extraordinary occurrence is taking place outside of the characters' field of experience. It is, importantly, a play on experience of narrative that is ambiguous, thanks in large part to the integration of intertextual referencing and diegetic interplay. This is an example of the suspension of the unknown, in narrative terms, and occurs simultaneously on a number of levels and specifically, in two orders: diegetic and extra-diegetic. Firstly, Dorothy is awakening to new knowledge of the unfamiliar and magical world of Oz. This could more properly be considered as intra-diegetic knowledge that exists in partial ignorance of the world of *Sky Captain* (but, of course with reference to our own – both New York and Kansas are real places after all). The main players in *Sky Captain* and Polly in particular are discussing backstory to a Nazi plot. At this level, the Radio City audience, who is perhaps experiencing Oz for the first time, is following the plot development of Dorothy's journey, but is also about to experience first-hand an invasion of New York by flying robots. The audience watching *Sky Captain* are experiencing narrative developments primarily connected to the *Sky Captain* plot, but with the amount of textual interplay occurring, this plotting is tied-in to extra-diegetic elements that none of the characters (from either film) are aware of, but that are nevertheless self-consciously present in the film's audio-visual make-up (such as the self-reflexive film poster already discussed). The material state of digital cinema, its textuality, and its culture of revelation and knowledge through fan practices, cinephilia, and connoisseurship of production techniques and practices, all foreground rational material explanations for such marvellous moving images as found in both *Sky Captain* and *Oz*. This is especially so, perhaps, through photorealist aesthetics deployed in the mise-en-scène. Digital cinema of this sort is often the principle focus of ephemeral promotion material and DVD special features as being *the* important element of the audio-visual experience. What is important to note is that, as Richard Maltby discusses, the negotiation of this abstraction has been established in film theory as being discernible in all conventional narrative cinema; it is therefore not too great a leap from conventional debates on traditional narrative cinema (especially in terms of the tension between narrative and spectacle) to speculate an indicative dialectical relation between narrative and narration common to both digital and celluloid formats in the history of narrative film. Maltby notes:

> The camera records a field of vision from a singular point of view, which is itself
> spatially contiguous to the space it records. In projection, however, the camera's

point of view is abstracted from its original spatial context and universalized for the audience, who, wherever they are sitting in the cinema, see the field of view from the same, by now abstracted, point of view. (1983: 12)

However, in the example from *Sky Captain*, we should note that there is a further abstraction in that the CGI elements of digital films approximate (or simulate) the very conventions of camera movement, mise-en-scène, depth-illusion, and two-dimensional abstraction that Maltby describes as 'abstracted point of view'. The 'recording' element is only ever partial, as most of the elements present on-screen never shared a space contiguous with the camera, and were added in post-production. It should also be noted, however, that in the context of a cinema screening, this partiality is then remediated through projection technologies that abstract point-of-view in similar ways to traditional film projection. Indeed, the CGI 'film' simulates conventional fields of filmed vision in order to approximate this effect through the use of conventional storyboarding and blocking. A case in point here would be the CG-animation feature *Shrek* (Andrew Adamson & Vicky Jenson, 2001). The sequence that springs to mind is the wrestling scene, in which 'blocking', 'camera' movements, and shot composition all adhere to conventions of televised wrestling, simulating an 'authentic' bout experience. Indeed, one may even go so far as to speculate that this type of cinema, and the particular pleasures that it evokes, illuminates Maltby's analysis of film in general, retrospectively. He speculates that: 'At the same time that they are most obviously viscerally associating with the image before them, the spectators are most concretely aware that they are watching an illusion' (1983: 19). This suggests that cinema in general, but CGI film in particular thanks to its simulational (in addition to representational) capacity, enables what David Chaney has described as the fulfillment of the audience's 'desire for vicarious authenticity' (1979: 130).

In turn, an affective response in film spectatorship materializes, one that Clement Greenberg claims existed in modernity long before Telotte's 'machine age': dating back to the industrial revolution and the urban acculturation of the proletariat that accompanied it. Greenberg defines kitsch as, among other things, 'vicarious experience and faked sensations. Kitsch changes according to style, but remains always the same' (1961: 10). And yet, for all its fake-ness, and vicarious distanciation, one may draw an element of pleasure in affective responses, such that kitsch tends to evoke. In this example, the kitschy element comes in the form of a spectacle of multi-layered narration strategies – visual, audial, and emplotted. For Chaney, 'the spectacular provides an opportunity for a member of the audience to participate in and yet be distanced from someone risking his life crossing the Niagra falls' (1979: 130).[3] This, for all the elitist protesting that Adorno offers in this chapter's second opening epigraph, is a crucial concern in terms of what cinephilia is, what it does, and how it works. Broadly speaking, in narrative cinema the suspension that exists between material condition and two-dimensional abstraction is the arena in which the interplay between textual elements, cultural knowledge, and dialogue between different narratives converge into a larger hypertext. This is borne out in our example from *Sky Captain*.

The sequence raises a number of questions that may be familiar to readers acquainted with debates on cinematic spectacle, special effects, and their tension with narrative in the most conventional sense. Although some of these questions have already been addressed in superficial terms, it is useful to highlight these explicitly, in relation to feature films that extensively use CGI in their textual make-up. For example, what makes self-conscious effects so self-conscious? How can we tell? How are such visual effects presented? What relationships do such spectacles have with the narrative of the films in which they appear? How are these elements formally organised or constituted on the screen? Can we say that such spectacles are constituted by the consumer (or do we still need to rely on somewhat old-fashioned theoretical notions of the spectator as constituted by the text)? In any event, in what ways might we speculate that the consumer's sensibility is addressed or solicited? Can we say, therefore, that an aesthetic intention of the producers of such films is made public through control of CGI elements? And finally, what role does intertextuality play and how is it perceptible in such self-conscious uses of CGI? The rest of this chapter will be devoted to addressing these questions in relationship to cinephilia.

The first thing that is noticeable about these questions is that they are tied to specific themes – most notably, spectacle, consumer knowledge and sensibility, and perceptibility. Theoretically speaking, the unifying notion for these themes might well be considered that of 'excess'. Spectacle is an excessive element of the text that allows it to be differentiated from other elements through an excess of (extra-filmic) knowledge, for example, or certain cultural practices such as connoisseurship and fandom that rely on excess for their very existence and differentiation from the mainstream. Leger Grindon, in 'The Role of Spectacle and Excess in the Critique of Illusion', has noted that 'As critical concepts the broad range and ambiguous nature of spectacle and excess have hindered precision in thinking about the cinema and in especially studying the film image' (1994: 42). However, my own approach to excess as a unifying notion emphasises the way excess is related to vicariousness, vicarious experience, and the pleasures invoked through the consumption of Chaney's 'vicarious authenticity'. By vicarious authenticity, I suggest that Chaney is addressing the pleasure of the disposable, the everyday or the superficial that film spectacles can bring to the consumer. There are precedents to this concept. Pierson has identified within contemporary discourses of spectacle, a 'spectatorial economy in which spectators experience visual display and illusion as something so overwhelming that they are completely at a loss to make critical or evaluative judgements' (2002: 7).

However, I agree with her critique of this discourse, in that the vicariousness of such spectacle does not necessarily negate the pleasures and felt experiences gained through their consumption. My previous work on CGI posits the perspective that CGI is perceived as a marker by and for which evaluative judgements are made by audiences who are by-and-large accustomed to such aesthetics:

> Through exposure to documentary footage of the film's production, or access to the director/producer's commentary on the meaning of the images on screen, a system of revelation and contemplation is set in motion: the spectator's eye is trained to 'spot' the CGI. (Singh 2007: 543)

Very often, this is informed by an 'excess', signified by the CGI element of the filmic material itself. However, following Pierson's (and Grindon's) persuasive argument, the term 'excess' is by itself far too simplistic and mechanical to describe the phenomenological affective element that is being demonstrated through this kind of aesthetic and cultural recognition. It suggests that such elements be *in excess of something*, a standard, which necessitates certain subjective criteria and value judgements that are impossible to maintain universally. 'Excess' is the discursive twin of 'spectacle' in this sense, and the two concepts are remarkably intertwined in theoretical traditions. However, the practice of communicating (and reading) such signification is a complex relationship that needs to be addressed. As Pierson states, film theorists have tended to stick to a formulation about spectacle that draws from two assumptions. Firstly, spectacle 'elicits an emotionally regressive, primarily sensory response from spectators'; secondly, spectacle 'draws attention to itself as a self-conscious mode of visual display that is recognised in those terms by spectators themselves' (2002: 8). It is this second assumption that forms the basis of questions asked in this chapter, as the self-conscious element is arguably the thing that puts the 'special' into special effects, and is often the thing that fans enjoy looking for and debating. Otherwise, following critics such as Tom Gunning (2004 [1989]), Stephen Prince (2004) and others, we may counter that all filmic effects (including the very basic abstraction of point-of-view effect) are 'special' in some way, as they involve 'tricks' of some kind – optical, phenomenal, affective, or epistemic.

This suggests that the first assumption noted by Pierson is only ever partially supported: emotional regression is one possible state that emerges from the emotional objects of film experience, which then potentially elicit affective responses from audiences.[4] There have been, of course, several attempts over the years to theorise these assumptions as a viewing relation within which the film pre-exists the audience and the cine-subject is constituted as an effect of the film text. However, as Richard Maltby suggests, rather than convert this relationship into a determinist one between film-cause and spectator-effect, 'We should try to preserve the paradox that the camera's presentation encourages the viewer's participatory identification with the performances it presents at the same time that it demonstrably reveals itself as artificial' (1983: 20–1).

In this sense then, the artificiality of the events and textual elements on-screen does not take away from the vicarious pleasure experienced through their consumption, and, if anything, add to the specific pleasure of consuming film spectacles. The 'performances' that Maltby discusses here have fundamentally more to do with film's ability to suspend fiction and the real world, rather than those of the actors performing roles in front of the camera. That said, this kind of performance (by actors, in a character role) itself engages specific viewing practices such as those theorised as species of fandom. The pro-filmic elements to which Maltby refers include the mise-en-scène, camera movements, and textual layers existent at both the perceptible and imperceptible level. It is largely the role of the spectator to piece together the spatial and phenomenal differences between the two-dimensional screen space and the three-dimensional space in which the spectator exists. It is even evident at the level of narrative, as David Bordwell and Kristen Thompson suggest: 'The story ... is a mental reconstruction *we* make of the events in their chronological order and in their presumed duration and frequency' (1979: 52; emphasis in original). To this extent, the 'process of constructing a fiction is formally retrospective: it requires a distance between the fictional events and the spectator who puts them to use' (Maltby 1983: 22). This is largely a matter of consenting to the formal conventions of cinema-going but may also be contingent upon knowledge of the film in particular, and of film (and film culture) in general.

In this regard, my position is deeply indebted to Christian Metz and his essay '*Trucage* and the Film'. Metz expands significantly upon the notion of the 'trick' film in early cinema, usefully positing it within a cultural and industrial framework. Following Metz, in a sense all film is a vast *trucage*, or special effect, and the spectator is not only constituted as a viewing subject through a linguistic (or discursive) system of the cinema, but also through participation in an epistemic event. As we have already seen, this is a theoretical perspective related to the illusory nature of cinematic point-of-view, but this aspect is not necessarily fundamental to the notion of cinematic *trucage* as a whole. This is because Metz crucially demarcates a difference between 'various optical effects obtained by the appropriate manipulations, the sum of which constitutes *visual*, but not *photographic*, material' (1977: 657; emphasis in original). We may also say then, that *trucages* are inclusive of the photographic, and therefore, incorporate the cinematographic. It is a wide remit that Metz allows for in his definition of what constitutes the *trucage*, and the translator's note of his article on this is quite revealing: 'The word "trucage" usually translates as "trick photography" in the singular and "special effects" in the plural. But Metz places many terms, including these, under the rubric of *trucage*, and I am therefore retaining the French word' (François Meltzer in Metz 1977: 657).

Metz cites the wipe, the fade, the dissolve and so on as examples of visible optical effects that are not images or representations by themselves; whereas, soft focus or slow-motion are examples of effects that are manipulations of images. Both, however, come under the rubric of *trucage* as elements of the 'image track' that are not representational images themselves. I have discussed specific examples of some of these above, all of which may be simulated through CGI technology – very often as kitschy homage to obsolete technologies. Francis Ford Coppola's *Bram Stoker's Dracula* (1992) demonstrates interesting examples of this throughout. The film's narration feeds off notions of authenticity of experience (old film stock, sepia tones, burlesque film shows) reminiscent of the earliest cinema, and fidelity to the novel (in both content and the way that content is delivered). The novel contains myriad references to media technologies, and attempts to simulate these in both the kinds of things referred to (typewriters, picture shows, dioramas, etc) and the way that it is written (simulation of letter writing, etc). This again suggests the role of simulation in traditions of film – this time, with the additional example of cross-media similarity (literary film adaptation, in this case). Quentin Tarantino's *Death Proof* is a more recent example (2007), using CGI post-production to simulate cheap film stock of the kind that many independent filmmakers used in Grindhouse exploitation movies in the 1970s. This effect is used in this case to invoke a nostalgic register for the audience, as a visual signifier for a film production process of the past that no longer exists and therefore attempts to signify some sort of authentic homage. Similarly, *Sky Captain*'s overall aesthetic is clearly an attempt to simulate the soft-focus look and feel of the classic Hollywood period.

After Metz's brief outline of the conceptual ground, he then moves on to an insightful statement in relation to this, worth quoting in full:

> The 'visible material of transitions', to quote Etienne Souriau, is always extra-diegetic. Whereas the images of films have objects for referents, the optical effects have, in some fashion, the images themselves, or at least those to which they are contiguous in the succession, as referents. (1977: 657)

As already noted above, visible CGI elements within live-action film are doubly abstracted in this process. They are not contiguous with the spatial location of the camera and recording medium (data is transferred from recording hardware into editing packages as digital information). They are equally in common with traditional optical effects such as visual transitions, not contiguous with the filmed images themselves. There are exceptions to this: CGI manipulation (computer-manipulated, rather than generated, imaging) allows for certain contiguity, as with the soft-focus effect on the two faces in profile, as well as the sepia-like tone within the colour scheme in the aforementioned two-shot in *Sky Captain*. The film screen in the background and its images are added separately, and are therefore of a different order. Nonetheless, according to Metz's definition, both effects may be considered *trucages*. This in itself presents its own problems. For example, and as the translator of '*Trucage* and the Film' notes, Metz uses the flexible term *trucage* to discuss all kinds of process effects, printing, celluloid, camera, and editing effects in his argument. Whereas this may cause problems in terms of generalist versions of what the *trucage* is and does, we may say that CGI technology is often found at every stage of the production process in contemporary film culture, and therefore may be included in the discussion. In fact, Pierson has noted this factor on a number of occasions, in discussions on manipulation, generation, and post-production image assembly (1999a, 1999b, and 2002). Usefully, Metz anticipates this generality in his definition by giving names to different types of *trucage*. For example, the dissolve is an effect that utilises two images superimposed upon one another to generate the effect, but 'at no time will the spectator see the optical effect *only*; he will see images *affected* by a special effect, like a type of semiological exponent' (1977: 660).

Therefore, in terms of dissolves as *trucages*, affect is an aesthetic category suspended only for as long as image and manipulation are simultaneous. Again, this may be simulated by CGI, as in the title sequence of *Sky Captain*. Here we see an amalgam effect comprised of familiar fade-in/circular dissolve/iris effects, of a kind common to both science fiction films and to films of the classical period more generally. What is interesting here, however, is that it is all CGI-rendered: images and effect. It is true that the effect would not be visible without the images, and yet, because the images were created within a virtual space, the successive frames that feature in the transition make up a 'third' image themselves. With this type of optical effect, Metz concludes that they are 'enunciation markings' accumulated through the history of cinema. In this argument, one senses that Metz is to an extent pre-empting the narrative vs. spectacle debate:

> They belong to the narrative, not to the story; to the telling process, and not to the told. And yet we shall see that, despite this principle, the real working of the film often brings them into play, at least in part, for the benefit of the diegesis. (1977: 663)

This suggests that Metz thought of *trucage* as fundamental to, and not separate from, the storytelling process. Spectacle has both presentational and representational aspects, and therefore as mentioned earlier, narrative and narration, or story and discourse, are here conflated to an extent. The notion of cinematic spectacle (of cinematic 'tricks' in general) then, is inseparable from the notion of cinematic narrative in narrative cinema. What is most interesting here, in terms of cinephiliac practice, is that the self-consciousness inherent in many (if not all) special effects is, for Metz, constituted through knowledge of that effect, because of the proliferation of access to the film's production history through peripheral means. In other words, it operates as much extra-diagetically as it does diegetically.

This approach is not exactly new in Metz and has its roots in the critical theory of earlier thinkers such as Theodor Adorno. As Pierson points out:

> Adorno argued that Hollywood represents a particularly powerful ideological apparatus because the pleasure audiences experience through the consumption of cinematic spectacle reinforces their appreciation of the role that technology plays in the 'progress' of all industry (not just the film industry). (2002: 8)

As Adorno himself states in his essay 'The Schema of Mass Culture':

> A poetic tremor is expected of every example of emphatic objectivity. The 'Oh!' of astonishment which the objective close-up still stifled is blurted out by the lyrical musical accompaniment. The tremor lives off the excess power which technology as a whole, along with the capital that stands behind it, exercises over every individual thing. This is what transcendence is in mass culture. (2002a: 63)

More recently, work on fan cultures and fandom (for example, Jenkins 1992; Hills 2002) has addressed the power of fan communities and activities to disseminate knowledge about cultural objects such as films down to the finest details. Arguably, one aspect of this approach to fandom negates the idea of a systemic base of ideology. Instead, a more fluid system is evident, engaging what de Certeau describes as 'secondary production' or 'tactics' of use that go against the grain of exploitative production strategies of corporate or institutional bodies; he goes on to suggest that 'strategies are able to produce … and impose … whereas tactics can only use, manipulate' (1984: 30). Tactics are articulated in everyday life, in everyday use, and there is a kind of 'poetics' in making do, adapting, cannibalising and customising that feeds off the very same excess power discussed by Adorno. What is interesting to note here is the vicarious nature of such excess that seems to lie in the ground somewhere between these two theoretical positions that provides the material for the cultural practice of audiences engaged with special effects. This vicariousness stems from the self-consciousness that draws the audience to it in attention – it is not that we are, in aesthetic terms, necessarily conscious of the effect, but that it is itself self-conscious.

Pierson's work usefully centres on the specialised knowledge afforded the connoisseur or 'buff'. She suggests that the desire of the buff to cultivate technical knowledge about the way cinematic spectacle is produced is a desire to break from the institutional convention of the cinematic spectator as passive consumer. However, she also points to the articulation of ideology in this desire, by returning to Adorno: 'He also saw in this desire the work of ideology, which simply functions to reproduce more appreciative consumers without bringing them any closer to having "even the slightest influence" on the production process' (2002: 8). There are a couple of facets to Adorno's position (a position that Pierson does not necessarily subscribe to, incidentally) that should be noted here. One might argue, quite legitimately, that most cinema-goers have no desire or will to actually influence film production in a direct sense. One of the pleasures specific to the experience of attending the cinema theatre is that conventional premise of letting the film 'happen to you'. It is an ostensibly passive form of spectatorship, and yet, Adorno has indicated a contrary impulse in certain cinema-goers, or buffs, in that they desire to break from this passive mode and engage critically. Still, there is no guarantee that even this kind of 'specialised' spectatorship pre-empts a desire to affect the production process. It is an *active* spectatorship without an *interactive* participation (a subtle but complex difference, demonstrated for example, in the very different ways consumers engage with film and videogames respectively, in the most general sense). It is a sign of the intricacies of fandom and different aspects of 'general' and 'specialist' audiences (who cannot be identified in any meaningful way, because people tend generally to be fans of different things at different times or simultaneously) that the terms active and passive are not mutually exclusive. What is usefully exposed through Adorno's approach, however, is an internal contradiction of consumption, as well as the central contradiction of commodity fetishism that suggests both passive and active consumer practices are sometimes engaged in simultaneity.

It is a classic tendency of the Marxist formulation of commodity fetishism that the relationship that consumers have with commodities within the specific mode of consumption known as late capitalism is characterised as fundamentally *affective*. The commodity itself is given a value beyond its use; the consumer is defined through his/her phantasmagorical relationship to the product in this formulation yet this relationship which defines the consumer is nonetheless felt to be a real relation. This felt, 'real' relation is an aspect of film spectatorship that is rarely given space in contemporary theoretical discussion, possibly because of the undue importance of projection models and mechanical identification processes that defined 1970s Apparatus Theory. The shortcomings of such models in considering the relation between film and spectator, understandably, have often been the focus of criticism. However, as stated by the editors of this current volume, a more thorough-going engagement with the notion of cinephilia as a practice to usefully deal with such questions in a more immediate, relevant or meaningful way, is long overdue. In no small part, the technological innovations of the last couple of decades (and particularly of broadband availability in telecommunications) have meant that the need for this meaningful engagement has a sense of urgency.

A number of technological developments have signalled the rise of digital cinema during the last twenty-five years or so, and which have contributed to its exponential growth in the industrial landscape of popular cinema. Digital sound configurations such as Dolby and THX have enabled filmmakers to design soundscapes to match spectacular visual creations. Digital, non-linear editing formats such as Avid and Final Cut Pro have utterly transformed the assemblage of the moving image, and have affected production decisions from storyboard through to post-production and promotion. More recently, the development of digital film distribution has addressed the commercial need for the conservation of copyright and the elimination of film and video piracy. Perhaps the most visible signifier of digital cinema for the spectator, however, can be found in the proliferation of CGI in mainstream film – both in spectacular and in 'realistic' uses. If spectacle may be considered kitsch's most encompassing or dialectical moment, then surely CGI is spectacle's least-kept secret.

While spectacle does perform a significant role in addressing the spectator, the issue that drives both demand for, and supply of, cinematic spectacles with ever-increasing impact, is the relation between the discerning consumer and the production of narratives. This is primarily articulated in what Paul Lunenfeld has described as the 'sheer plenitude of narrative, exemplified by the glowingly accessible archive of everything' (2004: 151). This relation is ultimately the felt real relation of spectator with text – in short, cine-subjectivity. However, this 'subject' has undergone a transformation, the specific nature of which is subject to remediation in both the technological sense, and in a 'distancing effect' sense. The contemporary relation between consumers and the narratives they consume is made accessible for the spectator, partly due to the excess of the CGI's spectacular tendencies, an excess that betrays 'kitschiness' through its very proliferation.

Approaching the problem of authenticity in relation to cinephilia (and, to an extent, the production of 'meaning' by which people in the most general sense try to make something of the narrative and imaginal strategies of a film), we need to start thinking about the CGI film as a manifestation of kitsch. Kitsch is a complex notion that accounts for the elision of critical engagement with cultural objects, and yet rests on the instantaneous emotional impact upon its consumer. To clarify, 'elision' in this context refers to the separation of critical reflection and consumption. This is to describe and elucidate the functionality of kitsch as an interpellative, dialectical phenomenon, without relying on outdated accounts of passive spectatorship or abstraction of spectator subjectivity by favouring the secondary meaning of 'elision', which would connote a straightforward suppression.

The subversion of 'distancing' or separation as a necessary element in critical thought (as well as Critical Theory), and its appropriation as an ideological affect, is crucial to understanding the role of perceived subjectivity in the everyday practice of critical spectatorship. Without this notion, we necessarily fall back into Max Weber's *wertfreiheit*, or 'value free work'. This is not a tenable position in a discussion of value and valuation, especially when kitsch may be used as both critical adjective and as a signifier of value. Several critics have discussed this notion of the separation of reflection and consumption in light of movements in popular culture (for instance Adorno, Calinescu [1987], Sontag [1982]) but these discussions are few and far between. They are separated by more direct attacks upon kitsch by art historians and critics (for example, Greenberg [1961], Burgin [1986], Kulka [1996]) in the sphere of high art production. Therefore, what is needed to engage with the feeling of subjectivity, and the felt relations between consumer and commodity in the light of kitsch affect, is a reconciliation of the dialectical nature of authenticity as both jargon for the 'real' and as manifestation of the imaginary.

Here, of course, I refer specifically to Theodor Adorno's essay *The Jargon of Authenticity*, a criticism of Heidegger's essentialist existentialism and more importantly, a development of, and play with, Benjamin's notion of the authentic. What becomes apparent in any discussion of the felt relations between consumer and commodity in the light of kitsch affect, is that one of the most immediately available kitsch commodities on offer within popular culture is the contemporary CGI film. The aforementioned scenes from *Sky Captain* function as exemplars of the ways in which the notion of authenticity may be both reconciled with and alienated from its relationship with reality and imagination in simultaneity.

As implied earlier in this chapter, it matters very little, it seems, whether or not the central problem for the filmmaker remains to be the task of convincing the audience that the images they are consuming are of real-world events, or that there is an indexical relationship between what we are seeing and the real world. Instead, authenticity in contemporary CGI films refers to the integrity of the film's aesthetic viability, its appropriateness to the film's story-world, and therefore its immediate apprehension on those terms. It is highly unlikely that spectators who would mistake the action sequences in *Speed Racer* (Andy and Lana Wachowski, 2008), for example, with the observable real-world phenomenon of Indie-car racing. Therefore, to reiterate a previous point concerning the materialisation of creative experience within fantastic milieu, we are already factored as an audience into that specific relationship via immediate emotional impact as typified by the affective properties of kitsch consumables.

The tension between the two drives of authenticity within CGI production (simulation and realism) as outlined by Pierson (1999a) appears now to be outmoded. The economy of knowledge associated with the relationship spectators have to CGI films now moves to the forefront in a kind of literal and figural mani-festation of what Marx called the 'appearance-form'. It is worth repeating here that knowledge of the value/valuelessness of the commodities that we consume is largely dependent upon that consumer relationship being a comfortable and pleasurable one. Of course, when it is (as it frequently is), the value shifts focus and is centred on that consumer relationship itself – that is, the site of *exchange*. Thus, the process of film consumption takes on the appearance-form of critical evaluation within discourses of authenticity (especially narrative plausibility) and usefulness (entertainment), whilst simultaneously valorising the simulational as an economic signifier (commercial success).

Sean Homer (2005) has argued that an historical materialist notion of the film as commodity is necessary to give full account of the *process* of the fetishisation of that commodity. That is, the investiture of value in the commodity, giving the commodity properties beyond the commodity as a thing-in-itself. It follows that film is not *just* film and requires that, whilst we do not have to necessarily say what it means, we are bound to the notion that it probably means some things to some people, that it is meaningful. In other words, it has the power to *move* its audience. If, in this common turn of phrase, this includes the idea that the film need not mean anything beyond being entertaining spectacle, it is still vital in negotiating the relation between the commodity (film) and the consumer (spec-tator-subject). This is the nature of that negotiation, the *felt* relation between consumer and commodity that enables the valuation of both film and spectator, and the pleasures that are engaged within that process. While spectacle does perform a significant role in addressing the spectator, the issue that drives both demand for, and supply of, cinematic spectacles with ever-increasing impact, is the relation between the discerning consumer and the production of narratives. As I hope to have demonstrated throughout this chapter, the contemporary rela-tion between film consumers and the narratives they consume is made acces-sible for the spectator, partly due to the very excess of the CGI's spectacular tendencies in popular cinema – an excess that betrays a 'kitschiness' through its very proliferation, and a pleasurable one at that.

NOTES

1   We should allow, of course, for the fact that not everyone who has seen this film has also seen *The Wizard of Oz*. An interesting case in point: I ran a workshop on spec-tacle at Bucks New University in 2007 using *Oz* and its evocation in this scene as an example. Out of a small class of around 20 students, average age 19, only two of them

had seen the film. Whether this phenomenon is largely based on a generation-shift or a shift in film culture itself is difficult to summarise. Inevitably, the intertextual reference was lost on most of the participating students. However, the overall reaction to the scene discussed was that something was going on here, largely to do with 'old films', childhood fairy-tales (and our recollection of them as adults) and the time that has passed since the 'olden times' of filmmaking (the students' own words). These students were clearly attempting to articulate the concept of nostalgia in relation to the representation of the passing of time, knowing it, and yet finding difficulty in expressing it – precisely one of the main points of this chapter.

2   He introduces himself by using a hard 'J' at the beginning of 'Jennings' instead of the expected soft 'Yu' – yet he still attempts to pass as a German national. This odd discrepancy feeds into the suspicious nature of the character, but may be put down to something as inconspicuous as having to use American phonetics in order to play successfully within the large US market. This is, granted, a speculation, but does call into question the visual and audio discourses on 'authenticity' that the film is attempting to express through its representational choices.

3   This is an issue I touch upon in *Film After Jung* in relation to Torben Grodal (1997)'s cognitive approach to the 'reality-status' of screened events. There, I discuss emotional response to Hitchcock's *Psycho*: 'Through a series of ingenious cuts and imaginative camera positioning, a naked and vulnerable Marion Crane has been murdered in cold blood before our eyes, and yet we know that she has not. This attitude is somewhat linked to Grodal's term, 'reality-status': an evaluation that enables us to make distinctions as to whether apparent phenomena are reality, fantasy, fiction, dream and so on' (Singh 2009: 109).

4   The theoretical differences between emotional objectivity and affective response in the phenomenology of film experience are issues that I discuss in detail in Chapters 4 and 5 of *Film After Jung* (2009).

REFERENCES

Adorno, T. W. (1997) *Aesthetic Theory*. London: Continuum.

_____ (2002a) *The Culture Industry*. London: Routledge Classics.

_____ (2002b) *The Jargon of Authenticity*. London: Routledge Classics.

Barthes, R. (1977) *Image/Music/Text*, London: Fontana.

_____ (1981) *Camera Lucida: Reflections on Photography* (trans. Richard Howard). New York: Hill and Wang.

Baudrillard, J. (1983) *Simulations*. London: MIT Press.

Bordwell, D. and K. Thompson (1979) *Film Art: An Introduction*. Reading, MA: McGraw Hill.

Burgin, V. (1986) *The End of Art Theory*. London: Palgrave Macmillan.

Calinescu, M. (1987) *Five Faces of Modernity*. Durham, NC: Duke University Press.

Certeau, M. de (1984) *The Practice of Everyday Life*. London: University of California Press.

_____ (1986) *Heterologies*. London: University of Minnesota Press.

Chaney, D. (1979) *Fictions and Ceremonies: Representations of Popular Experience*. London: Edward Arnold.

Davis, R. (2001/2) 'What WOZ: Lost Objects, Repeat Viewings and the Sissy Warrior', *Film Quarterly*, 55, 2, 2–13.

Greenberg, C. (1961) *Art and Culture: Critical Essays*. Boston: Bacon Press.

Grindon, L. (1994) 'The Role of Spectacle and Excess in the Critique of Illusion', *Post Script*, 13, 2, 35–43.

Grodal, T. (1997) *Moving Pictures: A New Theory of Film Genres, Feelings, and Cognition*. Oxford: Clarendon Press.

Gunning, T. (2004 [1989]) 'An Aesthetic of Astonishment: Early Film and the (In)Credulous Spectator', in L. Braudy and M. Cohen (eds) *Film Theory and Criticism: Introductory Readings*, sixth edn. Oxford: Oxford University Press, 862–76.

Hills, M. (2002) *Fan Cultures*. London: Routledge.

Homer, S. (2005) 'Cinema and Fetishism: The Disavowal of a Concept', *Historical Materialism*, 13, 1, 85–116.

Jameson, F. (1991) *Postmodernism, or, The Cultural Logic of Late Capitalism*. London: Verso.

Jenkins, H. (1992) *Textual Poachers: Television Fans and Participatory Culture*. London: Routledge.

Kulka, T. (1996) *Kitsch and Art*. University Park, PA: Pennsylvania State University Press.

Lunenfeld, P. (2004) 'The Myths of Interactive Cinema', in D. Harries (ed.) *The New Media Book*, second edn. London: BFI, pp. 144-56.

Maltby, R. (1983) *Harmless Entertainment: Hollywood and the Ideology of Consensus*. London: Scarecrow Press.

Metz, C. '*Trucage* and the Film', trans. F. Meltzer, *Critical Inquiry*, 3, Summer, 657–75.

Pierson, M. (1999a) 'No Longer State-of-the-Art: Crafting a Future for CGI', *Wide Angle*, 21, 1, 29–47.

_____ (1999b) 'CGI Effects in Hollywood Science-fiction Cinema 1989-95: The Wonder Years', *Screen*, 40, 2, 158–76.

_____ (2002) *Special Effects: Still in Search of Wonder*. New York: Columbia University Press.

Prince, S. (2004) 'True Lies: Perceptual Realism, Digital Images, and Film Theory', in L. Braudy and M. Cohen (eds) *Film Theory and Criticism: Introductory Readings*, sixth edn. Oxford: Oxford University Press, 270–82.

Singh, G. (2007) 'CGI: A Future History of Assimilation in Mainstream Science Fiction Film', *Extrapolation*, 48, 3, 543–7.

_____ (2009) *Film After Jung: Post-Jungian Approaches to Film Theory*. London: Routlege.

Sontag, S. (1982) 'Notes on "Camp"', in *A Susan Sontag Reader*. Harmondsworth: Penguin, 105–19.

Sperb, J. (2008) 'Cinephilia and History, or The Wind in the Trees By Christian Keathley' review, *Scope* 12, October. Available at: http://www.scope.nottingham.ac.uk/bookreview.php?issue=12&id=1077 (accessed 07/09/09).

Telotte, J. P. (1999) *A Distant Technology: Science Fiction Film and the Machine Age*. Hanover, NH: Wesleyan University Press.

CHAPTER ELEVEN

TURN THE PAGE:
FROM *MISE-EN-SCÈNE* TO *DISPOSITIF*
Adrian Martin

> The representational chamber is an energetic *dispositif*. To describe it and to follow
> its functioning, that's what needs to be done.
>
> – Jean-François Lyotard (1993: 3; translation amended)

GRAPHICS, STACKS AND MATERIALITY

It is always fascinating and instructive to return to a moment in history when a
change in the conditions of culture loomed on the horizon. In terms of international film culture – and the mode of it with which we live today – such auguries
reared up in the early 1990s. Thomas Elsaesser, in a position paper on the 'the
state of research and the place of cinema', spoke of 'the rapidity, apparent anar-
chy, and explosive force with which the so-called media and information "revolutions" have swept the cinema along with them'; he was thinking at the time
mainly of 'TV [and] the VCR', with a mere abstract nod, at the time, to the kinds
of 'virtual space' that computer technologies were to bring (1993: 44). Elsaesser
was atypical, in that period, for refusing to produce the standard, pessimistic
reflex as to the much-touted and entirely overrated 'death of cinema'; he speaks
instead of 'oxygen' (1993: 41), of revitalisation, of new possibilities. One particular research question, however, crystallises in his account: the nature of the
photographic image in an increasingly post-photographic world.

> As long as celluloid was its only basis, the image retained a physicality whose
> deceptiveness the electronic media underline from an altogether non-academic
> perspective. In front of the computer, for instance, no one speaks of images: only of
> graphics and animation. [...] With images reaching us as the analog video, and more
> recently, in a digitised form that is indifferent to its material manifestation, it becomes
> difficult, and therefore once more necessary to think of the image. (1993: 46–7)

In this period of the early 1990s, mainstream television still (as throughout much
of the advanced work in cultural studies of the 1980s) showed the way to critics

and theorists for the possible destinies of the image in the contemporary and future audiovisual landscape. Television formed a shared horizon for audiences and commentators alike – all of us more or less watching the same things on the same box-format – in a way that seems unimaginable, even quaint, from the far more dispersed and tactical vantage point of today's YouTube, Facebook and iPhone culture. In that period, cable or pay TV, and the new or exacerbated formats it invented, seemed like the cutting edge of a mass culture which could still bear that descriptor – before the termites of digital fragmentation well and truly went to work on textual forms and spectator-groupings alike. What may have seemed to commentators of the time as the cutting edge can now look to us, with hindsight, as a last gasp of a particular configuration of technologised popular culture. However, it remains for us to return to this moment of critical writing in the early 1990s and see whether, indeed, some sign of the times was being cannily intuited and formulated there.

For my part, I find such a sign not only in Elsaesser's far-reaching meditation on his profession, but also a remarkable text by Margaret Morse, 'An Ontology of Everyday Distraction: The Freeway, the Mall, and Television', which first appeared in the collection *Logics of Television*. The piece has a broad, cultural aim: to grasp the ways in which 'television is similar or related to other, particular modes of transportation and exchange in everyday life' (1990: 193). What grabs me, particularly in retrospect, is the concrete detail of Morse's analysis of the 'principles of construction and operation' (ibid.), and especially of '*passage* amid the *segmentation*' (1990: 200), at work in that last great bastion on broadcast television on the cusp between cable and digital: the news-magazine program.

> Television discourse typically consists of 'stacks' of recursive levels which are usually quite different in look and 'flavor'. These stacks are also signified at different spatial and temporal removes from the viewer and have different kinds of contents. Thus a shift of discursive level is also a shift of ontological level, that is, to a different status in relation to reality. Television formats then amount to particular ways of conceptualising and organising 'stacks' of worlds as hierarchy of realities and relationships to the viewer. (1990: 206)

We shall later consider the enormous prescience of this analysis of new-fangled television formats. For the moment, I want to juxtapose her superb word-picture of an audiovisual medium as a stack of worlds with Elsaesser's musing about the post-photographic image, fast becoming a matter of graphics and animation:

> Now it is not so much the reality-effect, but the materiality-effect of the cinema that is at stake, and with it, the questions of film theory, of the apparatus, of ideology and subjectivity may need to be rethought. (1993: 47)

Not the reality-effect but the materiality-effect? Not the tradition of the photographic index as classically associated with André Bazin, but rather the notion of cinema as fundamentally *artifice* – an artifice geared to the arousal of spectator-affects – as expressed, for example, in Daniel Frampton's trailblazing book *Filmosophy* (2006)? The idea, it seems to me, is so radical that contemporary theory today mounts a sophisticated rearguard action against it, as in the more recent work of Laura Mulvey. For her, the digital era – with its genuine potentiality to conjure or retouch absolutely anything – paradoxically 'allows a cinephilic meditation on the cinema's relation to reality … to continually rediscover the beauty, that Bazin compared to the flower or snowflake, of the indexical sign' (2009: 193). This is not mere nostalgia on her part for the 'lost cinematic'; for, as Elsaesser remarked, cinema's 'relation to the existence of objects and bodies in time and space, in this time and this space' (1993: 47) must also be considered a key part of any aesthetic, political or ethical commitment to mapping what he (among many others) has called *material culture*.

Nonetheless, it is precisely *materiality* – the ways in which we define it, and deploy it, in relation to cinema – which is at stake, and in flux, today. To pose it bluntly (at least at the outset), is materiality a matter of the reality registered within the film frame, or the reality of the frame (and everything we could include within the complex process of framing) itself? In response, I choose, polemically, to seize upon the following, somewhat gnomic pronouncement from Nicole Brenez, also first written in 1993, when she called in the pages of *Art Press* for (*après* Godard) a 'Bazinian exigency maintained at the heart of a type of non-Bazinian analysis that no longer takes the real as second nature or as the second nature of film'; in this avant-garde quest, Brenez estimated that, in fact, 'we remain still a little behind Bazin' (1997).

Are there any tools lying around for us to pick up and use in this non-Bazinian analysis? It is always a mistake to assume that new theory must always begin from a scorched-earth policy – which is the mistaken character of so much cyber-theory in the digital age – rather than scouring at ground-level for those glimpses of past models that have been overlooked, forgotten, or were never allowed to develop a future. The premonitory rumbles of a revolution in thought always come from far away and long ago; at last, from the vantage point of the present, we are able to hear and understand their echoes.

Morse's 1990 article provides one such example. In that text, Morse was attempting to define a (then) new media form in television which 'involves two or more objects and levels of attention and the co-presence of two or more different, even contradictory, metapsychological effects' (1990: 193). She distinguished this from a regime of 'split belief' and of 'sinking into another world' that characterises, in her view, 'the apparatuses of the theater, the cinema, and the novel' (ibid.). Her approach is richly useful for us today in the way it combines a very recognisable, but now rather forgotten, feature of 1970s film theory – the treatment by Jean-Louis Baudry (1978) and Christian Metz (1982) of *metapsychology* – with the manifold industrial and economic elements (and constraints) of a material culture case study. It is also uncannily prophetic in seizing upon another 1970s buzzword that has returned to us in a resurrected, newly energised way: the *apparatus* or, as I will call it for reasons that will soon become clear, the *dispositif*. Recall that Elsaesser, too, called for 'the apparatus ... to be rethought' (1993: 47). The time and opportunity for this rethink is now at hand.

CONTRAPTIONS

Two snapshots from the dawn of 2010:

1. A negative review of Abbas Kiarostami's *Shirin* (2008) in *Cahiers du cinéma* by Patrice Blouin – a perceptive critic who has been attentive, since the 1990s, in the pages not only of *Cahiers* but also of *Art Press*, to 'new media', post-TV forms like video games. Blouin recalls the way in which Kiarostami began the 2000s, in *Ten* (2002), with the 'audacious gesture' of attaching cameras to the left and right sides of a car and simply letting his cast members drive off to improvise their conversation, thus seeking precisely to 'do away with mise-en-scène' (2010: 74). And what replaces the traditional procedures of mise-en-scène – staging, dressing the décor, setting the lights, choreographing of the camera, guiding and cueing of actors? In a word: a *dispositif*, a fixed and systematic set-up or arrangement of elements (bodies, cameras, sightlines, moving object, passing cityscape) that enables what Blouin describes as an 'automatic recording' (ibid.).

2. Alongside all the 'best films of the year' lists run by cinema magazines the world over, a new sort of poll has started to gain prominence: it is geared to 'moving image highlights', and draws upon not only theatrical or festival screenings but also, and increasingly, Internet platforms. Here is what I contributed to one such poll: my delighted discovery of the website maintained by the group Pomplamoose (2010), on which Nataly Dawn and Jack Conte unveil a VideoSong (as they term it) for each of their new musical recordings. Pomplamoose offers a disconcertingly light-hearted flipside to the gloomy vision Jean-Luc Godard concocted, 35 years previously, for *Numéro deux* (1975) – wherein the shut-in, working-class inhabitants of a high-rise apartment complex are viewed only ever on unglamorous video footage framed within domestic TV sets positioned in the darkness of the full 35 millimetre image. For Dawn and Conte, the 'total environment' apartment has become a DIY home-studio (we rarely see anything beyond it), and this studio seems more like a children's playground than a prison or a hell. Their VideoSongs adhere to two exact rules of self-determined construction:

'What you see is what you hear (no lip-syncing for instruments or voice); and if you hear it, at some point you see it (no hidden sounds)' (theBestArts 2009). This *dispositif* – for that is exactly what it is – generates amusing gags: whenever Nataly overdubs herself singing (as she frequently does), we instantly jump to multiple split-screens – naturally, to maintain the integrity of the rules of the game. ('I'm a rule dogma kind of guy', remarks Conte in Dag 2009.) Fixed digital video cameras, set positions, restrictions on place and action: who could have guessed, in the days of *Numéro deux*, Chantal Akerman's severe *Jeanne Dielman, 23 Quai du Commerce, 1080 Bruxelles* (1975), or even Kiarostami's combative *Ten*, that a *dispositif* could be this much fun?

The mention of fun brings us immediately to a perhaps unlikely or surprising source for theorisation on the nature of current audiovisual *dispositifs*: the droll, often deliberately naïve or primitive French filmmaker and critic since the 1950s, Luc Moullet. In a 2007 article titled 'Les dispositifs du cinéma contemporain', he enumerates the strategies and tactics of the many films that are, in one way or another, as rule bound as Pomplamoose's VideoSongs or Kiarostami's recent films. A *dispositif* film – to fit Moullet's own idiomatic voice, I almost feel as translating it, in this context, as a *contraption* – is both a *conceit* (like the literary conceits of Georges Perec or other members of the Oulipo group [see Mathews 2003], writing an entire novel under the pre-set constraint of not using a particular letter of the alphabet), and a *machine*. Above all, it is a conceptual film (in the vein of conceptual art), a disposition (as the word is sometimes translated) that usually announces its structure or system at the outset, in the opening scene, even in its title, and then must follow through with this structure, step by step all the way to the bitter or blessed end.

Once regarded as an eccentric aberration of Peter Greenaway movies or avant-garde exemplars like Hollis Frampton's *Hapax Legomena* (1971/2), such procedures are now at the centre of the international art cinema – one need only look, among the progressive Asian films of the past two decades, at the work of Hong Sang-soo or Hou Hsiao-hsien, or (in Eastern Europe) the prodigious feature experimentation of Kira Muratova. Numbered sections (and even titles: *Five*, *Ten*, *Three Times*, *Three Stories*); intensive restrictions on camera angle and point-of-view; entire narrative structures built on a formal idea and its eventual, long-delayed pay-off (as in the final face-off of two close-ups concluding the Akermanian repetitions of Masahiro Kobayashi's *The Rebirth* [2007]); films built up from parts and layers and sections (a pop example being Todd Haynes's *I'm Not There* [2007] with its multiple Bob Dylans)...

This movement (if it can be called that) finds a succinct summary in one of the video-letters that Kiarostami contributed to the remarkable exhibition *Correspondences: Erice-Kiarostami* (2006/7): a lengthy series of digital images, landscape and urban views, filmed through a rain-spattered car window; each one slightly animated with a small, digital zoom-in reframing (but a reframing that shows or reveals nothing not immediately visible or evident); and a final image in the series announced as final precisely by having the windshield wipers erase the rain drops and cancel the *dispositif*. (Kiarostami is, as we have seen, fond of car *dispositifs*, as in the system of framings, entries, exits, scene dramaturgy, and cuts generated by the two-camera set-up on the front seats in *Ten*.) *Shirin* offers another bold *dispositif*: a lush Persian historical-mythological epic begins, we see its start and end credits, but for its entire unfolding we only hear this imaginary film off-screen, while we gaze at the faces of the many spectators – all women – who are watching it and reacting in their diverse ways. No matter – this is in fact part of the work's beguiling charm – that the women are not really sitting all together in a movie theatre (each was set up, separately, in Kiarostami's house), and that their reactions are triggered neither by watching nor even hearing the off-screen film-within-the-film named *Shirin*!

Cinematic *dispositifs* are often generated (Perec-style) from exclusions – refusals to play by this or that convention deemed corrupt or ossified by the filmmaker – and thus, to devotees or masochists, the immediately recognisable stylistic traits of many a modern director: the adherence to direct sound recording in Straub and Huillet, the de-dramatisation of performance in Pedro Costa, the absence of typical soundtrack scores in Tsai Ming-liang (where music only bursts forth in exaggerated song-and-dance sequences), the resolutely fixed camera in Sohrab Shahid-Saless ... In the vein of Moullet's article, we might also pinpoint predictable *dispositifs* that run out of steam and fall flat long before their finishing point (*I'm Not There*), or anti-contraptions like *Masculin-féminin* (1965) by that eternal, cheeky anarchist Godard, which announces 'fifteen precise facts' in its subtitle – and then proceeds to deliberately scramble the numbering, forget the conceit, and alter the structure mid-flight. (Numbers, including the dates of history, are always a lure, and a gag, in Godard, all the way to *Histoire(s) du cinéma* [1988–98] and its many film/video off-shoots.)

But we must immediately insist that a *dispositif* is not a mechanistic or rigid formal system: it is more like an aesthetic guide-track that is as open to variation, surprise or artful contradiction as the filmmaker (who sets it in motion) decrees. And it is not necessarily tied strictly or exclusively to the familiar style of an auteur: some directors change their *dispositifs*, slightly or radically, from work to work. The workings of *dispositifs* are often subtle and singular; and this approach allows us to move beyond the paralysing, shorthand designations that conventional criticism most often falls back on when casting a glance at post-1960 modernist cinema, labelling such films either Brechtian, minimalist, collages, or embroidered with a parametric narration (a notion which has been critically useful but rarely extends far or deeply enough into a complex film's textual logic).

A THOROUGHLY HETEROGENEOUS ENSEMBLE

The term *dispositif* is popping up in many places in English-language theoretical writing at present. Its feed-in to film studies is coming, simultaneously, from at least five sources – sometimes with overlaps, sometimes with confusions. But all these sources help to feed the richness of the concept: the theory of *dispositif* is itself a methodological *dispositif*! Indeed, it is useful to keep in mind that, in fields such as urban planning and in various branches of the social sciences, *dispositif* is a term used to describe such mundane set-ups in the everyday world as the operation and maintenance of traffic lights, or the organisation of rituals such as funerals (see Kessler 2006a) – and, thus, an entire social 'flow'.

Here are the main lines of *dispositif* inquiry feeding into cinema theory at present. Firstly, there is a return (for instance, in Kessler 2006b) to the meaning of the term in the foundational film theory texts of Jean-Louis Baudry where the term has a richer, more diverse sense than is often realised – partly due to a problem of its linguistic translation, as we shall see. Secondly, and perhaps most prevalently, there is a political-cultural deployment of the term that originated with Michel Foucault (most eloquently outlined in a 1977 interview), was taken in a particular direction by Gilles Deleuze (1992), and has been recently revived and expanded by Giorgio Agamben in his short book *What is an Apparatus?* (2009). Thirdly, and least cited, is Vilém Flusser's suggestive, shorthand use of the term, which seems to mix (without citation, and possibly purely instinctively) both Baudry and Foucault, especially in the sole major essay that this keen social commentator wrote (in 1979) 'On Film Production and Consumption' (see Flusser 2006; Martin 2009a). Fourthly, there is Jean-François Lyotard's (1993) enthusiastic and extensive deployment of the term to describe all manner of phenomena in the high period of his 'libidinal economy' theorising. Lastly, there is a use of the term that has crept in from art criticism, especially in relation to installation art since the pioneering work of Anne-Marie Duguet (1988), and this in turn has fed into recent film criticism addressing the film/art interchange.

Dispositif or apparatus? When film students imbibe second-hand, summary accounts of 'apparatus theory' (which is often cast out, in the same breath, as some outmoded relic from a delirious, continentally-infatuated moment of 'grand theory'), they are often learning (badly) to conflate two quite different, though necessarily overlapping, terms in Baudry's essays of the 1970s (English translations collected in Cha 1981), both of which came unfussily translated as apparatus. On the one hand, Baudry posed the *appareil de base*, the basic cinematic apparatus which consists of the tools and machines of camera, projector, celluloid, photographic registration, and the like. The *dispositif*, on the other hand, is instantly and necessarily more of a social machine for Baudry, a set-up, arrangement or disposition of elements that adds up to the cinema-going experience:

body in a chair, dark room, light from the projector hitting a screen. Baudry posed the movement between the two terms in this way: where the basic cinematic apparatus already includes the fact of projection, the *dispositif* adds in the spectator and all this implies. It has come to imply a great deal more since the era of Baudry's texts: to counter the somewhat abstract category of ideal or Platonic spectatorship, successive commentators have gradually added all the economic, architectural and social conditions in and around the movie theatre (single-screen or, more usually today, multiplex) – its proximity to or inclusion within a shopping center, for instance – that Flusser drolly outlined in his 1979 piece. However, where Flusser evokes a dark nightmare of social determinations, Jean-François Lyotard stresses the energetic, indeed libidinal dynamics of any given *dispositif*, from the human body itself to the 'representational chambers' of theatre, cinema and television.

It is on the broader level of political analysis that Baudry's formative contribution to film theory begins to intersect with Foucault and Agamben. Foucault did not get terribly far with the explicit or elaborated theorisation of his *dispositif* idea before his death in 1984, although much of his work, in retrospect, can be seen as developing it under other rubrics and through other models. In a long, much-cited interview, he proposed his plan of future research – especially as related to his projected, ultimately unfinished series on *The History of Sexuality* – defined as the study of a *dispositif*:

> What I'm trying to pick out with this term is, firstly, a thoroughly heterogeneous ensemble consisting of discourses, institutions, architectural forms, regulatory decisions, laws, administrative measures, scientific statements, philosophical, moral and philanthropic propositions – in short, the said as much as the unsaid. Such are the elements of the apparatus. The apparatus itself is the system of relations that can be established between these elements. Secondly, what I am trying to identify in this apparatus is precisely the nature of the connection that can exist between these heterogeneous elements. (1977: 195)

Agamben generalises the term even more decisively than this – while, at the same time, sharpening Foucault's fix on tracking the ways and means of subjectivisation, as well as what may fall beyond or resist such subject-making effects:

> I shall call an apparatus [in Italian, *dispositivo*] literally anything that has in some way the capacity to capture, orient, determine, intercept, model, control, or secure the gestures, behaviors, opinions, or discourses of living beings. Not only, therefore, prisons, madhouses, the panopticon, schools, confession, factories, disciplines, juridical measures, and so forth (whose connection with power is in a certain sense evident), but also the pen, writing, literature, philosophy, agriculture, cigarettes,

navigation, computers, cellular telephones and – why not – language itself, which is perhaps the most ancient of apparatuses – one in which thousands and thousands of years ago a primate inadvertently let himself be captured, probably without realising the consequences that he was about to face. (2009: 14)

The influence of art criticism on film analysis (as practiced by Bellour or Duguet [2002]) is important, because it aids in negotiating a fruitful passage between the vast social ensembles that Foucault and Agamben conjure, and those specific audiovisual works that also internally construct a system of relations between thoroughly heterogeneous elements. (Which is, by the way, exactly what Raúl Ruiz means when he refers to mise-en-scène in his work – or rather, the always multiple mises-en-scène that are possible in any staging or storytelling situation; see Ruiz 1999.) Erika Balsom, for instance, mixes Baudry with Foucault in order to discern, in the 16 millimetre projection-exhibitions of Tacita Dean, a 'new and different conception of medium specificity' created from the conjuncture of the 'economic and ideological determinations of the space of the gallery work in tandem with the material attributes of analogue film' (2009: 416).

When Morse cites 'the apparatuses of the theater, the cinema, and the novel' (1990: 193), or Bellour (2000a) invokes the contemporary 'quarrel of the dispositifs', they are ranging across all these working definitions of the *dispositif*. The cinematic *dispositif* today is no longer apprehended in the abstract or ideal terms elaborated by Baudry – it is not a matter of some totalised and totalising 'cinema machine' before or beyond the forms and contents of any specific film. Nonetheless, we must not lose sight of the essential elements of film production and consumption which Baudry (like Flusser) highlighted, and their basic metapsychological effects. These elements and effects are neither immutable nor all-determining, but they offer what we might call (after Kant and Eisenstein) a *Grundproblem* with which every film must work, whether it chooses to or is even aware of it. Thus, each medium (cinema, novel, theatre, art gallery/museum) has its broad *dispositif* – arising from a mixture of aesthetic properties and social-historical conditions – and each particular work can create its own rules of the game, its own *dispositif*.

Foucault's elaboration of the term, although not addressed to the nature of properties of aesthetic works, is in fact suggestive and helpful. According to him, in each *dispositif* there is both a *functional overdetermination* (each element in the heterogeneous ensemble 'enters into resonance or contradiction' [1977: 195] with the others, leading to constant and dynamic alteration), and a *strategic elaboration* – a need to recognise, deal with, and then take further the new, unexpected, unforeseen effects and affects produced by the essentially experimental, 'see what happens' workings of any *dispositif*. This is, as Lyotard stresses, the *positif* aspect of a *dispositif*.

SPATIALISING THE GAZE

Let us retrace, more slowly and gradually this time, the step that Patrice Blouin made in his *Shirin* pan from classical mise-en-scène to the modern *dispositif*. It is not a matter of declaring, in this progression, that mise-en-scène is dead, whether as a mode of filmmaking or of film criticism. Perfectly fine classical films are still made today (whether by Clint Eastwood or Lone Scherfig), and mise-en-scène criticism, as we have known and loved it, is far from exhausting the field, historical or contemporary, of its research (see Gibbs 2006; McElhaney 2009; Perkins 2009). Rather, the question is: has there been a certain tendency in cinema (and audiovisual production more generally), not necessarily only an invention of recent times, that has been marginalised or literally undetected by the protocols of *mise-en-scène* critique, with its inevitable, in-built biases and exclusions? A tendency which is not the opposite of mise-en-scène or its nega-tion, but a particular, pointed mutation of it? (Indeed, many auteur signatures – those of Bresson, Ozu, Angelopoulos, to take only a few classic art cinema examples – resemble the structure of a *dispositif*, even though auteurism, with its Romanticist attachment to a creed of unfettered creativity, has long fought shy of apprehending this intuition.)

Or – the most radical notion – does the concept of the *dispositif* name or point to something that is and has always been inherent in mise-en-scène – maybe even larger or greater than it, as an overall formal category? This is what Raymond Bellour suggested in 1997 when he proposed that *la-mise-en-scène* (as, with a literary flourish, he dubs it) is a classical approach that corresponds 'to both an age and a vision of cinema, a certain kind of belief in the story and the shot', but is ultimately only one of the available 'modes of organising images' in cinema (2003: 29). And if the *dispositif* idea should rivet our attention to anything, it is the modes of organising filmic materials: Christa Blümlinger, for instance, defines it as the 'spatial or symbolic disposition of gazes characterising a medium' (2010), where gaze refers to all manner of looks, orientations and perspectives (fictive, technological, spectatorial) – and this is a matter not only of our eyes but our ears, too. Naturally, within an art gallery – where directors including Akerman and Pedro Costa have literally disassembled some of their feature films and spatia-lised them across several screens in an architectural arrangement – the idea of *dispositif* as *installation* (and this can serve as yet another possible English trans-lation of the term) is obvious enough. But can we also project the concept, and everything it raises, back into the single-screen medium of cinema, illuminating this medium in a new way?

A key thrust of the machinic or systematic side of the *dispositif* concept is to remind us – a 1970s notion too quickly forgotten or repressed since then – that a *dispositif* is heterogeneous, that it is truly a matter of bits and pieces of very different substances brought into an often volatile working relation. For the great German critic Frieda Grafe (who died in 2002), all cinema – no matter how seemingly neutral or classical – came down to something resembling this: 'Only the calculated mingling of formative elements originating in various media, each with its own relative autonomy, generates the tension that gives the film life' (1996: 56). And she was, on this occasion, speaking not of any conceptual art installation but Joseph Mankiewicz's *The Ghost and Mrs. Muir* (1947)!

A televisual detour is again useful here. Again, Margaret Morse provided what was to be a prophetic vision of the audiovisual workings of our digital screen-media age:

> The representation of the co-presence of multiple worlds in different modes on the television screen is achieved via division of the visual field into areas or via the representation of stacked places which can be tumbled or squeezed and which, in visual terms, advance toward and retreat from the visual field of the viewer. Discursive planes are differentiated from embedded object-worlds via axes: the vector of eyelines and movements, and changes of scale along the z-axis of spatial depth indicate a proxemic logic of the shared space of conversation with the viewer. In contrast, embedded stories are oriented around x- and y-axes, actually or virtually by means of the field/reverse field of filmic, continuity editing. The primary logic of alternation in television segments is then not that of suture, as in filmic fictions, but rather that of communication with a spectator in various degrees of 'nearness'. (1990: 206–7)

Communication with a spectator, as theorised by Morse, is indeed a crucial aspect of the materiality of any audiovisual medium – a fact that is becoming increasingly evident to us today. At a conference on contemporary film and criticism at Reading University (UK) in September 2008, the brilliant cinema aesthetician Gilberto Perez, author of *The Material Ghost: Films and Their Medium* (1998), began his keynote address – which covered questions of point-of-view and direct address in movies from Buster Keaton to Andrei Tarkovsky – with a consideration of Barack Obama's spectacular stadium speech in the US. Perez, comparing Obama's mode of address with that of the typical television host or news reader, distinguished two glances or gazes in the then Senator's clearly very rehearsed performance: the look left and right to the stadium crowd, and the look straight ahead into the camera, thus addressed to the television audience. Obama's achievement, in Perez's estimation, was to fluidly draw together these two audiences – live and mediated – into the one mass.

Jacques Aumont's significant book *Le cinéma et la mise en scène* (2006) begins, in a similar vein, with a discussion of a key moment in the contemporary media politics of France: the farewell speech, on national television, of outgoing

President Valéry Giscard d'Estaing in May 1981 (2006: 6–11). (The best and longest YouTube snippet of this media event, labeled 'Giscard French President Goodbye France', is taken from a Raymond Depardon documentary.) It was an odd spectacle: from a mid-shot into a close-up of Giscard, before an indiscernible backdrop – and then suddenly a pull back, way back, by the camera, to show a rather unglamorous desk (complete with papers and flowers), an obvious set, and then Giscard awkwardly standing up, turning his back to the viewing audience, and marching off frame-left and off-screen – leaving the image bare and empty (like in an Ozu film) as the French national anthem played out to completion. It was a historic TV event that (as Aumont remarks) gave rise to numerous, popular, colliding interpretations: was it designed as an expression of Giscard's bitterness; was it an attempt by someone behind the scene to subvert the politician and his image; or was it a monumental example of overall ineptness and lack of planning?

Both Perez and Aumont present their televisual case studies as instances of mise-en-scène analysis – the kind of mise-en-scène which is (as Aumont puts it) *partout*, everywhere. A mise-en-scène of political speech – of the powerful addressing (unifying or dividing) the masses through the spectacle, based on the centuries-old model of the public rally, with its various modes of magnification (auditory, visual, architectural) of a central, authoritative figure; and a type of mise-en-scène common to televisual formats, from news broadcasts to variety shows. Species of mise-en-scène, in other words, that came into existence both before and after the advent of cinema, and now work alongside it, feeding into it. Indeed, for Aumont, the Giscard broadcast is an exemplary instance of at least two mise-en-scène: the politician's theatrical mise-en-scène overturned (wittingly or not) by the regard of the camera, by its movement in and out, by the commentative or interrogative mise-en-scène which this viewpoint introduces into the raw event that it renders.

This is a powerful displacement of traditional mise-en-scène analysis in the study of cinema – whether practiced by the French critics of *Cahiers du cinéma* and *Positif* in the 1950s, Andrew Sarris and his auteurist acolytes in America, or the British school that was first associated with *Movie* in the 1960s and is today enjoying a widespread, international revival, especially in relation to the magisterial work of V. F. Perkins. Traditional mise-en-scène analysis – precisely the kind that most university students are introduced to as a basic or essential tool of how to analyse a film – rests (as Aumont's 2006 book makes clear) on a simple but powerful assumption: that cinema is, above all, an *art*, an art form rather than (for example) a social discourse or a mass media form. No reasonable person today can doubt that cinema is indeed an art; but the real question is: is it *only* an art? And what would this question mean for its analysis and theorisation? However, even when cinema studies moves on (or up) to integrate historical, political and philosophical factors in its synoptic view of the medium, it tends to leave this area of close analysis (variously known as formal analysis, style analysis, detailed analysis or textual analysis) relatively intact and unquestioned at the art-medium level, as an aesthetic building block in our apprehension of cinema. It becomes a protocol, unquestioned and untheorised in any new or significant way.

TURN THE PAGE

One of the few texts to tackle the conceptualisation of mise-en-scène from other perspectives is Aumont's 2000 anthology, *La mise en scène*. Among the virtues of this book is its recourse to lesser-known histories of the discussion of film style, histories that differ significantly from the more rehearsed, enshrined and canonised histories emanating from France, USA or Britain. Instead, we are introduced to (for example) the work of Belgians Dirk Lauwaert and Frank Kessler; Shigehiko Hasumi and Tadao Sato in Japan; Sergei Eisenstein's overlooked theorisation of *mise-en-scène* in the Russian context of the 1930s and 1940s; brief but suggestive reflections by Pier Paolo Pasolini and Umberto Eco in Italy during the late 1960s; or the *Filmkritik* trajectory associated with Frieda Grafe and filmmakers including Harun Farocki and Hartmut Bitomsky.

Traditional mise-en-scène analysis is what I have elsewhere (Martin 1992 and 2009b) diagnosed as *expressive* in its orientation. When the poststructuralist revolution of the 1970s and beyond contested expressive theories, a new generation of critic-theorists tended to junk expressive tendencies *in toto*, replacing them with other models: an *excessive* model of film style, for example, derived from modern psychoanalysis and inspired by the unruly dynamism of psychic drives and processes, controlled or mastered by no artist (however great). It is not now a matter of turning back the clock to what film studies once was before the semiotic revolution. It is clear that the panoply of terms, functions and figures that derive from expressive aesthetics – artist, artwork, craft, masterpiece, artistic achievement – have never truly left us, never will, and never should. There is still – as Elsaesser once remarked – something powerful left over, some aesthetic force, some 'pleasure that seems to have no substitute in the sobered-up deconstructions of the authorless voice of ideology' (1981: 11). It is our duty to find an account that is worthy of the complexity of this artistic experience – an account which, at the same time, encompasses the manifold modernities and post-modernities of cinema that the theory of the 1970s (and beyond) primed us to grasp. This is where the notion of *dispositif* can help, and challenge, us in trying to bring these intellectual traditions together.

What is the central problem with traditional mise-en-scène analytics, of the kind bequeathed to us by the famous critical movements of Paris, London and New York, the kind that once upon a time illuminated for us so powerfully the works of a Minnelli or a Mizoguchi, a Visconti or a Sternberg? This problem has two aspects. As the Swiss critic-theorist François Albera has expressed it, classical mise-en-scène, at the height of the rhetoric associated with it, is meant to 'capture the invisible soul of things and manifest them in a form' (2000: 228). To put this in slightly more mundane terms, the classical *gesture* of cinematic creation – what is literally involved in the act of a director moving around actors and a camera and arranging the scenic elements on set or on location – is construed as one of 'organising, in some way, what is unorganised' (2000: 228), of *giving form to what is initially formless*, chaotic, dispersed. The director pulls together all these elements and, beyond a mere act of ordering or orchestration, transforms them through the regard of the camera and the way it defines the field before it. Hence, for example, Australian critic Barrett Hodsdon's notion (1992) of the epiphanic *transformative moment* in mise-en-scène (most often carried by a camera movement or a physical gesture), which is so crucial to the cult of cinephilia.

The idea of creating form from the formless is, properly speaking, a fully Romantic idea, and it corresponds, at this fundamental level, to the philosophy and ideology of grand Romanticism. And as far as film criticism may have moved, in many of its postures and assumptions, from the trappings of the Romantic code, it nonetheless remains beholden to and entrenched within it. In this sense, the legacy of Alexandre Astruc's famous notion of the *caméra-stylo* corresponds not only to the movement of the Romantic writer's pen, but also a displacement of the Romantic instant of the painter's inspired brushstroke. Yet, as Bellour (2000b: 119) has pointed out, there was always a stark cleavage between two ideas or tendencies in Astruc's thinking, as distinct from his filmic practice. Where the *caméra-stylo* was a concept projected into the future, mise-en-scène was for him a fully classical, even retro ideal: that was the only kind of cinema (often adapted from literature) he himself made. It is more on the side of the conceptual *dispositif* than the freewheeling *caméra-stylo* that the ex-cinema of the future – i.e. the cinema of now – is to be found.

The critique of this first aspect of the traditional concept of mise-en-scène thus opens one door: the challenge to think of what pre-exists the moment of shooting – whether we think of this along the documentary category of the profilmic, or some other distinct stage of the artifice of filmmaking – as itself already replete with all kinds of form (and meaning). One result of this line of thought has been the new concept of a *social* mise-en-scène that has been pursued, variously, by Albera (2000), Kessler (2000), Perkins (in his pathbreaking 2005 essay 'Where is the World? The Horizon of Events in Movie Fiction'), Jean-Louis Comolli (2004), Deborah Thomas (2005), and myself (2009c). I will not say much more about it here but, suffice to say, a social mise-en-scène is fully in play in the examples of mediatised public politics deployed by Perez and Aumont: the mass stadium rally and the 'intimate' Presidential farewell alike are already stagings as complex (if not quite as artful) as those by John Ford or Stanley Kwan.

The second aspect to the problem of classical mise-en-scène analysis has been tackled, in a far-reaching and rigorous way, by Raymond Bellour since the early 1990s, when he began co-editing *Trafic* magazine (founded by Serge Daney) and turned his attention back to cinema – sometimes quite classical cinema – after a long period attending to the revolutions in video and new media art. This work has culminated in his remarkable recent *magnum opus, Le corps du cinéma* (2009). Bellour, it is safe to speculate, was no doubt troubled by the limited scope and reach of the mise-en-scène tradition, especially as it filtered down to us many decades after its heroic age. Not only did it restrict itself to a rich but ultimately small body of classical works, especially associated with the 1950s; it also stopped short of those elements in otherwise classical works (those of Hitchcock, for instance, or Ritwik Ghatak) that were on the very border of classicism, or clearly broke free from it (see McElhaney 2006). Traditional mise-en-scène criticism had little purchase on much (even most) that had happened in cinema beyond the advent of 1960, all the New Waves of the world, not to mention its *avant-gardes* – thus burning altogether the longed-for bridge between cinema and the experiments of the new media. In this, Bellour recreated and pushed forward the critique once vociferously voiced by André S. Labarthe in a 1967 *Cahiers du cinéma* text ominously titled 'Death of a Word': for Labarthe, by that moment in cinema history, 'mise-en-scène is not only mise-en-scène, but also the contrary' of how it had been originally conceived in the days of Louis Delluc (1967: 66).

Bellour puts the matter succinctly (2000b: 112): in the cinematic history of the term mise-en-scène, too much attention has been paid to the *scène* – its theatrically-derived origin – and not enough to the *mise*, to the fundamental process of putting in place, the organising of elements. To think of (narrative) cinema, in a foundational gesture, as a matter of theatrical *scenes* – however transformed by the work of the camera and the expansive nature of the set or environment – is already a crippling limitation; yet it is one which much mise-en-scène criticism happily assumes. For with the assumption of the centrality of the scene comes a great baggage, which is precisely the baggage of classicism in the arts: continuity, verisimilitude, the ensemble effect in acting performance, narrative articulation, the necessity for smoothness and fluidity, centering, legibility and formal balance ... which can encompass the richest kind of classical expressivity (that of Jean Renoir, Max Ophuls or Nicholas Ray) or, just as easily, be shut down into a merely professional, functional-instrumental craft. At this point in 'expanded cinema' history, the definitional limitation of mise-en-scène as an old-fashioned tool – its almost fetishistic, quite unrealistic emphasis on the moment of the shoot in cinema, when the camera-take (as pen mark or brush stroke) transforms the scene – has become all too apparent. Where do pre-production and post-production – all the forms of preparation and montage – figure in this divine circuit of Romantic creativity? How can a theory of style or form in cinema – an aesthetic of cinema – ignore production design (in all its levels), picture editing, and the construction of a sound track? (Mise-en-scène criticism, at its simplest and most naïve, is indeed a relic of the – sometimes lamentably revived – 'film is a visual medium' era.)

Bellour's procedure post-1990 marks, in a sense, a return to the theories of Eisenstein: in cinema there are elements, and *intervals* between those elements, and hence a set or system of articulations. Let us note an important displacement here: where for many years the mystique of mise-en-scène – from Delluc right through to recent work on depth staging by David Bordwell (2005) or on the elasticity of the filmic scene by Alain Bergala (2000) – has rested on a holistic aesthetic of 'bodies in space', Bellour (2000b) prefers to speak of the more supple, variable and less continuous organisation of bodies and shots, particularly as defined by the constantly redefined and mutating interplay of camera movements, cuts, natural environment or built décor, and figure movements. Aumont (1982) made a similar methodological point in a groundbreaking 1978 essay on Godard's *La Chinoise* (1967) in relation to the protocols of textual analysis.

Cinema as a medium ceaselessly 'puts into place' (this is the most literal sense of the term mise-en-scène), arranges or articulates, many things: not just theatrical scenes, but also images, sounds, gestures, words produced as speech, passages of strongly marked rhythm or colour. And here, even the seemingly empty or inexpressive cadences of articulation – the black frames that can separate images, say – have a role to play which is just as aesthetically determining as the more obviously full or signifying ones. Hence Bellour's provocative spray of new concepts: *mise en phrase, mise en image, mise en page, mise en plan*, 'and above all' *mise en pli* (2000b: 126). Each corresponds to a certain strategy, technique or novel gesture of *placement* of a material element within a film: its weaving, 'spacing', particular emphasis – and, ultimately, its specific place and role within the logic of a cinematic *dispositif*. Here is where Elsaesser's intuition of cinema becoming an audiovisual apparatus 'only of graphics and animation' (1993: 46) comes home to roost: to that we can add Morse's image of stacking, and even (to use an old-fashioned trope become new again in the digital age) the turning of printed pages.

Brief examples of Bellour's categories must suffice here. Godard is the figure who has experimented with and demonstrated them all, in different combinations and with varying emphasis: think of the *Histoire(s) du cinéma* series, with its performative placement of still photographs (*mise en image*), sampled shots from hundreds of films (*mise en plan*), pictorial design layout (*mise en page*), and quotations that are written or spoken (*mise en phrase*). We can also take a far more mainstream, less essayistic instance: think of the phenomenon of 'explosive speech' which Australian artist-critic Philip Brophy (1992) has analysed in genre cinema, a vast machinery of image, performance and sound marshalled in order to prepare and deliver a dramatic utterance like Clint Eastwood's immortal 'do you feel lucky' in *Dirty Harry* (Don Siegel, 1971). *Mise en pli*, the textual process that Bellour describes as the 'folding of the physical body of the *mise en scène*' (2000b: 123), a pressure that can split or even efface the scene, is less common: he uses examples from the career of Alain Resnais, ranging from the celebrated montage sequence of ambiguous, intertwined bodies 'submitted' (2000b: 122) to the voiceover text in *Hiroshima, mon amour* (1959), to the hollowing out of a shot by the camera panning over a blurry bit of nothingness mid-scene in *Mélo* (1986) (2000b: 123).

CINEMA WITHOUT WALLS

A *dispositif* is not a writing or painting from a formless real; nor is it something arrived at, on the set, spontaneously, intuitively or mystically. It is a preconceived, or organically developed, work of form. In this sense, the idea of *dispositif* allows us to conceive of cinema in the holistic way that mise-en-scène analysis once promised, but failed to deliver: it is about the integrated arrangement of form and content elements at all levels, from first conception to final mixing and grading. Furthermore, its applicability to other audiovisual forms, both artistic and cultural, is immediately more extensive: the force of the analyses of television events by Aumont and Perez is that they identify not only an age-old political mise-en-scène, but also a very specific and very modern techno-assemblage or *agencement* of angles, gazes, televisual spaces, and the laws that govern (or the moves that unravel) them all. One need only look at Harun Farocki's gallery installations – which, as Blümlinger has noted, aim to reveal 'how moving pictures are formally organised' (2004: 61) – or the peculiar live performance of the re-editing process by Straub and Huillet in Pedro Costa's documentary *Where Lies Your Hidden Smile?* (2001), to see how a cinematic *dispositif* can be projected into other spaces and redistributed in new arrangements.

It is at this point that *dispositif* thinking intersects with another term that has become richly productive in recent years: *intermediality*. This refers to more than simply the sheer fact of a multimedia culture, or the mixing and copresence of many media forms within specific works (from Olympic Games Opening and Closing ceremonies to *Histoire(s) du cinéma*). Intermediality, as the crucial work of Belén Vidal (2002; 2006) has shown, takes us to the strange, hitherto unfamiliar heart of even the most seemingly classical and commercial films, like the heritage adaptations of beloved novels: here we see not the seamless blending of citations and allusions from literature, fine art, the history of costume, architecture and so on, but rather an evident spray – as in a catalogue – of all these items and levels, complete with implicit, allegorical tips as to how, where, and why to consume them in the modern world (hence the endless, heavily marked shots, in such movies, of characters reading books or looking at paintings). We are closer now to the floating, queerly spaced-out realm of popular culture evoked in Timothy Corrigan's prophetic book *A Cinema Without Walls* (1991) than ever before.

The realm today defined as World Cinema – critical surveys at last taking fuller measure of the work produced in Iran, Africa, India, China, Argentina, Romania, Portugal, and so on, beyond the tried and true Euro-Anglo centers – is also giving us an urgent impetus to understand filmic *dispositifs* as intermedial phenomena. In the productions of Manoel de Oliveira (*A Talking Picture*, 2003), Apichatpong Weerasethakul (*Syndromes and a Century*, 2006), or Miguel Gomes (*Our Beloved Month of August*, 2008), traces of so many diverse media (film, theatre, radio, installation, fiction, documentary) are set in relation to each other like so many levels, panels, screens or computer windows, not fused but held distinct and resonating precisely via their intervals. This is Bellour's conclusion about a new understanding of *mise-en-scène*: that it can be redefined as the 'proper power of the interval' to the extent that there is a 'readability of the interval between shots' as well as a 'readability of the work that operates a transformation of this interval' (2000b: 125).

It is not entirely a matter of inventing a new critical idiom in order to grasp all of this. In some ways, a tradition of such analytical work has long existed, in however fragmentary or unrecognised a form. There are elements of *dispositif* insight in the work of many critics usually associated with the expressive school. Manny Farber was an astute observer of what he called the 'ritualised syntax' and 'stylistic moves' (1998: 310, 324) in directors including Fassbinder and Duras. Jean Douchet (1993) invented a 'V Diagram' to decipher the characteristic mise-en-scène arrangements in Mizoguchi. In Perez's account (1998) of Straub-Huillet, everything that happens (dramatically, sensually and intellectually) from shot to shot in their films happens as a result of the establishing of, and subtle variation within, a *dispositif* of shot/counter-shot and eyeline relations – not in excess of or beside this *dispositif* (which would be the default position of much expressive criticism). Indeed, taking an approach to cinema via the *dispositif* may well allow us to overcome the contradiction pinpointed strongly in recent years by Ian Hunter in his critique of the contemporary 'moment of theory' (see King 2008): the tendency for criticism (even the most sophisticated) to swing, in an unconsciously opportunistic fashion, between the code (e.g. the code of classical narrative) and its excess or surplus. As I argued in Volume 1 of this project (2009b), it is, rather, the category of textual logic that we must reinvestigate and reinvigorate – neither the strict (structuralist) code nor its liberatory (poststructuralist) surplus.

Let us return, finally, to Brenez's challenge to produce a 'Bazinian exigency maintained at the heart of a type of non-Bazinian analysis' (1997). Bazin's work, as we shall see if we look at it closely again today, was always of a dual-edged nature: he has been taken as the spokesperson for transparent realism, but in truth his position (as clearly stated in his unfinished book on Jean Renoir) was that 'realism does not at all mean a renunciation of style' – going on to stake his ethical-aesthetic preference that 'cinematic expression must be dialectically fused with reality and not with artifice' (1986: 106). Yet this opens the possibility of precisely the opposing option: that cinematic expression can also be dialectically fused with artifice. Moreover, Bazin spoke with equal passion and conviction of the vocation of an *impure cinema* (2009), and it is to this idea that Bellour returned at the dawn of our new, digital twenty-first century:

> Thus, the cinema, this impure art as Bazin called it, since it is inspired by all the other arts while offering up reality itself, paradoxically gains in purity to the extent that its most active truth becomes the truth of its *dispositif*. (2000a: 52, translation mine)

The truth of cinema's *dispositif*: on one level, this thought returns us (as Duguet [1988: 240] has astutely pointed out) to the positions in art history and criticism concerning medium specificity, from Clement Greenberg to Michael Fried, that have been central to modernism. Greenberg's argument that 'what had to be exhibited and made explicit was that which was unique and irreducible not only in art in general, but also in each particular art', and that an art 'had to determine, through the operations peculiar to itself, the effects peculiar and exclusive to itself' (1982: 5) finds its echo today in Stephen Melville's assertion (made in relation to post-minimalist painting, but popular among some avant-garde filmmakers) that a work of art in a particular medium 'counts' as such when it only manages to define and make manifest its materiality 'where it is most in doubt', through a ceaseless 'work of measuring and discovery' (2001: 3).

On another level, cinema is surely a paradoxical object: its medium-specific possibility seems to have been well and truly overrun by its tendency to intermediality, its fundamental impurity. That is where its true materiality-effect, today, is situated: in the palpable aura of a mise-en-scène that is always less than itself and more than itself, not only itself but also its contrary, ever vanishing and yet ever renewed across a thousand and one screens, platforms, and *dispositifs*.

AUTHOR'S NOTE

This chapter is part of work funded by the Australian Research Council through Monash University for 2010–2012.

REFERENCES

Agamben, Giorgio (2009) *What is an Apparatus?*, trans. David Kishik and Stefan Pedatella. Stanford University Press.

Albera, François (2000) 'Mise en scène et rituals sociaux', in Jacques Aumont (ed.) *La mise-en-scène*. Bruxelles: De Boeck, 219–31.

Aumont, Jacques (1982) 'This is Not a Textual Analysis', *Camera Obscura*, 8/9/10, 131–60.

_____ (ed.) (2000) *La mise en scène*. Bruxelles: De Boeck.

_____ (2006) *Le cinéma et la mise en scène*. Paris: Armand Colin.

Balsom, Erika (2009) 'A Cinema in the Gallery, a Cinema in Ruins', *Screen*, 50, 4, 411–27.

Baudry, Jean-Louis (1978) *L'Effet cinéma*. Paris: Albatros.

Bazin, André (1986) *Jean Renoir*, trans. W. W. Halsey II and William H. Simon. New York: Simon & Schuster.

_____ (2009) *What is Cinema?*, trans. Timothy Barnard. Montreal: Caboose.

Bellour, Raymond (2000a) 'La querelle des dispositifs', *Art Press*, 262, 48–52.

_____ (2000b) 'Figures aux allures de plans', in Jacques Aumont (ed.) *La mise-en-scène*. Bruxelles: De Boeck, 109–26.

_____ (2003) 'Paris, 25 September 1997', in Jonathan Rosenbaum and Adrian Martin (eds) *Movie Mutations: The Changing Face of Contemporary Cinephilia*. London: British Film Institute, 27–34.

_____ (2009) *Le corps du cinéma. Hypnoses, émotions, animalités*. Paris: P.O.L.

Bergala, Alain (2000b) 'L'intervalle', in Jacques Aumont (ed.) *La mise en scène*. Bruxelles: De Boeck, 25–35.

Blouin, Patrice (2010) 'Shirin', *Cahiers du cinéma*, 652, January, 74.

Blümlinger, Christa (2004) 'Incisive Divides and Revolving Images: On the Installation Schnittstelle', in Thomas Elsaesser (ed.) *Harun Farocki: Working on the Sight-lines*. Amsterdam: Amsterdam University Press, 61–76.

_____ (2010) 'The Imaginary in the Documentary Image: Chris Marker's Level Five', *Image [&] Narrative*, 11, 1, < http://ojs.arts.kuleuven.be/index.php/imagenarrative/article/viewFile/51/32 >. Accessed 29 May 2011.

Bordwell, David (2005) *Figures Traced in Light: On Cinematic Staging*. University of California Press.

Brenez, Nicole (1997) 'The Ultimate Journey: Remarks on Contemporary Theory', trans. William D. Routt, *Screening the Past 2* (December 1997), <http://www.latrobe.edu.au/screeningthepast/reruns/brenez.html>. Accessed 29 May 2011.

_____ (2003) 'Paris, 18 August 1997', in Jonathan Rosenbaum and Adrian Martin (eds) *Movie Mutations: The Changing Face of Contemporary Cinephilia*. London: British Film Institute, 19–27.

Brophy, Philip (1992) 'Read My Lips', in Adrian Martin (ed.) *Film – Matters of Style*. Perth: Continuum, 246–66.

Cha, Theresa Hak Kyung (ed.) (1981) *Apparatus*. New York: Tanam Press.

Comolli, Jean-Louis (2004) *Voir et pouvoir. L'innocence perdue, cinéma, télévision, fiction, documentaire*. Paris: Verdier.

Corrigan, Timothy (1991) *A Cinema Without Walls: Movies and Culture After Vietnam*. New Brunswick: Rutgers University Press.

Dag (200) 'The VideoSift Pomplamoose Interview', December, <http://music.videosift. com/talk/The-VideoSift-Pomplamoose-Interview> Accessed 29 May 2011.

Deleuze, Gilles (1992) 'What is a dispositif?', in Timothy J. Armstrong (ed.) *Michel Foucault Philosopher*. New York: Routledge, 159–68.

Douchet, Jean (1993) 'Mizoguchi: la réflexion du désir', *Cahiers du cinéma*, 463, 24–7.

Duguet, Anne-Marie (1988) 'Dispositifs', *Communications*, 48, 221–48.

_____ (2002) *Déjouer l'image. Créations électroniques et numériques*. Nîmes: CNAP/ Jacqueline Chambon.

Elsaesser, Thomas (1981) 'Vincente Minnelli', in Rick Altman (ed.) *Genre: The Musical*. London: Routledge & Kegan Paul, 8–27.

_____ (1993) 'Film Studies in Search of the Object', *Film Criticism*, 17, 2/3, 40–7.

Farber, Manny (1998) *Negative Space*. New York: Da Capo.

Foucault, Michel (1980 [1977]) 'The Confession of the Flesh (interview), in Colin Gordon (ed.) *Power/Knowledge: Selected Interviews and Other Writings, 1972–1977*. New York: Pantheon, 194–228.

Flusser, Vilém (2006) *La Civilisation des médias*, trans. Claude Maillard. Belval: Circé.

Frampton, Daniel (2006) *Filmosophy*. London: Wallflower Press.

Gibbs, John (2006) 'Filmmakers' Choices', in *Close-Up 01*, eds John Gibbs and Douglas Pye. London: Wallflower Press, 1–87.

Grafe, Frieda (1996) *The Ghost and Mrs. Muir*. London: British Film Institute.

Greenberg, Clement (1982) 'Modernist Painting', in Francis Frascina and Charles Harrison (eds.) *Modern Art and Modernism: A Critical Anthology*. London: Harper and Row, 5–14.

Hodsdon, Barrett (1992) 'The Mystique of mise-en-scène Revisited', in Adrian Martin (ed.) *Film – Matters of Style*. Perth: Continuum, 68–86.

Kessler, Frank (2000) '''Les Américains ne connaissent pas le mot schreiten…''. La mise-en-scène du corps de l'étranger', in Jacques Aumont (ed.) *La mise-en-scène*. Bruxelles: De Boeck, 47–58.

_____ (2006a) 'The Cinema of Attractions as Dispositif', in Wanda Strauven (ed.) *The Cinema of Attractions Reloaded*. Amsterdam: Amsterdam University Press, 57–70.

_____ (2006b) 'Notes on dispositif', <http://www.let.uu.nl/~Frank.Kessler/personal/ notes%20on%20dispositif.PDF>. Accessed 29 May 2011.

King, Noel (2008) '''Another Way of Being an Intellectual'': An Interview with Ian Hunter', *Communication, Politics & Culture*, 41, 1, 47–62.

Labarthe, André S. (1967) 'Mort d'un mot', *Cahiers du cinéma*, 195, 66.

Lyotard, Jean-Francois (1993) *Libidinal Economy*, trans. Iain Hamilton Grant. London: The

Athlone Press.

Martin, Adrian (1992) 'Mise-en-scène is Dead; or The Expressive, The Excessive, The Technical and The Stylish', in Adrian Martin (ed.) *Film – Matters of Style*. Perth: Continuum, 87–140.

_____ (2009a) 'Vilém Flusser', in Felicity Colman (ed.) *Film, Theory and Philosophy: The Key Thinkers*. Durham: Acumen, 31–9.

_____ (2009b) 'Beyond the Fragments of Cinephilia: Towards a Synthetic Analysis', in Scott Balcerzak and Jason Sperb (eds) *Cinephilia in the Age of Digital Reproduction: Film, Pleasure and Digital Culture, Vol. 1*. London: Wallflower Press, 30–53.

_____ (2009c) ('At Table: The Social Mise en scène of How Green Was My Valley', *Undercurrent*, no. 4, <http://www.fipresci.org/undercurrent/issue_0509/how_green. htm>, accessed 29 May 2011.

Mathews, Harry (2003) *The Case of the Persevering Maltese: Collected Essays*. Urbana-Champaign: Dalkey Archive Press.

McElhaney, Joe (2006) *The Death of Classical Cinema: Hitchcock, Lang, Minnelli*. State University of New York Press.

_____ (ed.), *Vincente Minnelli: The Art of Entertainment* (2009: Wayne State University Press, 2009).

Melville, Stephen (2001) 'Counting/As/Painting', in Philip Armstrong, Laura Lisbon and Melville (eds) *As Painting: Division and Displacement*. Cambridge, MA: The MIT Press, 1–26.

Metz, Christian (1982) *The Imaginary Signifier: Psychoanalysis and the Cinema*, trans. B. Brewster, C. Britton, A. Guzzetti and A. Williams. Bloomington: Indiana University Press.

Margaret Morse, 'An Ontology of Everyday Distraction: The Freeway, the Mall, and Television', in *Logics of Television: Essays in Cultural Criticism*, ed. Patricia Mellencamp (Bloomington and Indianapolis: Indiana University Press, 1990), pp. 193–221. Reprinted in *Morse's book Virtualities: Television, Media Art, and Cyberculture* (Bloomington: Indiana University Press, 1998).

Moullet, Luc (2007) 'Les dispositifs du cinéma contemporain', *Esprit* 337, 121–30.

Mulvey, Laura (2009) 'Some Reflections on the Cinephilia Question', *Framework*, 50, 1/2, 190–3.

Perez, Gilberto (1998) *The Material Ghost: Films and Their Medium*. Baltimore: The Johns Hopkins University Press.

Perkins, V. F. (2005) 'Where is the World?: The Horizon of Events in Movie Fiction', in John Gibbs and Douglas Pye (eds) *Style and Meaning: Studies in the Detailed Analysis of Film*. Manchester: Manchester University Press, 16–41.

_____ (2009) 'Le Plaisir', *Film Quarterly*, 63, 1, 15–22.

Pomplamoose website, <http://www.pomplamoose.com/ >. Accessed 29 May 2011.

Ruiz, Raúl (1999) *Entretiens*. Paris: Hoëbeke.

theBestArts, 'Pomplamoose Music – Nataly Dawn and Jack Conte', 2009, < http://www.

thebestarts.com/pomplamoose/default.aspx >. Accessed 29 May 2011.

Thomas, Deborah (2005) '"Knowing One's Place": Frame-breaking, Embarrassment and Irony in *La Cérémonie* (Claude Chabrol, 1995)', in John Gibbs and Douglas Pye (eds) *Style and Meaning: Studies in the Detailed Analysis of Film*. Manchester: Manchester University Press, 167–78.

Vidal, Belén (2002) 'Classic Adaptations, Modern Reinventions: Reading the Image in the Contemporary Literary Film', *Screen*, 43, 1, 5–18.

_____ (2006) 'Labyrinths of Loss: The Letter as Figure of Desire and Deferral in the Literary Film', *Journal of European Studies*, 36, 4, 418–36.

SELECTED BIBLIOGRAPHY

Andrew, Dudley (2009) 'The Core and Flow of Film Studies', *Critical Inquiry*, 35, 879–915.

Andrew, Dudley and Mary Anne Lewis (2009) '"Writing on the Screen": An interview with Emmanuel Burdeau', *Framework: The Journal of Cinema and Media*, 50, 1/2: 229–34.

_____ (2000) 'The Three Stages of Cinema Studies and the Age to Come', *PMLA*, 115, 3, 341–51.

Arnheim, Rudolf (2004) *Art and Visual Perception: A Psychology of the Creative Eye*. Berkeley: University of California Press.

_____ (2004) *Visual Thinking*. Berkeley: University of California Press.

Balcerzak, Scott and Jason Sperb (2009) 'Presence of Pleasure', in Scott Balcerzak and Jason Sperb (eds) *Cinephilia in the Age of Digital Reproduction: Film, Pleasure and Digital Culture, Vol. 1*. London: Wallflower Press, 7–29.

Barthes, Roland (1972) *Mythologies*. New York: Hill and Wang.

_____ (1975) *The Pleasure of the Text*. New York: Hill and Wang.

_____ (1978) *Image, Music, Text*. New York: Hill and Wang.

_____ (1979 *Lover's Discourse: Fragments*. New York: Hill and Wang.

_____ (1980) 'Upon Leaving the Movie Theatre', in Ed. Theresa Hak Kyung Cha *Apparatus. The Cinematographic Apparatus: Selected Writings*. New York: Tanam Press.

_____ (1982) *Camera Lucida: Reflections of Photography*. New York: Hill and Wang.

Benson-Allott, Caetlin (2011) 'The Chora Line: RealD Incorporated', *South Atlantic Quarterly*, 110, 3, 621–44.

Buchsbaum, Jonathan and Elena Gorfinkel (2009) 'Introduction', *Framework: The Journal of Cinema and Media*, 50, 1/2, 176–80.

Brenez, Nicole (2009) 'For an Insubordinate (or Rebellious) History of Cinema', *Framework: The Journal of Cinema and Media*, 50, 1/2, 197–201.

Baudrillard, Jean (1983) *Simulations*, trans. Paul Foss, Paul Patton and Philip Beitchman. New York: Semiotext(e).

Bazin, Andre (1967) *What is Cinema? Volume 1*, trans. Hugh Gray. Berkeley: University of California Press.

Belton, John (2002) 'Digital Cinema: A False Revolution', *October*, 100, 98–114.

Benjamin, Walter (1969) 'The Work of Art in the Age of Mechanical Reproduction', in *Illumi-*

nations, trans. Harry Zohn, ed. Hannah Arendt. New York: Shocken Books, 217–52.

Bode, Lisa (2010) 'Posthumous Performance', *Cinema Journal*, 49, 4, 46–70.

Bolter, J. David and Richard Grusin (2000) *Remediation: Understanding New Media*. Cambridge, MA: MIT Press.

Buckland, Warren (1999) 'Between science fact and science fiction: Spielberg's digital dinosaurs, possible worlds, and the new aesthetic realism', *Screen*, 40, 2, 177–92.

Bukatman, Scott (1999) 'The Artificial Infinite: On Special Effects and the Sublime', in Annette Kuhn (ed.) *Alien Zone 2: The Spaces of Science-Fiction*. New York: Verso, 249–75.

_____ (1993) *Terminal Identity: The Virtual Subject in Postmodern Science Fiction*. Durham, NC: Duke University Press.

_____ (2003) *Matters of Gravity: Special Effects and Supermen in the 20th Century*. Durham, NC: Duke University Press.

Campbell, Zachary (2009) 'On the Political Challenges of the Cinephile Today', *Framework: The Journal of Cinema and Media*, 50, 1/2, 210–13.

Cavell, Stanley (1979) *The World Viewed: Reflections on the Ontology of Film*. Cambridge, MA: Harvard.

Charney, Leo (1998) *Empty Moments: Cinema, Modernity and Drift*. Durham, NC: Duke University Press.

Cubitt, Sean (1998) *Digital Aesthetics*. London: Sage.

_____ (1999) 'Phalke, Méliès, and Special Effects Today', *Wide Angle*, 21, 1, 115–30.

_____ (2005) *The Cinema Effect*. Cambridge, MA: MIT Press.

De Baecque, Antoine and Thierry Frémaux (1995) 'La Cinéphilie ou L'Invention d'Une Culture', *Vingtième Siècle*, 46, 133–42.

De Valck, Marike and Malte Hagener (eds) (2005) *Cinephilia: Movies, Love, and Memory*. Amsterdam: Amsterdam University Press.

Deleuze, Gilles (1986) *Cinema 1: The Movement-Image*, trans. Hugh Tomlinson and Barbara Hammerjam. Minneapolis: University of Minnesota Press.

_____ (1989) *Cinema 2: The Time-Image*, trans. Hugh Tomlinson and Robert Galeta. Minneapolis: University of Minnesota Press.

_____ (1994) *Difference and Repetition*, trans. Paul Patton. New York: Columbia University Press.

Deleuze, Gilles and Felix Guattari (1987) *A Thousand Plateaus: Capitalism and Schizophrenia*, trans. and foreword Brian Massumi. Minneapolis: University of Minnesota Press.

_____ and Felix Guattari (1994) 'Percept, Affect, Concept', in *What is Philosophy?* trans. and eds. Hugh Tomlinson and Graham Burchell. New York: Columbia University Press, 163–99.

_____ (2000) *Anti-Oedipus: Capitalism and Schizophrenia*, trans. Robert Hurley, Mark Seem, and Helen R. Lane. Minneapolis: University of Minnesota Press.

Dinsmore-Tuli, Uma (2000) 'The Pleasures of "Home Cinema", or Watching Movies on Telly: An Audience Study of Cinephiliac VCR Use', *Screen*, 41, 3, 315–27.

Doane, Mary Ann (2002) *The Emergence of Cinematic Time: Modernity, Contingency, the Archive*. Cambridge, MA: Harvard University Press.

Durgnat, Raymond (1971) *Films and Feelings*. Cambridge, MA: MIT Press.

Eisenstein, Sergei (1949) 'About Stereoscopic Cinema', *Penguin Film Review*, 8, 47.

Elsaesser, Thomas (2005) 'Cinephilia or the Uses of Disenchantment', in Marijke de Valck and Malte Hegener (eds) *Cinephilia: Movies, Love and Memory*. Amsterdam: Amsterdam University Press, 27–43.

Elsaesser, Thomas and Warren Buckland (2002) *Studying Contemporary American Cinema: A Guide to Movie Analysis*. New York: Oxford University Press.

Epstein, Jean (1978) 'Essence of Cinema', in P. Adams Sitney (ed.) *The Avant-Garde Film: A Reader of Theory and Criticism*. New York: New York University Press, 24–5.

_____ (1978) 'For a New Avant-Garde', in P. Adams Sitney (ed.) *The Avant-Garde Film: A Reader of Theory and Criticism*. New York: New York University Press, 26–30.

_____ (1984) 'Cine-Mystique', trans. Stuart Liebman, *Millennium Film Journal*, 10–11, 192–3.

Erickson, Steve. (1999) 'Permanent Ghosts: Cinephilia in the Age of the Internet and Video, Essay 1', *Senses of Cinema*: http://www.sensesofcinema.com/contents/00/4/cine1.html.

Flavell, Bill (2000) 'Cinephilia and/or Cinematic Specificity', *Senses of Cinema*, 7, June: http://www.sensesofcinema.com/contents/00/7/cinephilia.html.

Foster, Stephen C. (1998) *Hans Richter: Activism, Modernism and the Avant-Garde*. Cambridge, MA: MIT Press.

Fujiwara, Chris (2009) 'Cinephilia and the Imagination of Filmmaking', *Framework: The Journal of Cinema and Media*, 50, 1/2, 194–6.

Gunning, Tom (1990) 'The Cinema of Attractions: Early Film, Its Spectator and the Avant-Garde', in Thomas Elsaesser (ed.) *Early Cinema: Space, Frame, Narrative*. London: British Film Institute, 56–62.

Harvey, Sylvia (1978) *May '68 and Film Culture*. London: British Film Institute.

Hillier, Jim (ed.) (1985) *Cahiers du Cinéma: The 1950s. Neo-Realism, Hollywood, New Wave*. Cambridge, MA: Harvard University Press.

Hills, Matt (2002) *Fan Cultures*. New York: Routledge.

Jarvie, Ian (1960) 'Bazin's Ontology', *Film Quarterly*, 14, 1, 60–1.

Jenkins, Henry (1992) *Textual Poachers: Television Fans and Participatory Culture*. New York: Routledge.

_____ (2006) *Fans, Bloggers, and Gamers: Exploring Participatory Culture*. New York: New York University Press.

_____ (2006) *The Wow Climax: Tracing the Emotional Impact of Popular Culture*. New York: New York University Press.

_____ (2008) *Convergence Culture: Where Old and New Media Collide*. New York: New York University Press.

Keathley, Christian (2000) 'The Cinephiliac Moment', *Framework*, 42: http://www.frameworkonline.com/42index.htm.

_____ (2006) *Cinephilia and History; or The Winds in the Trees*. Bloomington, IN: Indiana University Press.

Kehr, Dave (2006) 'The Real Web Critics', *DaveKehr.Com* (21 May): http://davekehr. com/?p=84.

Klinger, Barbara (2006) *Beyond the Multiplex: Cinema, New Technologies, and the Home*. Berkeley: University of California Press.

Kuhn, Annette (1999) 'Introduction', in Annette Kuhn (ed.) *Alien Zone 2: The Spaces of Science-Fiction*. New York: Verso, 1–8.

Lambert, Jeff (1999) 'Permanent Ghosts: Cinephilia in the Age of the Internet and Video, Essay 4', *Senses of Cinema*: http://www.sensesofcinema.com/contents/00/4/cine4. html.

Lesage, Julia (2007) 'The Internet Today, or I got involved in Social Bookmarking', *Jump Cut*, 49: http://www.ejumpcut.org/currentissue/links.html.

MacCabe, Colin (1976) 'Theory and Film: Principles of Realism and Pleasure', *Screen*, 17, 3, 17–27.

Manning, Erin (2006) *Politics of Touch: Sense, Movement, Sovereignty*. Minneapolis: University of Minnesota Press.

Manovich, Lev (2001) *The Language of New Media*. Cambridge, MA: MIT Press.

Marks, Laura (2000) *The Skin of the Film: Intercultural Cinema, Embodiment, and the Senses*. Durham, NC: Duke University Press.

_____ (2002) *Touch: Sensuous Theory and Multisensory Media*. Minneapolis: University of Minnesota Press.

Martin, Adrian (2007) 'Responsibility and Criticism', *Cinemascope*, 7, Jan-Apr: http://www. cinemascope.it/Issue%207/Articoli_n7/Articoli_n7_05/Adrian_Martin.pdf

_____ (2009) 'Cinephilia as War Machine', *Framework: The Journal of Cinema and Media*, 50, 1/2, 221–5.

Martin, Adrian and Jonathan Rosenbaum (eds) (2003) *Movie Mutations: The Changing Face of World Cinephilia*. London: British Film Institute.

Metz, Christian (1977) *The Imaginary Signifier*, trans. Celia Britton, Annwyl Williams, Ben Brewster, and Alfred Guzzetti. Bloomington: Indiana University Press.

Michelson, Annette (1998) 'Gnosis and Iconoclasm: A Case Study of Cinephilia', *October*, 83, 3–18.

Mitchell, William J. (1992) *The Reconfigured Eye: Visual Truth in the Post-Photographic Era*. Cambridge, MA: MIT Press.

Modleski, Tania (1986) 'The Terror of Pleasure: The Contemporary Horror Film and Postmodern Theory', in Tania Modleski (ed.) *Studies in Entertainment: Critical Approaches to Mass Culture*. Bloomington: Indiana University Press, 155–66.

Moore, Rachel O. (2000) *Savage Theory: Cinema as Modern Magic*. Durham, NC: Duke University Press.

Morrison, James (2005) 'After the Revolution: On the Fate of Cinephilia', *Michigan Quar-*

terly Review, 44, 3, 393–413.

Mulvey, Laura (1975) 'Visual Pleasure and Narrative Cinema', Screen, 16, 3, 6–18.

_____ (2006) Death 24x a Second: Stillness and the Moving Image. London: Reaktion.

_____ (2007) 'A Clumsy Sublime', Film Quarterly, 60, 3, 3.

_____ (2009) 'Some Reflections on the Cinephilia Question', Framework: The Journal of Cinema and Media, 50, 1/2, 190–3.

Ng, Jenna (2005) 'Love in the Time of Transcultural Fusion: Cinephilia, Homage and Kill Bill', in Marijke de Valck and Malte Hegener (eds) Cinephilia: Movies, Love and Memory. Amsterdam: Amsterdam University Press: 65–79.

_____ (2010) 'The Myth of Total Cinephilia', Cinema Journal, 49, 2, 146–51.

_____ (2007) 'Virtual Cinematography and the Digital Real: (Dis)placing the Moving Image between Reality and Simulacra', in Damian Sutton, Susan Brind, Ray McKenzie (eds) The State of the Real: Aesthetics in the Digital Age. London: IB Taurus, 172–80.

Nichols, Ashton (1987) The Poetics of Epiphany: Nineteenth-Century Origins of the Modern Literary Movement. Tuscaloosa: University of Alabama Press.

Nin, Anaïs (1963/4) 'Poetics of the Film', Film Culture, 31, Winter, 12–13.

Norton, Bill (2003) 'Through a Glass Darkly', Cinefex, 93, 88–111.

Panayides, Theo (1999) 'Permanent Ghosts: Cinephilia in the Age of the Internet and Video, Essay 2', Senses of Cinema: http://www.sensesofcinema.com/contents/00/4/cine2.html.

Paul, William (1993) 'The Aesthetics of Emergence', Film History, 5, 3, 321–55.

_____ (2004) 'Breaking the Fourth Wall: Belascoism, Modernism, and Kiss Me Kate', Film History, 16, 229–42.

Perkins, Claire (2000) 'Cinephilia and Monstrosity: The Problem of Cinema in Deleuze's Cinema Books', Senses of Cinema 8: www.sensesofcinema.com/contents/books/00/8/deleuze.html.

Pierson, Michele (2002) Special Effects: Still in Search of Wonder. New York: Columbia University Press.

Porton, Richard (2002) 'The Politics of American Cinephilia: From the Popular Front to the Age of Video', Cineaste, Fall, 4–10.

Prince, Stephen (1996) 'True Lies: Perceptual Realism, Digital Images, and Film Theory', Film Quarterly, 49, 3, 27–37.

_____ (2004) 'The Emergence of Filmic Artifacts', Film Quarterly, 57, 3, 24–33.

Purse, Lisa (2007) 'Digital Heroes in Contemporary Hollywood: Exertion, Identification and the Virtual Action Body', Film Criticism, 32, 1, 5–25.

Ray, Robert (1985) A Certain Tendency of the Hollywood Cinema, 1930–1980. Princeton, NJ: Princeton University Press.

_____ (2001) How a Film Theory Got Lost and Other Mysteries in Cultural Studies. Bloomington, IN: Indiana University Press.

Rehak, Bob (2007) 'The Migration of Forms: Bullet Time in Circulation', Film Criticism, 32, 1, 26–48.

Robnik, Drehli (2005) 'Mass Memories of Movies: Cinephilia as Norm and Narrative in Blockbuster Culture', in Marijke de Valck and Malte Hegener (eds) *Cinephilia: Movies, Love and Memory*. Amsterdam: Amsterdam University Press, 55–64.

Rodowick, D. N. (2007) *The Virtual Life of Film*. Cambridge: Harvard University Press.

Rombes, Nicholas (2009) *Cinema in the Digital Age*. London: Wallflower Press.

Rosenbaum, Jonathan (2009) 'Reply to Cinephilia Survey', *Framework: The Journal of Cinema and Media*, 50, 1/2, 181–2.

_____ (2010) *Goodbye Cinema, Hello Cinephilia: Film Culture in Transition*. Chicago: University of Chicago Press.

Rosen, Philip (2001) *Change Mummified: Cinema, Historicity, Theory*. Minneapolis: University of Minnesota Press.

Sandifer, Philip (2011) 'Out of the Screen and Into the Theater: Film 3-D as Demo', *Cinema Journal*, 50, 3, 62–78.

Sarris, Andrew (ed.) (1963) Special Issue: 'American Directors', *Film Culture*, 28, Spring.

Shaviro, Steven (1993) *The Cinematic Body*. Minneapolis: University of Minnesota Press.

_____ (1997) *Doom Patrols: A Theoretical Fiction about Postmodernism*. New York: Serpent's Tail.

_____ (2004) 'The Life, After Death, of Postmodern Emotions', *Criticism*, 46, 1, 125–41.

_____ (2007) 'Emotion Capture: Affect in Digital Film', *Projections*, 1, 2, 37–55.

_____ (2010) *Post-Cinematic Affect*. Blue Ridge, PA: Zero Books.

Sobchack, Vivian (1991) *The Address of the Eye: A Phenomenology of Film Experience*. Princeton, NJ: Princeton University Press.

_____ (1998) *Screening Space: The American Science Fiction Film*. New Brunswick: Rutgers University Press.

_____ (2000) *Meta Morphing: Visual Transformation and the Culture of Quick Change*. Minneapolis: University of Minnesota Press.

_____ (2004) *Carnal Thoughts: Embodiment and Moving Image Culture*. Berkeley, CA: University of California Press.

Sontag, Susan (2001) 'A Century of Cinema' in *Where the Stress Falls*. New York: Farrar, Straus and Giroux, 117–22.

Sperb, Jason (2007) 'Sensing an Intellectual Nemesis', *Film Criticism*, 32, 1, 49–71.

Stern, Lesley (2001) 'Paths that Wind through the Thicket of Things', *Critical Inquiry*, 28, 1, 317–54.

Strauven, Wanda (ed.) (2007) *The Cinema of Attractions Reloaded*. Amsterdam: Amsterdam University Press.

Sterritt, David (1999) 'Permanent Ghosts: Cinephilia in the Age of the Internet and Video, Essay 3', *Senses of Cinema*: http://www.sensesofcinema.com/contents/00/4/cine3.html.

Tashiro, Charles Shiro (1991) 'Videophilia: What Happens When You Wait for It on Video', *Film Quarterly*, 45, 1, 7–17.

Taylor, Richard (ed.) (1999) *The Eisenstein Reader*. London: British Film Institute.

Trbic, Boris (2004) 'Contextualizing the Narrative: A Step Towards Classroom Cinephilia', *Australian Screen Education*, 34, 86–91.

Vogel, Amos (1974) *Film as a Subversive Art*. New York: Random House.

Whissel, Kristen (2010) 'The Digital Multitude', *Cinema Journal*, 49, 4, 90–110.

Willemen, Paul (1994) *Looks and Frictions: Essays in Cultural Studies and Film Theory*. Bloomington, IN: Indiana University Press.

Wollen, Peter (1976) 'Ontology and Materialism in Film', *Screen*, 17, 1, 7–23.

_____ (2001) 'An Alphabet of Cinema', *New Left Review*, 12 , Nov/Dec, 115–34.

INDEX

DATE DUE

Demco, Inc. 38-293